I knew that Stan Krippner had made vast contributions to the fields of scientific dream research, shamanism, psychedelics, transpersonal psychology, and more and that he had traveled all over the world making friends at every stop, and that graduate students had come in droves to study with him. I knew him as a wise and generous faculty colleague and keen-eyed co-author. But I didn't know he had hung out with rock musicians, played pranks, and organized amateur theatricals. This scholarly, artistic, and humorous autobiography offers proof that one may successfully combine rational thinking with openness to the beyond. His life's work is a witness to the best of both worlds.

Linda Riebel, PhD, co-author of *Understanding Suicide's Allure* and President of the Saybrook Chapter of the American Association of University Professors

Stanley Krippner's memoir, *A Chaotic Life*, is a fascinating read. Stan is a major researcher and scholar, and the book is filled with fascinating behind-the-scenes anecdotes and groundbreaking findings of his professional work. Stan has contributed to a vast array of approaches to human potential: clinical psychology, dream research, hypnosis, cross-cultural studies, parapsychology, mythology, post-traumatic stress disorder, and suicide prevention, to name but a few. The reader of this book is transported to the planet's most exotic corners and introduced to noted friends of Stan's—from Rational Emotive Therapy founder Albert Ellis to the band members of The Grateful Dead. He has lived an amazing life and has the story-telling skills to let you experience it.

Deirdre Barrett, PhD, Harvard University Author of *The Committee of Sleep*

Stanley Krippner has lived one of the most fascinating lives imaginable. Shamans, psychics, and psychedelic pioneers ... Stan has known most of them, been loved by many, and respected by all. Whether he was advising film directors, cavorting with rock stars, conducting solid research, or guiding students, Stan's approach has always been sincere, kind, and playful. He tells his story with courage and candor. This is a lovely book about an extraordinary man's life.

Christopher Ryan, PhD, Co-author of *Sex at Dawn* and *Civilized to Death* (and former student of Stan's)

Stanley Krippner is a true pioneer in not one discipline but several—psychology, anthropology, and parapsychology—all with a common thread of studying the nature of consciousness. His insights and mentorship have shaped at least two generations and this book recounting his personal path and life is one that I highly recommend.

Stephan A. Schwartz
Author of *Opening to the Infinite and The 8 Laws of Change*

Dr. Stanley Krippner is a giant in the field of humanistic psychology as well as personal and spiritual growth. Now in his elder years, he retains the acute memory, wit, and insight to share unique insights about the quest to understand ourselves and our world. As I read *A Chaotic Life*, I gained a passing acquaintance, through Stan's eyes, with other psychological and spiritual icons of the past century to the present day.

Dan Millman, author of *Way of the Peaceful Warrior*

Dr. Stanley Krippner is many things besides a beloved and brilliant teacher, researcher, and mentor. His expertise covers shamanism, dreamwork, consciousness studies, creativity, and much more. In his work and in his stories, he has helped open our eyes to a larger reality than most people realize. He delights in taking richness in the present moment. Stan knows people around the world and across cultures, as well as colorful people at home. Stan's memoir opens doors, enlarges experience, reveals special moments, and always entertains. He has shown ingenuity, bravery, nonconformity, and brilliant creativity in his explorations and expositions of the phenomenal worlds and realms drawn from his multicultural perspective. While writing over 1,000 articles and books, he has made friends globally as well as at home, and can tell a story like no one else. In these memoirs, he shares special moments from an extraordinary life well lived.

Ruth Richards, MD, PhD
Associated Distinguished Professor, California Institute of Integral Studies

In this memoir, the incomparable Dr. Stanley Krippner describes his life as "not too shabby." As befits a phenomenologist, the description says more about the speaker than about the person being described. We begin our story with a portrait of a man of modesty and authenticity. Most of us know him, on the other hand, as a magician, a nurturer of many generations of students all over the world, and a consummate academic. This book will continue to reach generations of students and colleagues, continuing Stan's legacy of humanistic education.

Ilene Serlin, PhD, Serlin Institute for the Healing Arts

In this majestic memoir, renowned consciousness researcher, psychospiritual explorer, and humanist Stanley Krippner takes us on a tour of his extraordinary life. This is the saga of a genuine pioneer that intersects with some of the key people, places, and ideas of the last 100 years. Krippner has incredible vivacity, boldness, and generosity of view, and his memoir beautifully illustrates his unique and brilliant journey.

Kirk Schneider, PhD
President of the Existential-Humanistic Institute
Author, *The Polarized Mind*, *The Spirituality of Awe*,
and *Life Enhancing Anxiety*

Stan has masterfully chronicled his memoirs that, at times, read like vignettes from a novel, invoking brilliant images of his incredible adventures. From his groundbreaking work in PTSD, dream research, parapsychology, and more, to his deep friendships with the likes of Albert and Debbie Joffe Ellis, Laura Huxley, Timothy Leary, Ram Dass, and Mickey Hart of the Grateful Dead, this amazing account documents, for the ages, a life truly well lived.

Rosemary Sword, PhD
Co-developer of Time Perspective Therapy

Stan has been a model for me, having one foot in the alternative transpersonal world and the other rooted deeply in mainstream psychological science. He has been a great influence on how I have approached my own career, emulating that quality of living in both worlds.

David Lukoff, PhD, Spiritual Competency Academy

A Chaotic Life is the astonishing—and I don't use that word lightly—memoir by Dr. Stanley Krippner. The book tells of a recurring theme in Stan's life, where apparently incidental or minor events resulted in major personal transformations that ultimately affected hundreds of others in positive ways. The word "chaos" in the title refers to subtle or hidden forms of order described by complex systems theory, and not to disorder or confusion. By magically surfing upon this orderly chaos, Stan transformed from a shy intellectual kid into a true force of nature, helping to shape the lives and careers of hundreds of scientists, scholars, and professionals across dozens of disciplines, some of which he co-founded. An enthusiastic world traveler into his late 80s, Stan's circle of friends has included famous actors, artists, musicians, political activists, scientists, shamans, psychics, and beyond, and he has gathered dozens of accolades and significant awards from professional and lay societies. This is a fascinating life story, well worth reading.

Dean Radin PhD, Chief Scientist, Institute of Noetic Sciences, Author of *Real Magic*

In these fascinating memoirs, Stan describes living his life like a blazing comet that has been wandering though the cosmos, dancing in Brazil, jogging in Spain, swimming in Hawaii, trucking with the Grateful Dead, and sweating and praying with Rolling Thunder in his sweat lodge. And the comet has yet to burn out!

Alberto Villoldo, PhD, author of *Shaman, Healer, Sage*

Stanley wrote one of the earliest and most profound reflections on creativity and altered states of consciousness. His presentations are always uplifting and encouraging, especially for the young and curious. Thank you, Stanley. We love you!

Alex Grey, co-founder, Chapel of Sacred Mirrors

Following along with the *chaos-theory-butterfly-effect* of Stanley Krippner's memoirs, you will likely feel amazed and reminded of the potentially unknown impact of every person you will ever meet, work with, or befriend. His book reads like a metaphor for the fulfillment of various precognitive dreams (and some parts, literally). His book, centered around the people he recognizes to have changed his life, speaks volumes about his loving and compassionate nature. Simultaneously, he shares numerous "behind the scenes" glimpses into his professional experiences and the legacy he has built in the fields of dream studies, transpersonal psychology, parapsychology and more, for the rest of us to learn from and build upon. As did Shakespeare, Dr. Krippner frames the story of his life as a theater, with dramatic entrances and exits of the most memorable characters, great journeys, dreams, personal mythologies, collaborations, partnerships, love ties and friendships. Among a plethora of other great stories, he shares his early involvement with the International Association for the Study of Dreams, his past presidency, and how IASD has been "doing its best to combat dreamism." His life theater consistently presents itself on these pages with "encores" of his world travels as well as reflections on the "encores" he would like to have fulfilled. Each chapter is an entire play.

Angel Morgan, PhD,
Past President, International Association for the Study of Dreams;
Founder, Dreambridge
Professor, Institute of Transpersonal Psychology, Sofia University
Past President, DAC Chair
International Association for the Study of Dreams

A Chaotic Life

The Memoirs of Stanley Krippner,
Pioneering Humanistic Psychologist

Volume 1

by
Stanley Krippner, PhD

Colorado Springs, CO
www.universityprofessorspress.com

Copyright © 2024 Stanley Krippner

A Chaotic Life: The Memoirs of Stanley Krippner, Pioneering Humanistic Psychologist (Volume 1) by Stanley Krippner, PhD

All rights reserved. No portion of this book may be reproduced by any process or technique without the express written consent of the publishers.

ISBN (Hardcover):   978-1-955737-47-0
ISBN (Paperback):   978-1-955737-49-4

The eBook version combines all three volumes and includes some additional chapters only available in the ebook.

University Professors Press
Colorado Springs, CO
www.universityprofessorspress.com

Cover Photo by George Berticevich © 2023
Cover Design adapted by Laura Ross

To Steve Hart, in appreciation for his years of dedicated assistance. And to Virginia Glenn, who introduced me to a network of cherished friends during what she fondly termed "happenings."

Table of Contents

Acknowledgments		i
Foreword	The Nonlinear Dynamical Life of Stanley Krippner by Tobi Zausner, PhD	iii
The Enduring Legacy of Stanley Krippner		vii
Preface	Not Too Shabby!	ix
Chapter 1	The Ordeal of Marcia Gates	1
Chapter 2	On Wisconsin!	16
Chapter 3	The Wisconsinites	32
Chapter 4	The Back of the Bus	46
Chapter 5	The Notorious Kent State Shootings	56
Chapter 6	My Uncle Max	72
Chapter 7	Mandrake Gestures Hypnotically	90
Chapter 8	It Started with Disney	105
Chapter 9	Seeking the Magic Mushroom	124
Chapter 10	Gifted Children	134
Chapter 11	Activism and Activists	152
Chapter 12	Bringing Order Out of Chaos	181
Chapter 13	Fran Dillon Comes to the Rescue	198
Chapter 14	A Turbulent Sea	212
References		225

Acknowledgments

Many friends have helped me pull these memoirs together, principally Phil Pollack, my archivist and co-editor. The other editor was Rosemary Coffey who prepared the final version of each chapter, making numerous improvements along the way. The copy editors for specific chapters included Deirdre Barrett, Etzel Cardeña, Leslie Combs, Suzanne Engelman, David Feinstein, Jim Hickman, Jim Jachim, Mason Peck, André Percia de Carvalho, Chris Ryan, Linda Riebel, Terje Simonsen, Ian Wickramasekera II, and Tobi Zausner. Technical assistance was provided by Scott Carpenter, Paris Duvall, and Michelle Piper. Additional gratitude goes to Jean Fox who facilitated various components of this publication. Special thanks goes to University Professors Press and its staff, notably Louis Hoffman, Steve Pritzker, and Shawn Rubin. I am profoundly grateful to Robert Frager, who created the impetus for me to begin the process. I also acknowledge the assistance I received on the Internet from Wikipedia and similar sources. Finally, I would like to thank Zohara Hieronimus, founder of The Ruscome Community, Inc., which has supported my work for many years, as well as Steven Halpern, Mary Stowell, and Richard and Connie Adams.

Foreword

The Nonlinear Dynamical Life of Stanley Krippner

Nonlinear dynamics, which includes chaos theory and complexity theory, is the study of systems that do not follow a straight line, never exactly repeat themselves, may appear chaotic, are unpredictable, and yet may keep their approximate form throughout constant change. This theory, which can be applied to the study of living organisms, describes the remarkable nonlinear dynamical life of Dr. Stanley Krippner.

In chaos theory, a profound change is marked by a bifurcation point to a new trajectory. Every chapter in this book begins with this type of sudden transformation that Krippner identifies as a "day my life changed." These bifurcations show the power of pivot points in daily life. In one chapter, the bifurcation point was an unfortunate family event.

As Krippner says, "it all started with the tragic news of my Uncle Max's death." He had a strong precognition about his uncle's sudden and unexpected passing moments before his tearful mother received the news by phone. This bifurcation point produced an entirely new world view. At that instant, Krippner recognized there were profound differences between unusual physical events with mainstream scientific explanations and anomalous phenomena that appeared to defy the known laws of physics.

Another aspect of chaos theory is sensitivity to initial conditions, which states that even a slight change at a crucial moment in a nonlinear system, such as a human being, can have lasting and profound consequences. Popularly called the *Butterfly Effect*, it comes from the meteorological work of Edward Lorenz, who said that a butterfly flapping its wings in Brazil could theoretically produce tornados in Texas.

Sensitivity to initial conditions appears in Krippner's insightful response to foreknowledge of his uncle's unexpected death. Realizing that experiences such as precognition and other forms of extrasensory perception (ESP) "were part of the human condition and worthy of serious study," Krippner went on to become one of the world's leading scholar/investigators of anomalous phenomena, eventually achieving directorship of the Dream/ESP Project at Maimonides Medical Center in Brooklyn, New York.

In chaos theory, fractals are sets of self-similar, size invariant, repeating patterns that retain their original proportions, no matter how large or small they may be. In mathematics, fractals are exact replicas of one another, like the fractals of a Mandelbrot set, yet in living systems, fractals are more approximate. They are like the fractal pattern of leaves on a tree or trees that fractally create a forest. In psychological processes, fractals are even more approximate. They can emerge, grow, and extend through time, sometimes producing intergenerational occurrences.

The fractal of compassionate action is a recurring pattern in Stanley Krippner's behavior. Modeled by his mother's concern for others, Krippner displayed acts of empathy and compassion throughout his life. On a segregated Virginia bus, Krippner gave his seat to a black woman who was pregnant, despite the angry bus driver who wanted her to remain standing; this incident led to his efforts to hasten desegregation in the Richmond public schools. The fractal of compassionate action also reveals itself through his strong history of activism, not only in protesting the War in Vietnam, but in promoting women's rights, the therapeutic use of psychedelics, the rights of LGBTQ people, AIDS awareness and prevention, and railing against antisemitism, among many other notable causes.

Krippner's activism can be modeled by complexity theory, which is the part of nonlinear dynamics that studies complex systems from molecules to biological and social aggregates. Here, multiple interacting variables organize themselves into a dynamic whole whose sum is far greater than its parts. Complexity theory models Krippner's interests in activism and altered states of consciousness as overlapping sets and interacting complex systems. Krippner's activist approach to the academic study of hypnosis and altered states of consciousness, made them more acceptable to mainstream science and accessible promoting mental health. As a very connected human being in complex social systems, Stanley Krippner's interactions with others changed him, changed them, and changed the world.

In nonlinear dynamics, an attractor is both an end goal toward which a system advances and the boundaries within which the system is contained. Nonlinear chaotic systems, such as human beings, are bounded by strange attractors, fluid borders that allow for growth and change while maintaining the integrity of the self. Stanley Krippner has evolved this way over his long lifetime. With a goal attractor of self-evolution and the evolution of others, Krippner sows the seeds of chaos and transformation wherever he goes.

    Tobi Zausner, PhD
    Author of *The Creative Trance: Altered States of Consciousness and the Creative Process*

Stanley Krippner's Enduring Legacy...

Stanley Krippner's influence continues to grow and expand. For a complete bibliography, a photo gallery, and information on new projects and contributions, visit Dr. Krippner's website at https://stanleykrippner.weebly.com.

Preface

Not Too Shabby!

On March 19, 2020, attempting to cope with the COVID-19 pandemic, the State of California issued an Executive Order that its residents should stay at home with very few exceptions. That is a day my life changed, as well as the lives of countless other people. In my case, it allowed me time to reflect and start writing these memoirs. One of the phrases that kept coming back to me was "not too shabby."

Apparently, that phrase first appeared in *Life* magazine in 1970. When something is "shabby," it is in a state of disrepair. When something is "not too shabby," it is fairly good, although not the best. I often use the term to describe my life incidents; although not necessarily the best that could have been hoped for, they are still "fairly good."

Of course, there are some incidents that were not shabby at all, experiences when I was "in the flow." And there were other experiences that were worse than shabby, or, in other words, they were absolute catastrophes.

For example, my life changed when I met my future wife, Lelie Harris, on July 17, 1965, and when she accepted my proposal on January 2, 1968. It changed again when she took the initiative to dissolve the marriage. But Lelie was the most private of people, and it would be an injustice to her memory to provide details of our 34-year-marriage. My life also changed when Saybrook University terminated my employment in 2019 but for various reasons I cannot discuss the termination or its conclusion.

Maybe someday someone will be able to discuss these matters in a way that does not entail untoward consequences. Until then, I hope that the days that changed my life will be of interest to my readers, and that they will find the results not too shabby.

I have titled my memoirs *A Chaotic Life,* referring to chaos theory, which postulates that a small perturbation can trigger an unpredictable chain of events. Early humans were able to create order out of this chaos, and this ability served an evolutionary purpose, helping them to survive. Indeed, their brains evolved to survive, not to find "truth," and they created myths and fables to explain such puzzling phenomena as lightning, earthquakes, plagues, childbirth, and the changes of seasons. These narratives can still be observed when one visits Indigenous people. In 1957, I read an article in *Life* magazine about a folk healer in Mexico who used mind-altering mushrooms in her practice. My fascination with that article led to several outcomes, among them a face-to-face encounter with the Mexican folk healer. Ten years later, a chance remark by a member of the Grateful Dead rock band led to an avalanche of unpredictable events, including an experiment in "dream telepathy" involving the band.

In each instance, a chaotic attractor emerged, one that guided my trajectory; in the first instance, the attractor was psychedelic science, and, in the second instance, it was dream science. Although some of my detractors would argue otherwise, my primary identification is that of a scientist. For me, the word science refers to disciplined inquiry, the organized and systematic collection, interpretation, and verification of data. Scientific inquiry involves procedures, guidelines, assumptions, and attitudes that can lead to the acquisition of knowledge. It is not perfect, but (at least in my opinion) it is the best approach to understanding and coping with the plethora of stimulation that surrounds every human, leading to the development of the most accurate worldview possible. If I were a psychotherapist, I would view life events through a different lens; the same would hold were I an artist or a member of the clergy. As an artist, I would probably see the world through an esthetic lens; as a pastor, it is likely that I would use the lens of "revelation" as laid down in "sacred scripture" and religious traditions. Neither of these frameworks appeals to me, however, as I rely on scientific methods to, in the words inscribed on a plaque designed by the University of Wisconsin's Class of 1910, engage in "fearless sifting and winnowing by which alone the truth can be found."

Chapter 1

The Ordeal of Marcia Gates
7 December 1941. A Day When My Life Changed

My parents' farm was located on Highway 12, between Cambridge and Fort Atkinson, Wisconsin. They subscribed to the *Daily Jefferson County Union*, which was published in Fort Atkinson, and the *Cambridge News*, a weekly newspaper published in Cambridge. I recall reading about the death of Sigmund Freud on September 23, 1939, which was featured on the front page of the *Union*; I suspect that it aroused my curiosity regarding dreams, the unconscious, and psychiatry. The only conversations about current events that I recall occurred during presidential elections; my father voted for Franklin Roosevelt twice, but switched to the Republican candidate, Wendell Willkie, in the 1940 elections. I do not recall family discussions about the Japanese attack on Pearl Harbor on December 7, 1941, but do recall reading about it in both newspapers. America's entry into the Second World War changed my life in many ways.

The War Effort

Some of our neighbors had sons who went into the Army and saw active duty. I was nine years old and did my part to support the war effort by collecting scrap metal; each week a cheerful fellow we called "The Junk Man" appeared to pick up what I had gathered. I added long-forgotten scraps of farm machinery to the collection and recall using a saw and hatchet to free metal from the wood to which it had been attached. I had no idea how much of the scrap metal went into the construction of weapons but suspect that truly little of it was of high-enough quality to serve the purpose. However, it did give me a feeling that I had done my part to defeat the enemy.

In addition, I put all my extra money into buying savings stamps. Once a booklet was filled, it could be converted into a war bond. The Junk Man paid me a pittance for the scrap metal I collected, and I used that money to buy savings stamps. At war's end, I decided not to cash in the war bonds as they were accumulating interest. I held on to them for decades, finally returning them when I needed the money to finance a house purchase following my marriage, in the early 1960s. The interest had accumulated, giving me almost $2,000.

I had my own vicarious experiences with war, viewing many popular patriotic films that were designed to boost morale and the war effort. I recall *So Proudly We Hail*, which depicts three heroic nurses serving in the Philippines. I also remember *Mrs. Miniver*, which depicted the triumphs and tragedies of an English family during the early days of the war. When Greer Garson won the Academy Award as best actress, she launched into a patriotic accolade that lasted seven minutes; I was listening to the ceremony on the radio. Garson's acceptance speech set a record that has yet to be broken.

A family friend, J. Leon Buchen (a professional magician known as "The Great Oscar") took me to see *This is the Army*, a star-studded musical featuring the future senator George Murphy and the future President Ronald Reagan. The film included a full-length version of "God Bless America" as well as Irving Berlin singing "This is the Army, Mr. Jones," a comical rendition of the travails of a new recruit. Buchen, who knew Irving Berlin, commented that he must have used bootblack to darken his greying hair. I recall another musical, *Thousands Cheer*, which featured even more stars, Judy Garland, Gene Kelly, and Kathryn Grayson among them, and was designed to raise and maintain the morale of U.S. troops and their families.

George Murphy also starred in another film from that era, *Bataan*, which portrayed American resistance to the Japanese invasion of the Philippines. Although the film was a commercial and critical success, it was banned in the Southern states because it depicted a racially integrated U.S. fighting force. I also recall *Mission to Moscow*, based on a best-selling book by Joseph E. Davies,[1] the wartime U.S. Ambassador to the Soviet Union. Although I did not realize it at the time, the movie was made at the request of President Franklin Roosevelt and put the U.S.S.R. in a favorable light, rationalizing the infamous "show trials" of the 1930s as a necessary attempt to rid the country of "fifth columnists." The film was not a box-office success and was soundly criticized during

---

[1] Davies, J.A. (1942). *Mission to Moscow: A Record of Confidential Dispatches to the State Department, Official and Personal Correspondence, Current Diary and Journal Entries, Including Notes and Comment Up to October, 1941.* Victor Gollancz Limited.

the years of the "Cold War" (the U.S.–U.S.S.R. confrontation). *Saludos Amigos* was another World War II film produced by Walt Disney at the request of the U.S. State Department; its goal was to acquaint Americans with their country's allies in Latin America, and it did very well at the box-office.

There were many other films from that era that I do not remember, but I had a special connection to *Bataan*, *So Proudly We Hail*, and other movies set in the Philippines. At the same time that those films were playing in U.S. movie theaters, my second cousin, Lt. Marcia Gates, a U.S. Army nurse, was languishing in a Japanese prison-of-war camp in the Philippines.

Enter Marcia Gates

Marcia Gates was my second cousin on my father's side of the family. Her parents and three siblings (including a twin sister) lived in Milwaukee until the collapse of her father's business, shortly followed by the collapse of her parents' marriage. Marcia's mother moved to Cambridge, taking her children with her, and put them all through college. In those days, there were two viable professions for female graduates, teaching and nursing; two of the girls became teachers and two—including Marcia—became nurses.

In 2011, Marcia's niece, Melissa Bowersock, published a splendid biography,[2] describing Marcia as "smart, sharp...the true partier, always up for the next dance, the next date." This is exactly how I recall Marcia when she visited our farm or when I met her at the home of my father's uncle, Carl Porter, a physician who lived in Cambridge. Marcia was cheerful, effervescent, a person who enjoyed a good joke. But Marcia wanted to see the world, so she joined the U.S. Army Nursing Corps in February 1941, hoping that she would be stationed in Europe, as she had always wanted to see Paris. However, she attained the rank of lieutenant and was assigned to the Philippines.

The Japanese invasion resulted in numerous casualties; Marcia and her unit went to the Bataan peninsula and set up a hospital that was so busy that it had to be extended into the nearby jungle. She later recalled that most of the supplies bore a date of 1917. She recalled that soldiers would come by the hospital, donate their blood to the wounded, and then return to battle. Marcia was taken prisoner with the fall of the Corregidor Island defenses in 1942 and was imprisoned in a makeshift

---

[2] Bowersock, M. (2011). *Marcia Gates: Angel of Bataan.* New Moon Publishing.

prison at Santo Tomas University in Manila. Marcia recalled that the Japanese troops thought that the nurses were similar to "geisha girls" and had to be disabused of that assumption. Once their actual role was fathomed, they were treated fairly well, at least while Japan seemed to be winning the war.

There were several worse prisoner-of-war camps, but the one at Santo Tomas posed special challenges. Marcia nursed prisoners whose health was at great risk until she fell ill with breast cancer and underwent a mastectomy. Conditions were passable in Santo Tomas until Japan started to lose the war; this was followed by a restriction of privileges and a diet consisting of rice mush, in which scraps of greens, fish, cat meat, and dog meat occasionally appeared. Marcia recalled searching for one grain of rice that had fallen to the floor in an attempt to assuage her hunger. Dysentery, beriberi, dengue fever, and malaria were rampant, and Marcia returned to nursing duty following her operation. Most of the nurses, Marcia among them, lost 30 percent of their body weight.

When General Douglas MacArthur returned to Manila, where he received word that the Japanese had been ordered to eliminate all prisoners, he sent troops to forestall the move. Marcia had been allowed to write only one letter during her years of internment, but on February 6, 1945, her name was on the War Department's list of those liberated. On the 23rd, Marcia was one of several nurses who received a letter from President Roosevelt praising their valiant service and welcoming them home.

Marcia's mother had never given up hope that her daughter was alive and well; she had even bought a cottage on Lake Ripley for Marcia's recuperation. In a letter to her mother and three sisters, Marcia described her experiences:

> The day that the army entered Manila was the greatest day of my life. It was the day we had waited for so long. I can't describe it. I'm still in a fog and numb with joy.... I keep getting up in the night and looking out of the window to see if it's true or just a dream.... I weigh 108 pounds now but it won't take long for me to gain weight. The past six months were really rugged. Several died each day of malnutrition and starvation, mostly old people. My spirits have been better than the average. I kept busy, resting only when I felt that I should. I was working in the main laboratory, which was extremely fortunate, as camp hospital nursing is very tiring.

> We worked under great difficulties on Bataan and Corregidor. I hated to leave my patients, even though the Japs were just down the road. I had charge of Ward 5, which was struck; "Tunnelitis," as we called it, was the hardest to bear. It was brought on by the lack of light and fresh air. We were moved to Santo Tomas in July and after that we just existed....
>
> There isn't a thing left in Manila, which is burning night and day. The Japs have stripped and destroyed property. If you see a picture of Army nurses, I am the one sitting on the bed, but you probably won't recognize me because I haven't had my hair cut in two years. I don't want to sleep, so much is going on, and I can hardly write, it's been so long since I've been able to.

Shortly after she was freed, a lieutenant from Marcia's hometown (Janesville, Wisconsin) came to take her to breakfast. She consumed six pancakes replete with maple syrup and gravy and drank what she called "real coffee." The lieutenant filled his helmet with water, so that Marcia could take a bath with "real soap." She was able to brush her teeth with toothpaste, even though she had forgotten what it tasted like. Later, the lieutenant brought her magazines so that she could check out "what the styles were like in the States." He gave her two "Victory bills" so that she could shop at the Army canteen, the first time she had used currency in years.

I saved several articles about Marcia. She was quoted as saying she had never thought that she would get out alive, and this is the reason why she did not collect souvenirs during her imprisonment. Two former classmates from her Cambridge, Wisconsin, high school located her and brought her copies of *The Cambridge News* that had her name on the front page.

Marcia was invited to give several talks and interviews about her ordeal; when asked what impressed her most on her return, she answered, "Freedom. Just freedom." She regaled her audiences with stories, such as when a group of prisoners bought a can of peaches for $40, when an imprisoned soldier built a radio from stolen parts, and when a Japanese soldier who molested one of the nurses was shot. In the latter instance, the Japanese soldier who had made the report was also shot; both were considered capital offenses. One newspaper article commented that the audience "couldn't seem to get enough of this slight girl who had come back to them from war."

In later interviews, Marcia advocated donating money to the Red Cross and for eligible women "to sign up for the nurses' cadet corps and help fill the vital need for more nurses in the Army and Navy." Marcia continued to say that she was "numb with joy" following her release and her return to the United States.

The Elusive Bluebird of Happiness
We were overjoyed when Marcia returned to Wisconsin; she brought me a collection of Filipino bills, overprinted with Japanese characters, that had been used as wartime currency. But Marcia was never quite the same. The joy and flamboyance that were an integral part of her personality appeared to have faded. She kept speaking of her search for "Mr. Right" and for her "bluebird of happiness." Family members thought that Marcia had found both when she married Captain Philip Hartman, whom she had met before the war commenced. They had served on opposite sides of the world, she in the Pacific and he in Europe, and reunited when they returned to the United States. The marriage was not preceded by a period of dating, and the couple soon became aware of their vastly different priorities and lifestyles; they parted after two years.

In the meantime, Marcia continued to give lectures and interviews about her wartime experience, took short-lived jobs as a nurse in California and Japan, and then returned to Wisconsin in 1954, where she joined the city health staff. I met Marcia one last time when I gave a lecture in Janesville, after which she greeted me. She seemed surprised that I remembered her so well, and I told her that she was unforgettable. She gave me a gift of hand-woven Filipino place settings that I took back to New York.

Marcia died in 1970 at the relatively youthful age of 55. I later discovered that she had become despondent and disillusioned, once attempting suicide by—in her words—"taking enough sleeping pills to kill a horse." Her mother collected all of her memorabilia, including letters and postcards she had written from overseas, and donated them to the Wisconsin Historical Society, where they are preserved in a special collection. In 2004, the Wisconsin State Department of Veterans Affairs dedicated a new residential facility in Union Grove, naming it Gates Hall. The plaque reads, "In honor of Marcia Gates, Army nurse, who provided compassionate care and selfless service to fellow servicemen and women while held captive in the Philippines during World War II." I paid Marcia tribute in the preface of my co-authored book *Haunted by Combat*, proposing that she had never fully recovered from the horrors of her internment. At that time, several observers used the term "shell shock" to describe Marcia's condition, but I soon began to use the new term, "post-traumatic stress disorder" (or PTSD). Other terms that were supplanted included "war neurosis" and "battle fatigue."

The Post-War Period

The Second World War ended on September 2, 1945, and I recall listening to the formal Japanese surrender on the radio. Massive reductions in U.S. military personnel followed, and we all hoped for an era of peace. However, the Cold War with the Soviet Union was initiated in 1947 when President Harry Truman enunciated "The Truman Doctrine" designed to "contain" Soviet expansion; it led to the founding of the North Atlantic Treaty Organization (NATO) in 1949. On June 25, 1950, North Korean troops invaded South Korea, and two days later, Truman sent U.S. naval and air force personnel to the peninsula. A few days after that he sent army troops to the front, as did some of the U.S. wartime allies, now members of the United Nations. General Douglas MacArthur, stationed in Tokyo at the time, was put in charge of the armed forces; he met with Truman in October 1950, following a brilliant military campaign that recaptured most of South Korea. However, MacArthur then invaded North Korea, the Chinese came to their ally's defense, and most of the gains were lost. MacArthur, who made several statements that contradicted official U.S. policy, was fired by Truman in 1951. I recall the intense arguments many of us engaged in at the university, where I was in the minority in supporting Truman's action.

At that time, I was a member of the Wisconsin Memorial Union Forum Committee and again found myself in the minority for supporting Dwight Eisenhower over Adlai Stevenson in the 1952 presidential campaign. In the closing weeks of the campaign, Eisenhower delivered his pledge: "I will go to Korea," a carefully crafted piece of rhetoric that had a significant role in winning the support of independent voters. One of the reasons why I supported Eisenhower was that the forthcoming truce would have been heavily criticized by voters if it occurred under Democratic leadership. In any event, Eisenhower was elected and went to Korea; the war ended in a stalemate on July 27, 1953, but was never officially ended by a peace treaty.

Soldiers suffering from "battle fatigue" were treated and sent back to the front, because it was thought that their condition was transient. This was not the case, and many combatants returned home with severe symptoms of PTSD. There were many contributing factors, such as the bitter, chilly winter months, the lack of strong public support for the war, and the inadequate training of troops—many of them simply reassigned from their bases in Japan. Once home, many of the veterans were reluctant to ask for counseling; those who did were met with practitioners who had little if any training in trauma treatment.

The Vietnam Conflict

Officially termed the "Vietnam Conflict," since there was no declaration of war, it reflected a long series of missed opportunities that could have saved numerous lives. During World War II, President Roosevelt called for the end of colonial rule in nations liberated from the Japanese. Ho Chi Minh, Vietnam's revolutionary leader during the war years, sent President Truman a telegram on February 28, 1946, in which he asked for America's support in establishing freedom from French rule, in accord with wartime declarations that promised independence for states that had been under Japanese occupation. Truman ignored the telegram, as well as subsequent requests for contact, thinking that if he objected to the return of French rule this would weaken the position of anti-Communist forces in France.

Nonetheless, the French forces were defeated in 1954, and the subsequent peace treaty divided Vietnam in two, calling for special elections in two years that would reunify the country. The date for the elections came and went; the leader of South Vietnam, Ngo Dinh Diem, feared that Ho Chi Minh would win the contest, and his decision not to cooperate was supported by President Eisenhower, who sent 500 advisors to help train the South Vietnam army. President John F. Kennedy sent even more advisors, was dismayed at the lack of leadership in South Vietnam, and reputedly agreed to the assassination of Diem, which occurred shortly before his own death. President Lyndon B. Johnson sent the first U.S. troops to Vietnam in 1965. He and his successor, Richard M. Nixon, made overtures to Ho Chi Minh, offering to provide compensation if the war could be concluded. These proposals were declined, as the Communists sensed that total victory was on the horizon. They were right; in April 1975, North Vietnam tanks entered the Presidential Palace in Saigon, as the last helicopters evacuated U.S. personnel. Ho Chi Minh had died in 1969; Saigon was renamed Ho Chi Minh City in his honor.

American losses during the Vietnam conflict exceeded 58,000, and there were additional losses of troops sent by such allies as Australia,

South Korea, the Philippines, and Thailand. Military and civilian losses among the Vietnamese exceeded three million. There were atrocities on both sides, as the Communists assassinated local leaders who supported the Americans, and U.S. troops engaged in ill-advised massacres, often not discerning who was a combatant and who was a civilian.

After joining the anti-war march in New York City, I found an even more effective way to save American lives. I was approached by the father of one of our research assistants at the Maimonides Dream/ESP Project. He asked me to meet with his son several times for counseling. After several sessions, I wrote a letter to his son's draft board, pointing out how unsuitable he would be for military service. My credentials were impressive, as I wrote on Maimonides Medical Center stationery and added PhD after my name. It worked, and I soon received other requests. I asked the young men if they wanted to be called "drug addicts," "homosexuals," or "mentally ill"—or a combination. Once they made their choice, I gave them instructions on how to behave when reporting for their exam. By writing my recommendations on Maimonides stationery, I took a great chance, since detection of my deeds would have led to my dismissal and possible imprisonment. There were psychiatrists and psychologists in New York City offering the same service for a $500 fee. I charged nothing; it was my patriotic duty. I was able to keep a dozen young men out of the army before the draft finally ended.

Enter Daniel Ellsberg
Many factors undercut public support for the conflict in Vietnam, support that had been almost universal at the beginning. The media had unparalleled access to activities in Vietnam, sometimes depicting actual scenes of combat. Thanks to television, the public also witnessed a plethora of body bags carrying the bodies of soldiers whose average age was 19 or 20. The instability of South Vietnam's government became apparent to the public, as did the lack of clear-cut objectives by American leaders. Protests became increasingly visible and drew larger and larger groups; my stepson, Bob Harris, and I participated in New York City's first major protest march in April 1967.

One cannot dismiss the role played by the publication of the so-called "Pentagon Papers,[3]" a collection of hitherto secret documents made public by Daniel Ellsberg. Ellsberg was a former Marine and Harvard graduate student who later worked as a special assistant in the Defense Department, then headed by Robert McNamara. He spent two years in South Vietnam on assignment from the State Department and joined the RAND Corporation as a strategic analyst on his return to the United States. He left RAND in 1970, joining the staff of the Center for International Studies at the Massachusetts Institute of Technology.

In 1967, Ellsberg had contributed to a top-secret analysis of documents regarding the Vietnam conflict. It was this assignment that totally changed Ellsberg's life. Information in the documents convinced him that government officials had lied to the public concerning events that led up to President Johnson's sending of U.S. troops to Vietnam, as well as his periodic reports on the war's course. Johnson offered North Vietnam a handsome monetary gift if they would cease military operations in South Vietnam, an offer that was rejected by Ho Chi Minh, who knew that his troops would win an eventual victory.

Ellsberg's tenure in Vietnam had convinced him that the war held "no promise of success," and in subsequent years he concluded that the war was "doomed" and "hopeless." Many of his colleagues who held "insider" jobs felt the same way, but felt powerless to make changes. Ellsberg began to attend anti-war events and, in August 1969, had an epiphany. He attended a meeting of the War Resisters League and heard a resister, Randy Kehler, say that he was "excited" to know that he would soon be joining his friends in prison. Kehler was referring to other members of the San Francisco War Resisters League, most of whom were already behind bars. Ellsberg left the auditorium, found a men's room, sat down on the tile floor, and began to sob uncontrollably for an hour, his life having been "split in two."

Kehler's statement left Ellsberg feeling "naked and raw," but resolved to act. It was apparent that President Richard M. Nixon would do no more than Johnson had done to conclude the war. Later in 1969, Ellsberg and a colleague began to photocopy the documents, knowing, as he wrote later, that this action "would probably put me in prison for the rest of my life." He used his security clearance to obtain—and

---

[3] Ellsberg, D. (2000). *Secrets: A memoir of Vietnam and the Pentagon Papers.* Viking/Penguin.

copy—all 7,000 pages of the "Pentagon Papers[4]" (the name that appeared on the cover of the top-secret government report). He shared portions of the report with colleagues at the Center for International Studies, with a few members of the U.S. Senate, and with a reporter from the *New York Times,* who wrote an article about the revelations.

In June 1971, the *New York Times* published the first of several sections of the Papers, and the Nixon administration issued a court order to stop further publication. The order was revoked by the U.S. Supreme Court a few weeks later and, in the meantime, Ellsberg gave a copy of the report to the *Washington Post* and later to several other newspapers. Several thousand pages of the Papers were entered into the *Congressional Record* by a sympathetic Senator, leaving members of both the Johnson and Nixon Administrations embarrassed. The result was the formation of the "White House Plumbers," a secretive group intended to prevent leaks of information. The Plumbers broke into the office of Ellsberg's psychiatrist, hoping to uncover material that would compromise his veracity. Finding nothing they could use, they left Ellsberg's file on the floor of the office, a mistake that became known much later.

Ellsberg surrendered in 1971 and faced a maximum sentence of 115 years; one of his colleagues, also arrested, faced a sentence of 35 years. The trial began in January 1973 in Los Angeles, during which the White House Plumbers break-in was revealed as well as several conversations Ellsberg had held with a government national security advisor, recorded by the FBI without a warrant. In May 1973, the presiding judge dismissed the case, calling the events "bizarre." Several members of Nixon's staff were arrested for their illegal actions, mostly related to efforts to undermine the Democratic Party. Some—including Nixon's Attorney General, John Mitchell—spent time in prison. Ellsberg continued his efforts to resist wars (this time in the Middle East), championed the actions of other whistleblowers, published another set of papers (revealing nuclear war threats and plans under most post-World War II Presidents), and received numerous accolades and awards.

It was inevitable that Ellsberg would be asked to write a first-person account of his involvement with the Pentagon Papers. In 1998, he signed a book contract and asked a few professional writers to provide him clues as to how to start his book. Their suggestions were not

---

[4] Ellsberg (2000).

helpful, and he sought the advice of a mutual friend, who told him, "Stan Krippner has written more books than anyone I know. Why don't you ask him for advice?" Ellsberg contacted me, and my advice was vastly different from the suggestions given to him earlier, which advised writing an outline, naming the chapters, and working down from there. In contrast, I suggested a "bottom-up" approach, in which he would describe one incident, just as fully as possible, polish it, and make a connection to another event. It worked, and his book *Secrets* became a best-seller.

I told only two close friends about our conversation, considering my discussion with Ellsberg to be confidential. However, in October 2002, I celebrated my 80th birthday at the home of Ingrid Kepler-May, in Berkeley. She invited the guests to briefly mention an encounter with me that was especially meaningful to them. Daniel Ellsberg told the group that I had been immensely instrumental in helping him begin writing his memoir. This came as a total surprise to everyone in the group, except the friend in whom I had confided years before. In the meantime, I was pleased that I had been of some small help in documenting Ellsberg's release of the Papers, an event that played a role in ending the war and saving both American and Vietnamese lives.

Coming Home from War

Upon returning to the United States, troops did not discover a hero's welcome. Instead, they were insulted, spat upon, and called "baby-killers." Some of this was due to the fact that they did not return as members of a larger force, as had been true at the end of the Second World War. They came back individually, with only family and loved ones to meet them if they were lucky. There were few benefits, unlike the rewards given to World War II veterans that spurred education, jobs, and an era of prosperity. Instead, the post-Vietnam economic malaise coincided with films that gave less than flattering portrayals of the war, *Coming Home* and *The Deer Hunter*, among them. Some of these films portrayed veterans with mental health problems such as PTSD.

PTSD was a term that was coined some five years after the U.S. withdrawal from Vietnam, a diagnosis applied to an estimated half-million service personnel. The third edition of the American Psychiatric Association's *Diagnostic and Statistical Manual of Mental Disorders*[5] defined it as a "fear-based anxiety disorder," characterized by half a

---

[5] American Psychiatric Association (1980). *Diagnostic and Statistical Manual of Mental Disorders* (3rd ed.).

dozen behavioral and emotional symptoms that last for at least six months. It supplanted earlier terms, which inferred that the person had a "neurosis" of some type, resulting from an internal weakness. Instead, *DSM-3* linked the condition to a stressor that was outside the range of ordinary human experiences, such as combat, rape, torture, internment in death camps, vehicle accidents, or natural disasters like floods, fires, and earthquakes. This reframing was very important in lifting some of the stigma that returning veterans faced. Emotional numbing was a prominent symptom, as were hyperarousal, "flashbacks," sleep disorders, and recurrent nightmares in which the trauma was re-experienced. As soon as I read this description, I connected the dots; the PTSD term described the changes we had noticed in Marcia following her return to the United States.

Because of my interest in the topic, I was invited to serve as an advisor to two groups of Vietnam veterans who had banded together to deal with PTSD: the Olympia Institute and Flower of the Dragon. These support groups counteracted the abysmal treatment of veterans, something I found personally abhorrent. My observations led to an article I wrote in 1989 with the director of the Olympia Institute, "Multi-cultural methods of treating Vietnam veterans with PTSD." One of my graduate students, Daryl Paulson, asked me to write an introduction to his book *Walking the Point*, his first-person account of PTSD and how he had to develop his inner resources to keep from killing himself.[6] In 2006, Paulson and I co-authored a paper, "PTSD among US combat veterans," for the volume *Mental Disorders of the New Millennium*.[7] That chapter led to an invitation for the two of us to author the book *Haunted by Combat: Understanding PTSD in War Veterans*,[8] published in 2007 and updated in 2010.[9] In 2018, I co-authored an article on humanistic

---

[6] Krippner, S. (1994). Foreword. In D. S. Paulson, *Walking the point: Male initiation and the Vietnam experience* (pp. ii–iv). Distinctive Publishing.

[7] Krippner, S., & Paulson, D. S. (2006). Posttraumatic stress disorder among U.S. combat veterans. In T. G. Plante (Ed.), *Mental disorders of the new millennium: Public and social problems* (Vol. 2, pp. 1–23). Praeger.

[8] Paulson, D., & Krippner, S. (2007). *Haunted by combat: Understanding PTSD in war veterans including women, reservists, and those coming back from Iraq*. Praeger Security International.

[9] Krippner, S., & Paulson, D. S. (2010). Epilogue: Still haunted. In D. S. Paulson & S. Krippner, *Haunted by combat: Understanding PTSD in war veterans* (pp. 149–174). Rowman & Littlefield.

and existential approaches in PTSD treatment for the book *Humanistic Psychology: Current Trends and Future Prospects.*[10]

Because I am not a clinical psychologist or a psychotherapist, I took care to author these articles in tandem with practitioners who had the authoritative credentials. This was especially important when I was asked to draft a book about PTSD for a series, "Biographies of a Disease.[11]" I enlisted the aid of Daniel Pitchford and Jeanine Davies,[12] the latter yet another former student who also had clinical expertise. In this book and other writing I did on the topic, I frequently referred to Marcia Gates, giving her credit for spurring my interest in the topic.

My co-authors and I made no great innovations in our books and articles on the topic, but did stress the importance of "post-traumatic strengths." We also emphasized the importance of dealing with PTSD nightmares, perhaps as the first step in treatment rather than the last. We described several methods of working with nightmares, such as "Imagery Rehearsal Therapy," which encouraged people to produce different endings to the nightmare, endings that were therapeutic rather than conflicted. For example, a veteran who had inadvertently killed a girl carrying a doll, mistaking the doll for a grenade, could imagine going back to Vietnam, apologizing to her family, telling them "something inside of me died, too," and vowing to work on behalf of abused children in their daughter's memory.

As often as I could, I described an intervention developed in Hawaii by Richard Sword, a former student, and his wife, Rose. They had read Philip Zimbardo's work on past/present/future time frameworks, discovering that their own clients typically showed a negative past, a fatalistic present, and a negative future.[13, 14] Treatment included several activities to shift all "time perspectives" to something positive. They received a grant to apply their model to a group of veterans, who not

---

[10] Krippner, S., & Pitchford, D. (2018). Humanistic and existential approaches in the treatment of PTSD. In R. House, D. Kalish, & J. Maidman (Eds.), *Humanistic psychology: Current trends and future prospects* (pp. 174–185). Routledge.

[11] Krippner, S., Pitchford, D. B., & Davies, J. (2012). *Post-traumatic stress disorder: Biographies of disease.* Greenwood/ABC-CLIO.

[12] Davies, J. A., & Pitchford, D. B. (Eds.). (2015). *Stanley Krippner: A life of dreams, myths, and visions.* University Professors Press.

[13] Zimbardo, P., Sword, R. K. M., & Sword, R. M. (2012). *The time cure: Overcoming PTSD with the new perspective of Time Perspective Psychotherapy.* John Wiley & Sons.

only reduced their number of PTSD symptoms but did so with no divorces and no suicides.

I also drew upon my background in general semantics to point out the problem with the term "traumatic event": The *event* is not traumatic; rather it is the *experience* triggered by the event that is traumatic. I drew upon Albert Ellis's statement that "It is not our outer events or circumstances that will create happiness; rather it is our perception of our events or of ourselves that will create, or uncreate, positive emotions.[15]" At most, an event can be "potentially traumatizing," as two people can react to the exact same event in vastly diverse ways.

In 2013, the fifth edition of the *Diagnostic and Statistical Manual of Mental Disorders*[16] spelled out causes and symptoms in greater detail, reclassifying PTSD as a "trauma and stressor-related disorder," and my subsequent writing used this definition as well. It is possible that I would have learned about PTSD without reflecting on my Cousin Marcia's ordeal and changed behavior. But would I have felt impelled to devote so much time and energy to alleviating this type of human suffering? Who knows? Nonetheless, I am gratified that my books on the topic have received better reviews from mainstream journals (including the prestigious *New England Journal of Medicine*) than my books on any other topic.

---

[15] Ellis, A., & Joffe Ellis, D. (2019). *Rational Emotive Behaviour Therapy.* American Psychological Association (p. 3).
[16] American Psychiatric Association (2013). *Diagnostic and Statistical Manual of Mental Disorders* (5th ed.).

Chapter 2

On Wisconsin!
2 September 1950. A Day When My Life Changed

> On Wisconsin! On Wisconsin!
> Plunge right through that line!
> Run the ball clear down the field,
> A touchdown sure this time![1]

The University of Wisconsin "fight song," written in 1909, was hailed as the ultimate fight song by John Philip Sousa, the renowned "American March King." It was originally written for a Minnesota contest, but its author was persuaded to give it to his alma mater instead. In 1919, it was adapted to become a state anthem and was officially recognized as such in 1959. The call "On Wisconsin!" dates back to the Civil War, when "On Wisconsin!" was Lt. General Arthur MacArthur's rallying call during the Battle of Chattanooga. MacArthur was the father of General of the Army Douglas MacArthur, another famous Wisconsinite. I had many opportunities to sing the song because I purchased season tickets for the football season every year I was at the university.

Leaving Home

On September 2, 1950, my father and I left home for Madison, where I had a room reserved in Frankenberger House, one of the university dormitories. There was no space for my mother to join us because my effects took up the entire back seat of his Nash automobile, but she gave us a cheery goodbye. My grandmother, Hattie Krippner, in contrast, was in tears. She was well aware of both the physical and symbolic import of the event.

Once we reached the dormitory, we began to unpack and soon were joined by other students, almost all of whom were freshmen, too. After

---

[1] Beck, W., & Purdy, C. (1909). *On, Wisconsin!* (song). Hillison, McCormack & Company

an early supper, my father left in order to get home before dark. I strolled around the campus, identifying the buildings in which I would be attending classes. I discovered a group of "temporary" buildings, most of them Quonset huts, constructed to provide classroom space for the World War II veterans who doubled the university enrollment at the end of the Second World War. These "temporary" structures remained in use during my four years at the university. I also discovered that the dormitory dining hall would open early, as some students—myself included—had 7:30 AM classes.

My roommate, Joe Hartz, arrived, as did a high school classmate, Glen Kaufman, who was assigned a room on the same floor as mine. Joe eventually joined a fraternity and was replaced by Dale Miller, who, in turn, was replaced by Gunter Laangebeck, an exchange student from Germany. My dormitory counselor discussed Gunter's placement with me, thinking I would especially enjoy keeping company with an overseas student, and he was right. After one semester, Gunter found another roommate and was replaced by Phil Reukert, a distant relative who had just begun classes at the university. He dropped out after a few months, much to my regret. Eventually, my request for a single room was granted, and I remained in Frankenberger Hall for the remainder of my stay at the university.

In the meantime, Glen's roommate, Hugh Burdick, introduced us to Tom Chalkley, a friend of his from Lake Geneva, Wisconsin, as well as to Larry Wiesner, another student from Lake Geneva. The four of us became a cohort with similar interests. We often double dated or triple dated and held parties at the home of Larry's brother, Warren Wiesner, a Madison resident, and his wife, Mary. Those parties continued even after Larry dropped out of school to join the Navy, and after Hugh dropped out to become a master repairperson for pipe organs, a unique occupation that was greatly in demand and did not require a college degree.

Frankenberger House was one of four dormitories in a quadrangle, known as the "Quad." Don Taylor was assigned housing in another Quad dormitory, and we soon made contact. I had met Don during my high school years at Presbyterian Church camps and also when Glen and I represented Fort Atkinson High School at "Badger Boys' State," a week-long program for young men whom adults deemed potential "future leaders." Don's political talents were obvious at Boys' State, where he became campaign manager for the "governor" of the state. His candidate was professionally qualified, gregarious, and a fine speaker. However, his opponent was African American, and Don shaped his candidate's campaign around a plea to ignore skin color! It did not work. I voted for the African American candidate, seeing the historic significance of the occasion. But Don's candidate went on to "Boys' Nation" as runner-up and was elected "president." In the meantime, I lost a local election, which was no surprise to me, given that I had lost every election in high school when I had been nominated for a class office.

There was a Quad post office, whose clerk was kept busy with numerous requests. Most of us had sturdy containers that we used to mail home our laundry when we needed clean clothes. My mother was very obliging, even though I felt bad for the extra work involved. But one day another student, Larry Levy, told me that he had a service that could do my laundry for a reasonable price, and I was happy to give him some business. Larry and I stayed connected, and years later he embarked on a remarkable career as a film and television director as well as an author. His wife, Marilyn, is the author of numerous well-reviewed books, and all of us have stayed connected over the decades.

Some of my fellow students knew that my aunt, Gertrude Munson, her daughter, and her daughter's family lived in Madison and thought that I should have had them pick up my laundry. To do so would have violated my ethics, as I never tried to take advantage of family members or burden them with requests that were better served by others.

Integrated Liberal Studies
When I was a high school senior, a recruiter from the University of Wisconsin spoke to several of us. Because my parents had already decided to send me to the university, the recruiter devoted his time to discussing several options, one of which was the Integrated Liberal Studies program or ILS. This program offered an interdisciplinary series of courses designed to meet the university's required "depth courses." Faculty members worked together to provide some coherence in the three basic areas covered—the natural sciences, the social sciences, and the humanities. Its precursor was a two-year experimental college organized by Alexander Meiklejohn that ran from 1927 to 1932, when it became a victim of the Great Depression as well as its own radicalism, unique for its time. I quickly decided to take this option, as did my friend Glen, and it was a wise decision.

During my two years in ILS, I became close friends with such outstanding professors as Walter Agard, who introduced us to the ancient Greek classical literature, and who founded the "Stick-Out-Your-Neck Club" that encouraged students to take unpopular positions in the face of the conformity of that time. I also befriended Robert Pooley, who introduced us to English literature, Paul Wiley, who introduced us to American literature, and Aaron Ihde, who taught the natural science courses. One of the social science courses was General Semantics, which was one of my most memorable classes. Our required text was *Language in Thought and Action* by S.I. Hayakawa, and I used what I had learned about general semantics throughout my professional career.[2]

Another social science course traced the interaction of geography and culture throughout history. I wrote an essay titled, "Why Portugal?" in which I asked why Portugal became one of the first European nation-states, when the rest of the Iberian Peninsula remained divided. My answer was that the Portuguese early developed a sense of identity, due in part to their expulsion of the Moors in 1249 (some 250 years before the invaders were expelled from the rest of the peninsula) and a long-standing monarchy that established an alliance with England in 1386, the longest standing European alliance. There were other factors, such as the boundary set, in part, by the Tagus River, and a long-standing distrust of Spain. The teaching assistant for the course was so impressed with my essay that he arranged for me to meet Professor Richard Hartshorne, perhaps the country's leading political geographer. Hartshorne took special interest in my translation of old Portuguese historical records on file in the university library. While I was enrolled in ILS, I took two years of Portuguese to fulfill the language requirements, required at that time by the university. This was a wise decision. During my professional career, I was able to use Portuguese on my several trips to Portugal and Brazil, sometimes delivering part of my lectures in that language.

Theater and Forensics
The university offered a wide array of extra-curricular activities. Always interested in the theater, I volunteered to paint backdrops for the Wisconsin Union Theater's production of *Ethan Frome*, a theatrical adaptation of the celebrated novel by Edith Wharton. Coincidentally,

---

[2] Hayakawa, S. I. (1949). *Language in thought and action.* Harcourt, Brace.

the play was re-created on radio a few weeks after it was performed at the university.

I interviewed for *Something Human*, a production in the small Wisconsin Union Play Circle. It was one of three prize-winning student-written plays, and the reviewer for *The Daily Cardinal* hailed it as "the best of the lot." I was cast as Ned McCoy, a maintenance worker who installs a switchboard for a small community, essentially putting the long-time telephone operator out of business. I had a total of 18 lines but it was enough to provide me a first-hand theatrical experience and to appreciate the directorial skills of Terry Wells, who went on to become a successful director in New York City.

In high school, Glen and I had been members of the debate and forensics team, going to various parts of the state for tournaments. We continued this work at the University, participating in discussions on such topics as the "Communist threat," the presidential primaries and campaign, and the claims that Communists had infiltrated the government proffered by Senator Joseph McCarthy (another Wisconsinite). Once again, we traveled to various parts of the state for these events, finding them quite stimulating, especially when we were asked to take the opposite side of an issue for which we had taken our preferred stance. In Milwaukee, Glen and I won a debate on a "counterplan to end all counterplans," a controversial proposal for high-level integration of government services. Our group also attended a regional tournament in Iowa City where we won a few and lost a few. My most notable achievement occurred at a Big Ten Discussion Tournament on April 7, 1954, when I received the highest score of any Wisconsin participant and the third highest score for the entire group of participants. After Glen moved on to work in the university's theatrical productions, I partnered with Don Taylor, with whom I won three out of four debates at a tournament at the University of Illinois. During a practice debate, Don and Jerry Lepp took different sides regarding the positive effects of McCarthy and McCarthyism. My sentiments were with Jerry but I did think that Don had put the best possible face on a phenomenon that was both grotesque and harmful.

My record sufficed to win me membership in a national forensic fraternity, and in 2021 I was approached by the Wisconsin Speech and Debate program, requesting my reminiscences, which I was happy to provide. I was delighted to hear that its activities had expanded over the decades to become of one the nation's leading forensic programs.

The Wisconsin Union Forum Committee

In 1927, the Wisconsin Student Union was initiated by Porter Butts, known as the "godfather of the student union movement," who went on to advise dozens of other student unions, both in the United States and abroad. Activities are initiated and supervised by the Union Directorate, in which students play the leading role. On March 27, 1952, I interviewed for membership on both the Union Forum Committee and the Union Film Committee and was accepted by both. I chose the Forum Committee, which proved to be a felicitous choice as I ended up becoming chair of the committee. I was able to meet and interact with the public figures we invited to speak at the university, among them Frank Lloyd Wright, Eleanor Roosevelt, former United Nations Secretary-General Trygve Lie, historian Arthur Schlesinger, Jr., political columnist Marquis Childs, novelists James T. Farrell and John Dos Passos, author and columnist William F. Buckley, Jr., British diplomat Sir Roger Makins, anthropologist John Gillim, parapsychologist J. B. Rhine, six-time Socialist presidential candidate (and Presbyterian minister) Norman Thomas, and anthropologist William McGovern. We also invited Supreme Court Justice William O. Douglas and biologist Sir Julian Huxley, both of whom accepted, and I returned to the campus the following year to join committee members for dinners and their lectures.

Thomas and McGovern were opponents in the committee's Wisconsin Union Debates, which the previous committee chair, Robert Tehan, and I organized. It staged free monthly debates that drew respectable numbers, even in the time of what is known as the "Silent Generation." The debates linked two well-known speakers with two university students; for example, Gaylord Nelson, a member of the state legislature, and his partner won the debate on vote reapportionment; Nelson went on to become a U.S. Senator and to create what is now a national holiday, Earth Day. When McGovern and Thomas debated the proposition "Resolved: That the United States implement a policy of socialism," Thomas and his partner narrowly won the debate when the show of hands was counted.

A few years later, I heard Norman Thomas speak in Chicago and reminded him of our previous meeting, which he was gracious enough to acknowledge. During his presentation, Thomas remarked that the happiest day of his long life was January 20, 1953, when Dwight Eisenhower was inaugurated as U.S. President. As Thomas listened to his inaugural address, it became clear to him that Eisenhower was not about to curtail the human welfare programs that had been a part of Roosevelt's New Deal or Truman's Fair Deal. In fact, he intended to broaden them.

My three years on the Forum Committee were to leave a lasting impression. I learned how to become at ease with celebrated men and women from various occupations. I learned how to organize large-scale events. I learned how to coordinate a team that often consisted of people with different opinions and backgrounds from my own. And I learned how to do my homework, so that I could speak intelligently with our distinguished guests. On one occasion, I found myself in disagreement with a speaker—namely, John Dos Passos, whose *U.S.A.*[3] trilogy ranked (in my opinion) with *Huckleberry Finn, Moby Dick,* and *The Great Gatsby* as "The Great American Novels." Later in his career, Dos Passos was criticized for making an apparent political reversal, but he maintained that he had always held libertarian positions and that it was politics that had changed, not him.

Anne Minahan was an invaluable asset to our committee, keeping us out of trouble and assisting our endeavors. For example, she helped us secure a display case in the Wisconsin Union lounge for an exhibit that highlighted Dos Passos' career, including his work as an ambulance driver during World War I, his defense of the anarchists Nicola Sacco and Bartolomeo Vanzetti, and his membership in the American Committee for the Defense of Leon Trotsky (a group chaired by the philosopher John Dewey and joined by the socialist Norman Thomas, the philosopher Sidney Hook, the theologian Reinhold Niebuhr, and others). Sacco and Vanzetti were executed, and Trotsky was assassinated, but Dos Passos felt the struggle had been worthwhile. He frequently described the United States as being "two nations," one rich and one poor, and many of his writings focus on this theme, especially in his *DC* trilogy, a follow-up to his *U.S.A.* trilogy.

Dos Passos' lecture was an erudite account of the role played by Thomas Jefferson in the founding of the Republic and the need for a decentralized "bottoms up" policy on governmental services. But in private conversation, Dos Passos expressed his admiration for Joseph McCarthy and his extravagant claims of Communist infiltration of the federal government. Another student and I took Dos Passos to task, explaining how most of McCarthy's allegations were unfounded and actually were undercutting the very foundations of the democracy that

---

[3] Dos Passos, J. (1937). *U.S.A.* Modern Library.

Dos Passos had just described. Taken aback, Dos Passos could not offer a counterattack that made sense. Instead, he promised to consider our position and would visit Washington, DC, and observe McCarthy in action at the public hearings of his subcommittee. I discovered later that Dos Passos' ardor for McCarthy dissipated once he had seen him interrogate witnesses.

Dos Passos' perspective was diametrically opposed to that of our other literary luminary, James T. Farrell, the author of the Studs Lonigan and Bernard Carr trilogies and the Danny O'Neil quintopoly. Farrell was a supporter of Norman Thomas's bids for the Presidency and an unabashed opponent of Senator McCarthy's machinations. Norman Mailer once recalled immersing himself as an undergraduate in works by both Dos Passos and Farrell, leading to his winning a competition that cemented his desire to become a writer. The Modern Library ranked *U.S.A.* as the 23rd best novel of the 20th century and *Studs Lonigan* as the 29th.[4] I had read all six books and heartily agreed with their high rankings.

Farrell's lecture focused on pornography and censorship. I designed a post that featured a sensuous woman in a slit skirt, triggering alarm in some quarters. However, it served the purpose, and Farrell did not disappoint his audience. Farrell asked me why he didn't meet any beautiful co-eds, as he had just lectured at the University of Minnesota, where he claimed to have been entertained by a bevy of blue-eyed blonde undergraduates. I replied that what our co-eds lacked in beauty was more than compensated for by their brain power.

It was inevitable that members of our committee discussed politics with Farrell. He called Eisenhower "the Republican George Marshall. They both are dumb generals." I later discovered that Farrell had urged the Socialist Party to support the Marshall Plan, which helped to rebuild Europe following the Second World War. In retrospect, I think Farrell was right when he discussed censorship and his opposition to it, but wrong regarding his assessment of Eisenhower and Marshall.

Our committee also sponsored a number of lectures by university faculty members, held in the Library, a small venue. We invited my philosophy professor, A. Campbell Garnett, to make a presentation on the topic of science and religion; Farrington Daniels, a pioneer in solar energy, was another of our speakers.

---

[4] Farrell, J. T. (2004). *Studs Lonigan.* Library of America.

When I chaired the committee, I was invited to several memorable Union Directorate functions, including a festive banquet on October 7, 1989, honoring the 50th anniversary of the Union's founding. During this memorable event, I sat with Robert and Audrey Tehan. Robert, my predecessor as committee chair, was the son of a prominent Milwaukee judge, and we were to become lifelong friends. When he and his wife, Audrey, were married, I was invited to become a member of the wedding party. Later, we all attended the annual Beefeaters Banquet. The original Beefeaters were guards at the Tower of London, so named because part of their salary was paid in slabs of beef. The Wisconsin Union appropriated the name and the costume; I still have the statuette given to me at one of the events. I even donned a Beefeaters costume for a documentary about the Union, where I had the only speaking role—a call, "Hear Ye, Hear Ye," that brought the group to order. The film went on to win first place in a cinema documentary competition.

During my years at the university, I dated furiously—once having three dates during the same weekend. I even scored a date with Pat Flom, the most elegant girl in my classes. Glen Kaufman called her "the elite chick," and he meant it as a compliment. She met me wearing fashionable attire and carrying a pink tulip. Once we graduated, she married a millionaire and went on to live happily ever after, or so I assume. Unlike my friends, I never spent an "all-nighter" studying for an exam the next day. I spent a great deal of time in the Wisconsin Memorial Union building, especially the outdoor Terrace, the indoor Rathskeller, and the Play Circle, which brought outstanding films to the campus. My friend Glen became chair of the Union Film Committee and made sure I received tickets for popular movies. I was especially fond of *Peter Pan*, and our friend Hugh, when he manned the projection booth, made me a tape recording of the entire movie, one that I enjoyed for years afterward. An ice cream concession stand, later named "The Daily Scoop," featured concoctions from nearby Babcock Hall, many of them unique because they were being "test marketed." At the Union Craft Shop, I learned silk-screening—cutting stencils, and then applying ink that would appear only in the non-stencil areas upon printing. One year, I silk-screened dozens of Christmas cards in the craft shop, surprising the recipients who had been used to commercially produced greetings.

Not all my initiatives during my time on the Forum Committee were successful. I had been following events in the Middle East with great interest and wanted to hold a forum with students from Israel and its neighbors participating. I was able to obtain agreement from an Israeli student and three students from Egypt and Jordan. On May 12, we all held a meeting to plan the program. Much to my dismay, the group could not agree on an agenda. I suggested that they could simply present their points of view and then hold a discussion. No luck. They could not even agree on the wording that would be used to open the program, and the Israeli student walked out. The best I could do was to hold a program in which the students from Egypt and Jordan presented their perspective, and then the Israeli student responded from the audience, not from the platform. The Egyptian student told me, "That is the way they won their country, playing the underdog!" After that experience, I was never surprised when negotiations over the status of Israel and the Palestinians broke down, even after months of preparation.

Robert Tehan encouraged me to run for president of the Union Directorate, which I did, again losing an election. But my opponent, Ted Crabb, went on to succeed Porter Butts as union director, so to have lost an election to Ted was not too shabby! On May 30, 1953, I joined Ted and several members of the Union Directorate for an end-of-semester canoe trip down 36 miles of the Wisconsin River. Gretchen Hardt, a Forum Committee member, joined us at my invitation, as did Glen's girlfriend, Charlene "Char" Page.

We had a truck drive us and the canoes to a launching site north of Madison. We launched our four canoes, and the first part of the trip was scenic and placid, but then we noticed storm clouds. It began to rain, and the water became turbulent. The canoe carrying Glen and Char overturned and I heard her scream, "I can't swim! I can't swim!" Having just recently passed three swimming tests in my gym class, I jumped into the river. Despite my confidence, I found the current too strong for me to make much headway to where her head was bobbing up and down. Suddenly she said, "I can stand up!" I discovered that I could stand on the river bottom as well. Another crisis averted.

We pulled up on shore, put our wet clothes on tree branches to dry, changed into the dry clothes we had brought with us, and prepared dinner, finding enough dry wood to build a campfire. We all had sleeping bags and retired for the night. But we awakened with a start. A herd of cattle was heading straight for our encampment! Glen grabbed a large shirt from the branch where it was drying and made his best bullfighter's gestures, yelling and screaming as he did so. The cattle stopped dead in their tracks, then made a turn that avoided our campsite. Yet another crisis averted.

The next morning, we prepared breakfast and then entered the canoes for the remainder of our journey. Gretchen Hardt, another friend, and I had a sudden rush of energy, and soon outstripped the other three canoes. We arrived at the dock of the Wisconsin Memorial Union, where a crew was waiting to retrieve the canoes. We did our best to move the canoes to dry land, but Gretchen simply was not as strong as her two compatriots. The young man who was supervising the project called out to her, asking her to exert more force. Then I realized that the ordeals of the trip had left Gretchen rather unkempt, and she had been mistaken for a man! I let the crew know, and they became a bit more civil. The other canoes soon arrived, and we congratulated ourselves on completing a short but memorable journey.

A Caper

January 20, 1953, might have been the happiest day of Norman Thomas's life but it was a poignant event for Robert Tehan and the other members of the Union Forum Committee. During our next meeting, Robert asked everyone to stand up for a minute of silence to honor Adlai Stevenson, the losing candidate. Of course, I had to stand as well, but I began to plan a way to strike back. During the campaign, I paid several visits to the local "I Like Ike" campaign headquarters, signing in as a volunteer, and picking up campaign buttons, leaflets, and other paraphernalia. It was no surprise when, on November 28, I received a form letter from a federal election agency asking me to detail my contributions, which I was happy to do.

But I did not throw away the letter or the envelope that held it. Very carefully, I cut out my name as it appeared on the envelope, replacing it with a glassine patch, which I secured with glue on the reverse side. I found a typewriter with a font that closely matched the font of the letter and typed in "The Wisconsin Union Forum Committee." There was no postage stamp on the envelope because this was official government business, only the mailing date. I had a friend in the Union mailroom who placed the envelope in the Forum Committee's mailbox.

The very next day, Robert called me aside and told me about the letter, which he had taken very seriously. I said that I was not surprised, given the predominant Democratic membership of the committee but sympathized, nonetheless. He took the letter to Anne Minahan, our faculty advisor, and Porter Butts, the Union director. Butts was especially alarmed, as he had always tried to keep the Union from taking a political stance. He swore Anne, Robert, and me to secrecy. I told nobody about the letter, but the news leaked out, probably due to my friend in the mailroom, and soon the campus newspaper requested details. Even worse, one of the Madison daily newspapers (the one with a pro-Republican stance) heard about the incident and wanted to run a story to demonstrate the Democratic regime's vengeance on its opponent, who had won the presidential election.

Everything became magnified, and Porter Butts scheduled a meeting with the university president to discuss the matter. At this point, I decided that my caper had gone far enough and was getting out of control. I asked Robert if I could see the envelope and the letter, which he had been carrying with him ever since he received it. I looked at the envelope and told him that the glassine seemed to have been taped onto the envelope's inside. Robert replied that this was widespread practice in mass mailings when there is a flaw in the production line. I then pointed out how the typed font of the address was slightly different from the font of the letter itself. At this point he said, "If this is a joke, I will murder the perpetrator." I told him he would have to murder me! Robert regained his composure, started laughing, and asked me to sign the letter and the envelope so he could save them as souvenirs. Within the hour he had alerted Porter Butts, and before the end of the day all crisis points had been resolved. Members of the Forum Committee were informed and took the revelation in stride; most of them congratulated me for the ruse.

Did I regret my support of Eisenhower? My support was quite rational. Only a moderate Republican could have guaranteed the continuation of the welfare policies initiated by Roosevelt and Truman. Only a moderate Republican could have ended the Korean War without being accused of "selling out to the Communists." Only a moderate Republican could have taken steps to undercut McCarthyism. Eisenhower's success in doing so was attributed to the "hidden-handed" way he often operated. Eisenhower also initiated the Interstate Highway System, bolstered science education, sent troops to Arkansas to support racial desegregation, and left office warning about the "industrial-military complex." Surveys conducted by the American Political Science Association and similar groups usually list Eisenhower as number seven in their rankings of presidential greatness. Not too shabby!

Entering the School of Education

On August 1, I received notification that I had transferred from Integrated Liberal Studies to the School of Education, where I would begin taking courses that would prepare me for my role as a speech therapist. I began to take the required classes, learned how to administer an audiometer to check people's hearing acuity, and gave several tests, notably the Stanford-Binet, the leading "intelligence test" of its time. I recruited the children of friends and relatives, much to the surprise of my instructor, Professor Gwen Arnold, who said I had completed my quota more quickly than anyone else in the class. Another favorite professor was Gladys Borchers, who recruited me for her ambitious project "Speech Makes the World Go Around." One day Professor Arnold asked me to stay for a few minutes after class. She told me that she and Professor Borchers had been discussing me and strongly advised that I should go to graduate school. This news took me by surprise; until that moment, I had not seriously considered such a move. But she had planted the seed, which took a few years to germinate but eventually blossomed.

Professor Borchers lived past her 100th birthday, as did Professor Warren Southworth, from whom I took several courses in health education, which was my minor concentration. At that time, I was kept busy seeing clients in the speech and hearing clinic, diagnosing several types of articulation problems, and learning about special needs of those with cerebral palsy, cleft palates, and mental challenges. Special attention was given to those who stutter, approximately one percent of the adult population. We were taught the differences between speech repetitions, prolongations, and stoppages. My background in general semantics was helpful; Wendell Johnson, a prominent leader in the field, had pointed out that giving a child the label of "a stutterer" added to the problem. It is made worse when well-meaning adults tell the child to "slow down," "speed up," or "think before you speak." Johnson advised patience and avoiding bringing ordinary dysfluencies to the child's attention, noting that at least five percent of children repeat or prolong words and that societies that have no word for "stutterer" lack individuals who would be labeled thus by other societies. One of our classmates had received a grant to administer an experimental drug to his "stuttering" clients, a procedure that most of us found doubtful. I used two different approaches—having clients sing, and having them speak to animals and young children. Both approaches appeared to break the pattern and give them confidence that they could speak fluently.

A close friend in those days was Honey Swinder, who took the same speech therapy classes that Glen and I took. She helped to host J. B. Rhine during his Forum Committee appearance and kept in touch with him, often sharing family experiences that seemed to have parapsychological implications. He graciously answered all her letters and carved out time to meet with her and her family when they visited North Carolina. Honey and I took several courses with Professor Harvey Irwin, one of our favorite instructors. We were appalled to find out that he supported Senator McCarthy's attempts to "purge" the government of "spies" and "Commie sympathizers." After class, we regularly took him to task, and were surprised to discover that we were better informed than he was. When McCarthy was censured by the U.S. Senate, Professor Irwin finally relented—but maintained that there had been a need for "a McCarthy," as he was still impacted by the "Red Scare." Neither Honey nor I claimed that there had been no attempt by the U.S.S.R to influence American policy, but that other government agencies had identified and removed the suspects. And that is where the controversy ended when we graduated in 1954.

One of the most prominent members of the department was Professor Fred Haberman, the man who had judged our high school forensics contest in 1949. He had liked my presentation, but observed my lateral lisp, noting that I said "thcool" instead of "school" and "Thanley" instead of "Stanley." He showed me the correct placement of my tongue, and within a few weeks I had made the correction. Earlier, I had been puzzled when some of my classmates teased me and imitated me. My mother insisted that the speech pattern was "a Norwegian brogue," and thought nothing of it. But the short lesson changed my life for the better and was pivotal in my decision to become a speech therapist so that I could help others.

I took one class with Professor Haberman, which gave me another chance to thank him for changing my life. I received an "A plus" from him for my talk on McCarthy and McCarthyism, and later he gave a memorable address when President Truman relieved General MacArthur of his command during the Korean War. MacArthur returned to the United States and was invited to address Congress, ending his talk by citing an army ballad, "Old soldiers never die, they just fade away." Haberman quoted one attendee who stated, "We have heard God speak to us today," and another who called the talk "demonic." Haberman's presentation was brilliant and set a standard that few others of my professors have ever matched. It also reflected MacArthur's mixed legacy. Personally, I agreed with Truman, feeling that MacArthur's intent to broaden the war actually lengthened it because Truman was about to negotiate a truce. However, I gave MacArthur credit for advising Presidents Eisenhower, Kennedy, and Johnson to avoid a major military intervention in Vietnam, advice that the latter two Presidents did not heed, with disastrous results.

One of my classes involved "practice teaching," and we were given a list of possibilities. I noticed that one option was teaching Sunday School at the Unitarian Church, one of Frank Lloyd Wright's memorable creations. I reported for duty, became a popular instructor, and continued with the class until April 30, 1954, just as I was about to leave Madison. I met the Reverend Max Gaebler, longtime pastor of the church, and we continued our friendship for years. My classes consisted of various discussions ranging from the history of the Unitarian movement to Eastern philosophies. I covered Biblical times, the origins of Christianity, the Catholic Inquisition, the Protestant Reformation, and much more. My students were all boys in their early teens—and I had to keep things active, or they would become bored and start to pester one another. I attempted to bring each lesson into their lives, asking how what I had related could affect their lives and beliefs. Most of their parents were university professors who were members of the congregation and attended services fairly regularly. One student, Daniel Mermin, stayed connected with me for years, crediting me, in part, for his decision to become a clinical psychologist. Another student, Larry Clinard, remained behind following my last class to wish me a personal goodbye. The following year, his father, Professor Marshall Clinard, informed me that Larry had died of a rare blood disease. Later, I used Professor Clinard's book on alienation as my text for a course on the topic that I taught at New York University. I visited him and his wife at their home in Santa Barbara, California, and we remained friends until his death.

When I entered the School of Education, my advisor suggested that I opt for a Bachelor of Sciences degree (B.S.) rather than a Bachelor of Arts degree (B.A.), as it would look better on my record. We planned my curriculum accordingly, and I was grateful for the advice. Over the years, I followed the activities of what became the Department of Communication Science and Speech Disorders, which soon was acclaimed as one of the best programs in the country. Currently, students can opt for either a B.A. degree or a B.S. degree, which have slightly different requirements. My advisor's efforts to provide me (and others) with a B.S. degree apparently laid the groundwork for this achievement.

In retrospect, my four years at the University of Wisconsin laid a foundation for most of my future activities. The Integrative Liberal Studies curriculum kept me from taking specialization courses too quickly and introduced me to both the humanities and the sciences. My forensic activities helped me to think quickly, to see various aspects of a controversial topic, and to speak clearly enough to be easily understood. The Union Forum Committee provided me with an opportunity to interact comfortably with celebrated men and women—despite our age and status differences. My teaching stint at the Unitarian Church helped solidify my religious convictions while providing me with the challenge of harnessing the attention of a group of bright but rowdy students. My course in General Semantics yielded a bonanza of gifts, insights that I have used ever since. My specialization courses segued into my first post-university job, namely, as a speech therapist for three public schools in northern Illinois. My work in the theater gave me insights into the massive preparations needed to pull off a memorable production, something I put to effective use when I directed the junior and senior class play for one of the aforementioned schools. Finally, I made long-lasting friendships that I cherished for the rest of my life.

On Wisconsin! My touchdowns were metaphorical in nature, but I often "plunged right through that line!"

Chapter 3

The Wisconsinites
29 October 1952. A Day When My Life Changed

Ever since I can remember, I have been proud to have been a "Wisconsinite," taking special delight when a fellow Wisconsinite was mentioned in the news. I made special efforts to see several of them in person when they appeared on stage, notably such entertainers as Don Ameche, Tyne Daly, Liberace, the "Incomparable Hildegard," and the iconic actor and director Alfred Lunt, whom I saw with his wife, Lynn Fontanne, in "The Great Sebastians" and "The Visit." Liberace acknowledged Hildegard's influence on him as the pioneer of both one-name entertainers and elegant costumes, calling her "perhaps the most famous supper club entertainer of all time." Both were from Wisconsin!

Enter Jack Carson

I attended the State Fair in Madison every year, helping my father enter his apples in one of the many agricultural contests. I even kept a collection of the blue, red, and yellow ribbons he would win. One year was especially memorable because Jack Carson, a prominent actor, had promised to make a guest appearance. Having made sure that we were in the audience, I was able to photograph Carson as he left the stage, entered an automobile, and was whisked away. Since he was the first Hollywood actor I had seen in person, I followed his career until his death in 1963. Born in Canada, he moved to Milwaukee when he was young. Carson attained success as a comedian while also winning acclaim for his dramatic roles in *A Star Is Born* and *Cat on a Hot Tin Roof*. He has two stars on the Hollywood Walk of Fame, one each for his film and his television work. In 1944, he had a central role in the black comedy *Arsenic and Old Lace*, a play later condensed into a 10-minute version that I performed in a high school dramatic contest in 1949. I also directed the play in 1955, when I worked in the public schools in Warren, Illinois. I took great satisfaction with this production because I found parts for everyone who auditioned, including one student whose voice could hardly be heard becoming a dead body. More girls than boys auditioned, so I turned all the policemen into policewomen.

Jack Carson made several films with Dennis Morgan, including "wo Guys from Milwaukee, a city regarded by both men as their hometown. Morgan was a popular romantic lead in such musicals as *The Desert Song* and *My Wild Irish Rose*, but he also played dramatic roles in *Kitty Foyle* and *In this Our Life*. In 1952, he headed a team of Hollywood cohorts (under the title of "Hollywood U.S.A.") that attempted to convince audiences movies could tell stories better than television could and that the large screen was superior to the small screen. When they stopped at the University of Wisconsin, I cut classes to hear them and to get autographs, not only from Morgan but from William Demarest, Catherine McLeod, Richard Arlen, and Adele Buffington, a co-founder of the Screen Actors Guild and a pioneering female writer with some 150 scripts to her credit. Demarest, whom I had seen in *Miracle of Morgan's Creek*, was known as a character actor and comedian who later had a successful career in television. I recall his short monologue at the event for his description of the oboe as "an ill wind that nobody plays good," not an original attribution but still clever. Richard Arlen starred in *Wings,* the first film to win an Academy Award. When I asked him about future films, he told me that he had just signed a contract to appear in half a dozen Technicolor productions. I saw several of these films, including *The Mountain,* with a cast headed by Spencer Tracy, another Wisconsinite. I also had a brief conversation with Catherine McLeod, who had starred in one of my favorite films at that time, *I've Always Loved You*. The junket had been organized to lure people away from television, but almost all the members of the group later appeared on television (or, in the case of Buffington, wrote for television). McLeod appeared not only in TV dramas but also in a commercial for Anacin, a pain medication, in which she protested, "Mother, I'd rather do it myself!"—a line for which she will always be remembered. Dennis Morgan stayed away from television because he did not think people should be able to see actors perform without paying for a ticket; he later regretted his decision.

Enter Joseph McCarthy

I did not find all famous Wisconsinites admirable, most notably Senator Joseph McCarthy, who had defeated Robert M. La Follette, Jr. in the 1946 Republican primary. McCarthy's first years in the Senate were lackluster, but in 1950 he alleged that some 200 Communists had infiltrated the State Department. I recall that, after I discussed these charges with a fellow student, Jerry Lepp, an active member of the campus Young Democrats, I adopted a "wait and see" stance. It was well considered because McCarthy never made good on most of his allegations. He went on to claim that the Voice of America and the U.S. Army had been infiltrated by Communists, the latter charge leading to the 1954 "Army–McCarthy Hearings," which I watched zealously on the public television set at the Wisconsin Union, the popular student center. At that point, I had finished most of my classwork, which gave me time not only to view the proceedings but to make sketches of the protagonists, creating an album of caricatures that would later be archived in the University of West Georgia's collection of my memorabilia.

Jerry Lepp was a prominent member of the university's Young Democrats; he brought James Roosevelt to the campus for a lecture and made a point of introducing me to him. Another of my classmates, Don Taylor, who was active in the university's Young Republicans, brought Senator McCarthy to the campus in December 1951. Taylor knew of my antipathy to McCarthy and made sure I was on hand for his speech, personally introducing us. McCarthy asked me to hold his newspaper, which he never reclaimed after his presentation. I tossed it in the trash as soon as I could, although his supporters would probably have venerated it as a treasure.

But Taylor did not give up. The following night, he took me to Milwaukee for a testimonial event honoring McCarthy. Because this was not an official campaign event, McCarthy had been warned that if he spoke he might be in violation of state law and could be prosecuted. Senator Karl Mundt and other notables spoke in praise of McCarthy, including William McGovern, a Northwestern University political science professor whom I would later befriend during my doctoral studies. Eventually, it was McCarthy's turn at the podium, and I recall his words, "My friends, my heart and my cup are both running over. I just can't speak to you tonight." Of course, it was a clever ruse to avoid prosecution.

In October 1953, Don arranged for some of us to join him for a Republican rally in Milwaukee, where we had reserved seats for Dwight Eisenhower's presidential campaign appearance. Sharing the platform was Wisconsin Governor Walter Kohler and other GOP luminaries, including McCarthy. During his presentation, McCarthy spoke of "twenty years of treason," claiming that Franklin Roosevelt and Harry Truman had allowed Communists to infiltrate the government. I recall that Eisenhower sat on his hands while others were applauding. I later discovered that Eisenhower had intended to defend his mentor, former Secretary of State George Marshall, but party leaders told him to delete that reference because he needed Wisconsin's electoral votes to win the election.

As chair of the U.S. Senate Permanent Subcommittee on Investigations, McCarthy had a platform to expand his accusations. The term "McCarthyism" was coined to refer to the practice of character assassination and unsubstantiated allegations. But taking on the U.S. Army led to his downfall, allowing millions of Americans to see how the Army's special counsel, Joseph Welch, skewered the Senator, concluding one line of questioning with the immortal phrase, "At long last, have you left no sense of decency, sir?" The ostensible reason for the hearings was to investigate whether the Subcommittee's chief counsel, Roy Cohn, had used undue influence on behalf of his unpaid assistant, David Shine, who had been drafted the previous November, to avoid the draft. The hearings, chaired by Karl Mundt, led to the conclusion that Cohn had crossed the line in demanding special privileges for Shine, but that McCarthy had not been responsible. It was a Pyrrhic victory for McCarthy; his popularity with the American public dropped, and, in December the Senate officially censured McCarthy and condemned his behavior. McCarthy continued to rail against the "Communist threat," eventually accusing hundreds of individuals of being Communists, until his death in 1957.

In retrospect, historians have concluded that there were, indeed, Communists and Communist sympathizers in the entertainment industry, academia, labor unions, and some branches of the federal government but not in the U.S. Army or the State Department. One of McCarthy's targets, Owen Lattimore, spoke at the University of Wisconsin; he was introduced by Richard Hartshorne, one of my professors. I had to walk through a picket line to hear his presentation, which focused on U.S. foreign policy. Lattimore did not mention his earlier endorsement of Stalin's infamous "show trials," an ill-advised move on his part, but something that did not warrant McCarthy's 1950 allegation that he was the "top Russian espionage agent in the United States." Many of McCarthy's targets had shown poor judgment during their careers, but a lesson I learned from these proceedings is that people who have been impacted by injustice are not always paragons of virtue. Nonetheless, this does not excuse the way they have been treated.

As a result of McCarthy's charges, Lattimore's career was ruined, but at least he survived. The same could not be said of those who took their own lives as a result of "McCarthyism." A U.S. Senator shot himself after McCarthy publicized his son's arrest for soliciting sex from an undercover police officer. In addition to McCarthy's allegations against purported Communists and "fellow travelers," he railed against homosexuals in positions of influence. Both the "Red Scare" and the "Lavender Scare" cost thousands of people their jobs, resulted in several hundred being imprisoned, and were implicated in several suicides (more due to the latter than the former). Following his work for McCarthy, Roy Cohn embarked on a 30-year career as an attorney, during which time he was Donald Trump's personal lawyer. Cohn, who was known as a "political fixer," was eventually disbarred by the New York Supreme Court. Cohn and I once crossed paths in the Frankfurt, Germany, airport. His visage was so menacing that I said to myself, "I have encountered pure evil," a judgment I had never made about another human being. Cohn died of AIDS-related complications in 1988.

Was I too extreme in my judgment? Perhaps. Cohn was known to have been kind to his friends and to have engaged in various philanthropies. In his autobiography,[1] he claimed that McCarthy's mistake was coming on like a "thug," even though he was genial in his personal relationships. These positive qualities assure us that Cohn and McCarthy were human beings, not total aberrations. After all, even Adolf Hitler had a soft spot for animals and children.

Members of his own party hastened McCarthy's downfall. Eisenhower cited "executive privilege" to keep him from sharing vital information that the Senator had requested during the Army hearings. Chief Justice Earl Warren and the Supreme Court made a number of rulings that curtailed McCarthy's investigations. Senator Margaret Chase Smith addressed the Senate in a "declaration of conscience" speech; it did not cite her fellow Senator by name, but the implications were obvious, coming only a few months after McCarthy's first accusations. When he expanded his charges to "twenty-one years of treason," his break with the Eisenhower Administration alienated many of his key supporters. As time went by, the derogatory term "McCarthyism" was used by members of both political parties. What an outrageous legacy for a Wisconsinite!

---

[1] Zion, S. (1988). *The autobiography of Roy Cohn*. Lyle Stuart.

Enter Frank Lloyd Wright

My first career goal was to become a harpist. I adored the sound that came from harps, having heard harp music in a Walt Disney cartoon. Eventually, I had a chance to meet a harpist and see the instrument firsthand. Immediately, I knew that the necessary skill was beyond my capabilities and switched my career goal to that of architecture. I did several drawings of prospective buildings and constructed a rabbit hutch that served its purpose quite well. My influence was Frank Lloyd Wright, another Wisconsinite, and I read anything about him that came my way. I learned that he had briefly been a student at the University of Wisconsin and that he had worked with Louis Sullivan in Chicago, from whom he borrowed the phrase, "form follows function." Wright went on to create a home and school near Spring Green, Wisconsin, naming it "Taliesin, "or "Shining Brow," to reflect his Welsh heritage. "Shining Brow" indicates that his residence was "of the land," not "on the land," a reference to his concept of "organic architecture." Taliesin was also the name of a Welsh bard whom Wright admired.

Wright had a tempestuous love life, marked by legal imbroglios and, tragically, the murder of his paramour, her children, and several residents in 1914, when he was out of town. The assassin, a Taliesin chef, set fire to Taliesin, which necessitated reconstruction. In 1925, shortly after the birth of Wright's daughter Iovanna, Taliesin burned to the ground again, resulting in "Taliesin III." His construction of the Imperial Hotel in Tokyo was followed by an earthquake that destroyed all the surrounding buildings; Wright had deliberately created a foundation for the hotel that would withstand tremors.

When Walter Kaufman asked Wright to design a home near a waterfall in Pennsylvania, he made the waterfall itself a part of the design. The result, "Fallingwater," is an architectural masterpiece, an example of Wright's "organic architecture," which holds that natural life manifests itself in a given space and that anything built on that space should flow into and co-exist with it. Wright took his students, the "Taliesin Fellowship," to Scottsdale, Arizona, in the cold winter months and built a school there using local materials.

On March 27, 1952, I applied for membership in the Forum Committee, a part of the Memorial Union at the University of Wisconsin. Once accepted, I suggested that we invited Wright to give a lecture and was given the task to write the letter. I was thrilled to receive a response that stated that there were only two possibilities: one was a thousand-dollar fee, the other was "nothing at all." I responded, saying that we were interested in the "nothing at all" option, and Wright agreed, on the condition that no admittance fee be charged. This was during the 1950s, a time noted for student apathy. Some of our other programs were free of charge, but Wright's appearance was the only one we held in the Wisconsin Union Theater to fill the house.

On October 29, Wright arrived with his entourage, consisting of his wife, Olgivanna, his daughter Iovanna, and a convoy of two dozen of his apprentices and students. They had dinner in the Wisconsin Union restaurant, while the Wrights and Forum Committee members dined in a private dining room. Wanting to "share the wealth," we arranged for Wright to sit with me at the head of the table, while his wife and daughter sat at the foot. Mrs. Wright, I discovered later, complained, saying, "A husband and wife should not be separated." The students were so shocked at being in Wright's presence that they did not say a word. In so doing, they missed out on conversing with a highly intelligent dinner companion. Olgivanna Wright, an accomplished dancer from Montenegro, taught courses at Taliesin on G. I. Gurdjieff's theosophical teachings as well as on fine arts. Olgivanna had studied "sacred dance" with Gurdjieff for eight years, a subject that was an integral part of Gurdjieff's philosophy, which held that people live their lives in a state of "waking sleep" from which they need to become "awakened." Olgivanna's daughter Svetlana, child of her first husband, Russian architect Vladimir Hinzenberg, would later become Wright's daughter-in-law.

Olgivanna happened to sit next to Wright at a Chicago performance of a Russian ballet company, and their marriage coincided with Wright's most productive years. She introduced Wright to Gurdjieff, but her husband did not share her enthusiasm, although they both used variants of the Bible verse "The Kingdom of God is within you," to describe their theology. Nonetheless, Wright allowed her and their daughter Iovanna to teach sacred dance and to arrange several musical productions at the school and the local community. In one of his autobiographies, Wright described their meeting: "I fell in love with her. It was as simple as that." After his death, Olgivanna ran the school until her demise in 1985. Olgivanna co-founded the Taliesin Fellowship in 1932 and the Frank Lloyd Wright Foundation in 1941. Wright's biographers generally give her credit for being a stabilizing force in Wright's life, ushering in his era of greatest creativity and preserving his legacy after Wright's death. On a minor note, it was Olgivanna who persuaded Wright to trim his long hair and to abandon his use of flowing ties, as both tended to make him seem stuck in the wrong century.

At our end of the table, the conversation was more animated. I sat on his right, and a visiting architect from London sat on his left. After being served tea, Wright asked for lemon, and the waiter brought a slice. Wright looked at it in disgust, saying "This is just a little rind. I want an entire lemon." The waiter soon brought back a lemon cut in half, and Wright squeezed both portions into his teacup, saying, "That is more like it!" He proceeded to place both halves in the teacup, spilling much of the tea in the process, but he did not seem to mind. Wright asked several of the students what they planned to do when they finished school. One student replied, "It is not up to me. There is a war going on, and I might be drafted." Wright asked, "Do you really want to go to war?" The student replied, "Of course not," and Wright responded, "Then become a conscientious objector, leave the country, or go to jail. Remember that you always have a choice." The reaction was electrifying. He had raised the consciousness of everyone who heard him, including me.

Years later, I remembered this conversation when a student feared being sent to Vietnam. His father paid for him to have faux weekly "therapy sessions" with me, after which I was to write a letter on Maimonides Medical Center stationery stating that he was in no condition to serve in the armed forces. This ploy was successful, and I soon repeated it with a dozen other students. I gave them a choice—they could be homosexuals, drug addicts, emotionally disturbed, or any combination. At the time, some psychiatrists were charging hundreds of dollars to write such letters. I charged nothing, as I felt that it was my patriotic duty to save these bright young men from serving in what I felt was an ill-fated war. My decision dated all the way back to that dinner with Frank Lloyd Wright.

The Lecture
Following dinner, we went to the theater where Wright was to speak. It was filled to—and beyond—capacity. Wright's students ended up standing against the wall; it was a violation of fire regulations, but nobody complained. My introduction was quite simple: "We have all heard of the master of ceremonies who claims that the speaker needs no introduction and then spends half an hour introducing him. Tonight the Union Forum Committee is going to break that tradition. We are proud to present Mr. Frank Lloyd Wright."

Wright spoke without notes, describing his approach to architecture and how his buildings were designed to be a part of their natural environment. He maintained that his houses were not *on* a hill, they were a *part* of the hill, the two joined in perfect unity. He also advocated a respect for the building materials and for the emotional and spiritual needs of his clients. Wright referred to Louis Sullivan, with whom he had apprenticed in Chicago, as "my lieber Master," not mentioning the stormy aspects of their relationship. He did comment on Sullivan's dictum that "form follows function," stating that the two are not separate but can work together. He pointed out that Sullivan broke with European architectural traditions, striving to create an approach that was typically American. Wright maintained that architecture was the "Mother Art," and that the best architects were poets who could project themselves and their works into the future. He handled questions deftly, often with a sense of humor that evoked laughter. The local radio station recorded his talk; when it was broadcast, I made a tape recording of it that I enjoyed for years to come. We saw the caravan to their cars, and they trekked back to Spring Green and Taliesin.

In June 1953, I was surprised to see Iovanna Wright and a companion in the university bookstore. I reminded her of our previous meeting, and she told me that the event was one of the highlights of the year for the Fellowship. Wright's students had never heard Wright speak to a large group, and his presentation added to his luster. Then I realized that Wright's "nothing at all" appearance served a personal agenda and teaching function as well.

Earlier that year, I had taken several members of the Forum Committee to Taliesin for a guided tour of the school. We were invited to inspect drawings and models of many of Wright's 1,000 structures, as well as designs of future works, many of which were never built. We visited the nearby town of Wyoming to see "Romeo and Juliet," a windmill that Wright had designed at the invitation of his aunts in 1897. For Wright, the structure resembled two lovers in an embrace, hence the name. We noted some of the "sprite statues" that had decorated the Midway Gardens, an outdoor plaza created in 1914 for a Chicago company. The project had a troubled history and was destroyed in 1929 but had been so solidly constructed that the wrecking crew went bankrupt. Wright and his family were nowhere to be seen during our visit, but I did see him at a campaign rally for Adlai Stevenson in 1954. He sat on stage with the presidential candidate and was introduced, receiving tumultuous applause.

In 1955, Wright returned to Madison to accept an honorary degree from the University of Wisconsin, the school from which he had dropped out during his sophomore year. I was invited to the event as well as to the banquet that preceded it, another memorable chapter in my ongoing saga with this celebrated Wisconsinite. This time there was no *faux pas*, as his wife, Olgivanna, was seated by his side.

In 1956, while I was doing graduate work at Northwestern University, I went to hear Wright lecture in Chicago, describing his plan for The Illinois, a mile-high building. He was introduced by Ellen Borden Stevenson, the former wife of Adlai Stevenson, the ex-governor of Illinois and Democratic candidate for President. I recall Wright describing the taproot foundation and the core of the building from which walls would be cantilevered like "branches and leaves from a tree." I was able to squeeze into the reception simply by positioning myself in back of Ms. Stevenson; once we were inside the room, the doors were closed. I stood in line to greet Wright and showed him a photo I had taken of the windmill he called "Romeo and Juliet." His eyes lit up and he smiled and signed his name. I reminded him that I had introduced him to the student audience at the University of Wisconsin. He smiled and said, "And you are still so young."

In October 1957, Wright returned to the University of Wisconsin, again filling the theater. Anne Minahan invited me to the event, and we joined the standing ovation both before and after his lecture. The topic was "A Study of Nature," in which he described buildings as "children of the Earth and Sun" and urged students to "stay close to Nature because it will never fail you." My friends Edgar and Betty Obma, who had driven down from Dodgeville for the event, drove me to the bus station shortly after it ended. I had two memorable encounters with Wright and wanted the new students to have similar opportunities. Notably absent on this visit was Olgivanna, who had made such an issue of being separated from her husband during his 1952 visit.

In 2017 I visited the Burj Khalifa in Dubai, the world's tallest building. Although only half as tall as the projected Illinois, it used some of the same ideas that Wright had proposed decades earlier, specifically the buttressed central core and cantilevered wings. Wright passed away in 1959. My aunt, Pearle Krippner, saw me shortly afterward and commented, "Your friend just died." She knew of my admiration for Wright and of my two personal contacts with him.

Aftermath

In 1960, I returned to Taliesin. Edgar Obma, who had taken Wright's favorite formal photographic "portrait," had arranged a "workday" for his son, Bob, and me. During these "workdays," people were assigned tasks commensurate with their architectural abilities. Bob and I had little ability to offer, so we spent the day digging ditches. However, we were allowed to have lunch with Wright's students and their families. I recall two people at our table, a member of the Fellowship and his handsome young son Tai (named after Taliesin, of course). Tai told us that he planned to go to Hollywood and become an actor. Later, Bob asked me how Tai could become an actor, since a bout of polio had left him with a misshapen leg and a severe limp. I told Bob that Alan Ladd became a leading man despite being only 5'6" tall, so perhaps Hollywood would work wonders for Tai as well.

Over the next several years, I persuaded my friends to join me in visiting a number of Wright's completed projects. In 1939, Wright designed the offices for S. C. Johnson's company in Racine, Wisconsin, after Johnson announced, "Anybody can build a typical building, but I wanted to build the best office building in the world." The Wisconsin Industrial Commission hesitated to give its approval, thinking that the tree-shaped columns could not bear the weight expected of them. Wright responded by piling weights on a column that exceeded the required weight sixty-fold. He also included air conditioning, an innovation at the time, and an open workspace. He made liberal use of "Cherokee Red," his favored color, in the bricks used in the construction. I was one of many members of the international group who took the regularly scheduled popular tour.

It took me fifty years to visit Fallingwater, but in between I was able to see Wright's Beth Shalom Synagogue in Elkins Park, Pennsylvania, which Wright called "a luminous Mount Sinai." I attended a friend's wedding in Wright's Unitarian-Universalist Unity Temple in Oak Park, Illinois. Completed in 1908, its use of reinforced concrete later evoked the title of "the world's first modern building"; later it was added to UNESCO's list of World Heritage Sites, an honor bestowed on several other Wright constructions. I also took a tour of the Robie House in Chicago, the last of Wright's so called "Prairie Houses," and one for which he twice campaigned to keep it from destruction. Later, I visited the Disciples of Christ Community Christian Church in Kansas City, Missouri, which won a spot on the National Registry of Historic Places. That appellation was also given to the First Unitarian Society building in Shorewood Hills, Wisconsin, completed in 1951. For my required internship at the University of Wisconsin, I taught Sunday School at the church, and became friends with Max Gaebler, the minister, who presided at Wright's funeral in 1959. I was able to visit several homes designed by Wright in Los Angeles and in or near Madison, Wisconsin, many of which became state or national historic sites. I also spent a day on the campus of Florida Southern College, for which Wright had designed all the major buildings, and which appears on the National Registry as well. The college is Methodist affiliated, and Wright was a member of the Methodist Church.

When I lived in New York, I made frequent visits to Wright's Guggenheim Museum, known for being wider at the top than at the bottom, and for its spiral ramp. Controversial when it first opened, it became a UNESCO World Heritage Site and a sought-after exhibit space for contemporary art. The museum was designed when Wright and his students were living at Taliesin West, near Scottsdale, Arizona. Following his physician's orders to avoid the Wisconsin winters, Wright paid $3.50 per acre to acquire the desert property, using local materials in its construction. When he found Native American petroglyphs among the rocks, he improvised on them to design the logo for the school. During my visit in 1960, I was especially impressed by the six-sided cabaret theater, renowned for its acoustic perfection.

When I moved to California, I wasted little time in visiting the V. C. Morris Gift Shop, which also boasts a spiral staircase and is sometimes called a "rehearsal" for the Guggenheim. San Rafael, where I had been living for several years, is the home of the Marin County Civic Center, which was Wright's final completed project as well as his largest. The adjoining post office is the only federal building he designed, and the nearby Veterans Auditorium was completed by Taliesin Associated Architects after his death. Wright borrowed ideas from his 1932 Broadacre City design, because the Marin County project was the size of a campus. When Wright visited the site in 1957 (at the age of 90), he immediately made sketches that served as the basis for the project. The pink stucco walls, the scalloped balconies, and the blue roof are distinctive features. Wright had hoped for a golden roof to match the surrounding fields, which turned gold during autumn. This turned out to be impractical, and his wife, Olgivanna, selected the distinctive shade of blue. Wright's son, grandson, and son-in-law also played roles in the construction and dedication of the project, and I delight in bringing overseas visitors there for my personally conducted tours. I also tell them how the project aroused considerable controversy, to the point where construction stopped for two years and only a vote for a new board of supervisors saved the day.

Years earlier, Wright had designed a county courthouse for Jefferson County in Wisconsin, where I grew up. The project, which had been intended to honor Thomas Jefferson, consisted of several adjoining buildings wedded to a rural setting. Local politicians scuttled the project, thus depriving the county of its place in architectural history. Some called his work "socialist architecture," while others objected to his support of the Soviet Union during the Second World War. Still others bemoaned the expense of his projects. The hostility to Wright's design that ruined his plan for the Jefferson County Courthouse in Wisconsin and that delayed for years building the Marin County Civic Center in California, also delayed the construction of the Madison, Wisconsin, Monona Terrace Community and Civic Center. Shortly after Wright's lecture at the Wisconsin Union, local newspapers were filled with descriptions of Wright's elaborate plans for a complex city center, complete with not only offices but theaters, shopping areas, a port for boats, and a railroad station. Originally proposed in 1938, it was voted down by the county board by a single vote. It was repeatedly resurrected and scuttled until Madison's mayor called for a referendum in 1992, at which time it was overwhelmingly approved. Voters who had objected to the cost remained silent when the Center brought in millions of dollars of revenue each year through conventions, meetings, weddings, and its restaurant and gift shop. I paid a visit shortly after its completion in 1997, some six decades after Wright had proposed it. I remarked to a friend, "When Katherine Hepburn won her fourth Academy Award, she mused, 'If you live long enough, anything can happen.'" I was gratified that I had lived long enough to complete the Wisconsin sojourn that had begun when our university committee invited Wright to give his celebrated "nothing at all" lecture.

In a 2012 compilation of the top Hollywood female actors, Katherine Hepburn was listed as Number Two. The Number Thirteen spot went to Anne Baxter, who was a granddaughter of Wright, which endeared her to me. I made a special point of seeing her films, especially *All About Eve*, which became *Applause*, a musical starring Lauren Bacall. Baxter took over from Bacall in 1971, and in 1974 returned to Broadway in *Noel Coward in Two Keys*, playing completely different roles in each play. I saw both productions and wrote Baxter a fan letter, mentioning my connection with her grandfather, and received a gracious reply. I prized that letter, and it is now in my archives at the University of West Georgia. In an interview, Baxter noted that her grandfather wore nothing but a red sash on his wedding night, most likely referring to his marriage to her grandmother. She commented, "That is real glamor!"

In retrospect, October 29, 1952, was a day that changed my life. My admiration for Wright would have persisted had we never met. But his advice to the draft-age student galvanized social activism on my part and inaugurated a number of activities that continued long after the Vietnam War ended. I have a framed copy of Edgar Obma's photograph of Wright on the wall above my desk, a constant reminder of his impact on my life.

Chapter 4

The Back of the Bus
1 September 1955. A Day When My Life Changed

Tennessee was one of the first states other than Wisconsin that I visited with family members. We had relatives living near Jackson, in the western part of the state, and they spent some time each summer vacationing at Lake Ripley, a popular tourist destination not far from my parents' farm. Each summer they asked us to return their visit, and in 1940 we were able to accept their invitation. I do not remember much about that visit, but I do recall driving by the fields where several African American workers were picking cotton. My mother told my father to stop the car. She gave me a sack of candy and asked me to give some to the "darkies" (as she called them), which I was happy to do. They were quite grateful, and soon I had distributed the entire supply. My parents took a photograph of me handing out the sweets, a photo that I have kept over the years. I spent most of my spare time reading, even while my mother kept telling me, "You need to meet all kinds of people." She invited friends my age to visit our home, enrolled me in various clubs, and took me to square dances. My father was in accord and also did his best to augment my social life, driving me to club meetings and social events.

"Inherently Unequal"

I went through elementary school and high school without having significant contact with people of color. During my high school years, I was one of half-dozen students sent to "Boys' State," a week-long program designed for "future leaders." Don Taylor, whom I had met previously at a Presbyterian Church camp, represented his high school in Waukesha. At camp he became an active politician, the campaign manager for one of two contenders for "governor." His candidate's opponent was African American; Don's campaign focused on asking voters to ignore skin color and evaluate the merits of the candidates. That appeal was ahead of its time and worked all too well, as far as Don was concerned: the African American won, creating a small historic record for that institution. Both of them represented Wisconsin in "Boys' Nation," where Don's candidate was elected "president."

When I entered the University of Wisconsin, everything changed. I interacted with a variety of students from African American, Asian American, and Latinx backgrounds, enjoying the cultural diversity that resulted. I recall being asked why I did not join a social fraternity, and my stock response was that I thought "hazing" was both juvenile and dangerous, and because fraternities did not open their membership to "Negroes" (the term used at that time). There was an African American freshman who went through fraternity "rush," and my friends and I admired his courage. From what we understood, he was treated politely but, of course, was not invited back and eventually joined the campus's African American fraternity. My friends and I formed our own "fraternity," Sigma Epsilon Xi (SEX), discovering much later that there actually was such a group.

Years earlier, in Tennessee, I was not aware of the strict racial segregation laws that encompassed all aspects of daily life—schools, theaters, churches, playgrounds, parks, public transportation, and even drinking fountains and restrooms. Supporters of segregation claimed that schools were "separate but equal," but common sense belied that fiction. The issue was brought close to home when a Black family bought a farmhouse not far from where my family lived. The matron of the family applied for membership in the local "ladies' aid society," which dated back to the days of the Second World War when it supported troops, often providing them with hard-to-find supplies. My mother, a long-time member, voted for admission, but she was in the minority. However, the family was not harassed or labeled with derogatory epithets and later became contributing members of the community.

I was glued to the television in the Wisconsin Memorial Union Lounge on May 17, 1954, when the U.S. Supreme Court announced its decision in the Brown v. Board of Education of Topeka case. Chief Justice Earl Warren announced that the "separate but equal" doctrine could not be supported because segregated schools "were inherently unequal." It was a unanimous decision, but much later I discovered how close the court had come to upholding the status quo, a position favored by Warren's predecessor. However, the predecessor died before the case could be heard, and President Eisenhower named Earl Warren to succeed him. Warren, the governor of California, used all his political acumen to produce a unanimous verdict, one that cited the 14th Amendment's protection of "equal justice under the law."

Perhaps it was hopelessly naïve on my part, but when the time came to look for a job placement, I opted for Richmond, Virginia, the former capital of the Confederacy, wanting to play a small role in desegregating the public schools. My application went unanswered, so I accepted a position as speech therapist in Warren, Illinois. No sooner did I send my letter of acceptance, than I received an offer on April 1, 1954, from Margaret Hudson, director of the Richmond Department of Special Education. Telling her that we would stay in touch, I spent a fruitful year in Illinois, honing my skills as a speech therapist while putting into practice what I had learned at the University of Wisconsin.

In the meantime, I had several more letters from Mrs. Hudson, as well as a visitor from her department who was in the area and who reiterated the invitation. Of course, it was flattering to receive so much attention, so I rented an apartment in Richmond, shipping my effects in a large black trunk, the one that I had used when leaving for Warren and that served a similar purpose for several later moves.

On September 1, I met Mrs. Hudson in an enormous school orientation at the Mosque Theater. Among the throng, there were some fifty special education teachers she had called together. Mrs. Hudson was wearing a jaunty hat with a bright red feather, making it easy to locate her. When we had gathered, I met Doris Sue Katz, who had been in some of my classes at the University of Wisconsin; Peg Lewis, who had graduated from the university a few years earlier; Rubye DeWitt, and Nancy Torkelson. This was the cadre of speech therapists with whom I would be spending the ensuing school year. And that was the day my life changed.

The Doctrine of Interposition

Interposition is the claimed right of a state, or group of states, to oppose action by the federal government involving measures that the state deems to be unconstitutional. In 1955, the Virginia Legislature attempted to interpose itself between the federal government and the citizens of the state in regard to school desegregation. The Commonwealth of Virginia General Assembly held that the May 17, 1954, Supreme Court decision was unconstitutional, defying many precedents that had established the "separate but equal" policy. Virginia Senator Harry S. Byrd announced a policy of "Massive Resistance" to the ruling, one aspect of which was the "Doctrine of

Interposition" supported by Governor Julian Stanley. The editor of the *Richmond News Leader,* James J. Kilpatrick, was another key supporter; his editorials were rallying cries for a continuation of school segregation. Kilpatrick changed his mind about school segregation later in his career, although he continued to advocate for states' rights.

In 1956, I read an article by H.O. Reid in the *Journal of Negro Education* that put this together in a clear perspective.[1] Earlier that year, Governor Stanley, as well as the governors of Georgia, Mississippi, and South Carolina, announced support for interposition. The governor of North Carolina, Luther Hodges, was at the meeting as an observer, so did not feel constrained to voice his support. This was a shrewd political decision, as it affirmed Hodges' reputation as a "moderate" and his selection by President John F. Kennedy, in 1961, to join his cabinet as the Secretary of Commerce.

I attended several of the public hearings when the governors had congregated in Richmond. I also was able to work my way into a not-so-public hearing, thanks to a page at the Capitol who told me where the governors were meeting. The rhetoric centered on "states' rights," and the topic of school segregation was rarely mentioned—at least not in the public hearings. However, Kilpatrick addressed the issue directly, and his rhetoric was cited by legislators in Texas, Arkansas, and Alabama, who evoked the doctrine of interposition. But Kilpatrick never thought that President Eisenhower would oppose interposition or send troops to Little Rock to enforce school desegregation. Kasey Pipes, writing in 2004, called Eisenhower the "key segregation figure" in the struggle; moreover, in 1958, the U.S. Supreme Court rejected the doctrine of interposition. In 2004, K.S. Pipes wrote a fine retrospective book[2] describing "Ike's Final Battle"; because of Eisenhower's "hidden handed presidency," he never received enough credit for it at the time.

In May 1954, Virginia's Superintendent of Public Education, Dowell Hurd, vowed to abide by the Supreme Court's decision. If Governor Stanley had shared Hurd's sentiments, it is likely that desegregation would have occurred more rapidly and smoothly than it did. In the meantime, Mrs. Hudson had arranged for speech therapists to spend one day a week at the school hearing clinic. There was no segregation there; students were tested in the order in which they arrived.

---

[1] Reid, H. O. (1956). The Supreme Court and interposition. *Journal of Negro Education, 25,* 109–117.
[2] Pipes, K. S. (2004). *Ike's final battle: The road to Little Rock and the challenge of equality.* World Ahead Publishing.

Sometimes a Black therapist would test a White student and vice versa. There was no segregation in the waiting room, and the students' mothers carried on amiable conversations with each other. Needless to say, we did not alert the news media about the clinic's *de facto* integration. We just carried out our tasks, and there were never any protests from parents or students. This taught me a lesson regarding how some good deeds should be unpublicized!

Several years later, on a visit to Richmond, Mrs. Hudson took me to the new school for children with orthopedic disabilities. When one enters the school, one sees a colorful mural. Indeed, it is colorful in more ways than one, with Black and White children playing together. Mrs. Hudson always said, "I am very liberal—for being a Southerner." Indeed, she was!

Mrs. Hudson and I were especially concerned with the fate of Kelly, a student with a club foot. I was able to help him improve his slurred speech, and she was able to schedule an operation at a local hospital that would correct his limp. When he did not show up for his surgery, we were both stunned. Kelly's mother, a single parent, explained that her only source of income was the sale of her handmade doilies. When Kelly went on the street to sell the doilies, people took pity on him because of his disability. If his condition were to be corrected, she feared that sales would drop. I told Mrs. Hudson that we simply had to face reality—"win a few, lose a few."

One case that we won concerned a mother whose 9-year-old son, Terry, had been diagnosed as autistic, a condition marked by impaired social interactions along with issues related to both verbal and non-verbal communication. The psychiatrist making the diagnosis attributed the cause to a dysfunctional mother–child relationship, which produced considerable guilt on the part of Terry's mother. I interviewed them both, finding Terry to be a delightful young man who took his time in expressing himself but who eventually was able to communicate with me, albeit using unconventional verbal responses. I told Terry's mother that there was no evidence that autism was linked to poor mothering; rather, it was the result of Terry's brain being wired in an unusual way. On receiving this news, she broke into tears, and we discussed ways in which Terry, an engaging and attractive youngster, could lead a happy and fulfilling life. Upon hearing the news, Mrs. Hudson was delighted, and congratulated me on my work. But this outcome reflected my personal perspective, which took a brain-based approach to problems in speech and communication skills.

One of my schools was in a low-income part of town, and my students were thrilled to receive the pictures I had created. I used "Sammy Swan" and "Thelma Goose" to help them differentiate the "S" and the "TH" sounds. I helped them distinguish between "SH" and "ZH" with two characters, "Sha-Sha" and "Zsa-Zsa." This was not as serious a problem as the "S" and "TH" confusion, but the students enjoyed making the two sounds. One day I arrived at school to discover that one of my students had been killed by a hit-and-run driver. I announced the news to our class, but they had already heard about it. One student lost no time in requesting her late peer's collection of drawings. When I asked if there were any objections, there were none. I acquiesced but said we would need to observe a minute of silence first.

In each of my classes, I demonstrated correct tongue, lip, and teeth placement for each sound, putting to use what I had learned in my university classes on phonetics. I would use a small mirror and would have them observe themselves articulating the sounds in the mirror. Then I had students put the sounds into words, and the words into stories. I had them use their pictures as the basis for their stories. They were especially eager to use the "V" sound, along with the picture of "Voo the Robber," with his bloody knife and his sack of loot. A few of the parents from other schools objected to the violence, and I quickly erased the bloody knife from "Voo." But the parents of students from the low-income areas never raised a protest, as they were absolutely delighted that someone was giving their children special attention. I made sure that all students were able to use their newly mastered sounds in words and sentences, often creating stories and skits to reinforce what they had learned.

Sometimes I needed to provide individual sessions, as was the case with children who stuttered or those with aphasia, a language challenge resulting from brain injury. However, I would integrate them into a group from time to time, especially when we were playing card games or engaging in role-playing. When taking on a role, many non-fluent children speak fluently, because they have not been conditioned to fail in such a situation. I took the position that most stuttering is brain-based; even so, the role enactment provided the opportunity for new neurological connections to be made. The same would be true when I gave homework assignments that asked them to converse with a pet, a sibling who had not mastered speech, or an imaginary character. I combined this with breathing and relaxation exercises that they could practice on their own, especially when facing a challenging situation that might raise their anxiety level and increase their stuttering. I had learned these procedures at the University of Wisconsin and was pleased to have a chance to put them into practice.

Sitting in the Back of the Bus

I was assigned to four schools and visited two of them each day, one in the morning and one in the afternoon. I took buses from one school to another, immediately observing that Black people were assigned to seats in the back of the bus. If seats at the front of the bus were filled, I did not hesitate to sit in the back of the bus, and the conductor did not make an issue of it. However, if a Black person sat in the front of the bus, the driver immediately stopped the bus and ordered the transgressor to move to the back. If there were no seats, that meant standing.

On one occasion, a Black woman who was visibly pregnant was ordered to move back, even if that meant standing. I immediately offered her my seat; when the driver protested, I asked him if he wanted to be held responsible if she went into labor when the bus hit a few bumps. This was an unexpected response, and he returned to his seat, grumbling. He could not blame it on "damn Yankees" because I used a Southern accent when engaged in my speech classes. One of my professors, Gladys Borchers, advocated using local terms and inflections that matched the part of the country where we were practicing speech therapy. I quickly learned the colloquialisms of the area and put my knowledge to good use on numerous occasions.

Richmond had built the world's first electric streetcar system in 1888 and boasted a fine public transportation system until the 1950s. At that time, every city expenditure was looked at through the lens of maintaining racial segregation. The Virginia General Assembly felt that de facto segregation could be maintained by hardening the judicial authority of the central city, ending the annexation of new areas. As a result, public transportation ended where the city ended, depriving workers of buses going into outlying areas where new stores were opening and where new jobs were becoming available. Richmond became the only city in the United States with a population of over one million that did not have full-service public transportation. Segregation by public transportation replaced laws requiring Black people to sit at the back of the bus. From being the envy of the world, Richmond fell to nearly the bottom of the list when U.S. public transportation systems were evaluated.

Racial segregation also was required in the case of interstate transportation. However, on November 7, 1955, the Interstate

Commerce Commission banned segregation on interstate transport vehicles, ending the use of "separate but equal" as a defense. The U.S. Supreme Court had made the same ruling in 1946, but Virginia had ignored that decision. This came as good news to the Greyhound Bus Line, because maintaining segregation was inefficient and costly, and the company began to remodel its terminal to reflect the new reality.

One change required consolidating restroom facilities in the Greyhound waiting rooms. One memorable day, I observed workers obliterating the signs "White Men," "Colored Men," "White Women," and "Colored Women" from the restroom doors. The restroom for "White Women" was closed for additional repairs when a middle-aged White woman arrived, looking desperately for relief. She had no idea which door she should open, so entered the restroom for "Colored Women." She quickly exited with an embarrassed look on her face and entered the next restroom, the one for which the "White Men" sign had been obliterated. She exited, even more embarrassed, and went to the one remaining door, the one leading to the restroom for "Colored Men." I heard a piercing scream, and the hapless woman went running out of the terminal into the street. In retrospect, I supposed that I could have intervened, but I simply wanted to see how the drama would play out.

Mrs. Hudson once told me that she was ashamed to admit one of her own behavior patterns, a hangover from her childhood. She simply could not enter a swimming pool if there were one or more Black people in the water. Like the tormented woman in the Greyhound terminal, close contact with Black people, especially Black men, was one privacy line that she could not cross.

Colonial Williamsburg

In 1903, the Rev. Dr. W. A. R. Goodwin became pastor of the Bruton Parish Church in Williamsburg, Virginia. He had visited the church earlier as a seminarian assigned to recruit students for the local William and Mary College, the second oldest institution of higher education in the United States (after Harvard), boasting three Presidents as alumni. On returning to the church, he found the congregation divided into factions on doctrinal issues and attempted to resolve the differences. One successful endeavor was to propose renovating the 1711 building, a task accomplished in 1907, just in time for the celebration of the Episcopal Church's 300th anniversary of its founding in the United States. The renovation was expensive, but Goodman proved to be an excellent fundraiser.

Goodwin accepted a call from St. Paul's Episcopal Church in Rochester, New York, where he pastored until 1923 when he returned to Virginia to work as a fundraiser for William and Mary College. In addition, he became pastor of Yorktown's Episcopal Church and a chapel in nearby Toano. Goodman's trips around the area saddened him, because of the deterioration of historic colonial buildings he witnessed; he began to work with the Association for the Preservation of Virginia Antiquities to rectify the situation. He saved one home from being turned into a gasoline station, making it into a faculty club; he preserved other landmarks by turning them into faculty and student housing.

In 1926, Goodwin again became pastor of the Bruton Parish Church. He acquired the neighboring George Wythe structure, turning it into the parish house. Wythe had been the first American professor of law, and Goodwin enlisted the support of John D. Rockefeller, Jr., and his wife, Abby Aldrich Rockefeller, in preserving this historic building. In 1927, the Rockefellers committed themselves to supporting Goodwin's plan to restore the entire area to what it had been in the 18th century, when it was capital of the Virginia Commonwealth.

Goodwin and the Rockefellers kept their plan a secret, fearing that property prices would explode if knowledge about their plan was revealed. Goodwin did not even tell his attorney about the Rockefellers' role. Property after property was acquired, papers were filed with the Virginia State Corporation Commission, and the project was formally revealed in June 1928. No African Americans were asked for their input, but the Rockefellers insisted that admissions should be open to all if their contributions were to continue. A fellow speech therapist, Rubye DeWitt, gave me this information and invited me to visit Williamsburg, where her husband, also African American, was the director of personnel.

On a free weekend, I took a bus to Williamsburg and, once there, hailed a taxicab and gave the driver Rubye's address. He was somewhat taken aback, asking, "Do you know that this is in the colored part of town?" I replied that I knew it quite well and that I would be staying with friends. The driver took me to "the colored part of town," dropped me off quickly, and made his exit. He had not taken me to the correct location, so I had to make inquiries before I finally found the DeWitt residence. There was a boisterous party going on in the next yard, and Rubye apologized for all the noise. I told her that the ruckus was fine with me because her neighbors seemed to be having fun.

The next morning, the DeWitts took me on a tour, showing me the buildings that had been restored (using what remained from the originals) or reconstructed (based on records, drawings, and photographs). The latter included the Governor's Palace and the Capitol, where Patrick Henry first spoke out against Britain's King George III. Over 700 buildings that had been erected after about 1800 had been demolished, so that the "Williamsburg Project" would enable its visitors to step back in time, both literally and figuratively. Restaurants served colonial fare, shops sold colonial crafts, and some 800 restored and reconstructed buildings were opened to tourists.

A number of "re-enactments" provided historical context, but Black and White "re-enactors" lived in separate quarters. On subsequent visits, I noticed an increasing number of Black re-enactors, many of them playing more varied roles than the enslaved people whom they were originally intended to represent. At the time of my first visit, privately owned hotels did not admit Black tourists, but some public accommodations were open to all—perhaps the only integrated sites of that nature in the state. The Williamsburg Project could not violate state law, but it found clever ways to honor the original agreement with the Rockefellers that would not attract notable attention. The authenticity of Colonial Williamsburg has always been a matter of debate, but more often than not common sense has prevailed.

Early on, I became a member of the Colonial Williamsburg Foundation and have taken several friends to the site for weekend visits. My weekend with the DeWitts was a highlight of my tenure with the Richmond Public Schools. The state's "Massive Resistance" policy formally ended in 1962, when racial terminology was dropped from the school district's reports. It had been most forcefully applied to public transportation and public education, and I had experienced both firsthand. By that time, many private schools had opened, siphoning resources from the remaining public schools, resulting in a somewhat modified segregated system. On the other hand, Mrs. Hudson had laid the groundwork for what became the Richmond Public Schools' Office of Exceptional Education, with services not only in speech therapy but in audiology, autism, aphasia, and a host of other areas. Once again, "win a few, lose a few" certainly applies.

Chapter 5

The Notorious Kent State Shootings
20 July 1961. A Day When My Life Changed

The notorious Kent State University shootings on May 4, 1970, resulted in the deaths of four unarmed students and the wounding of nine others by twenty-eight members of the Ohio National Guard. The shootings occurred during a rally protesting the expansion of military action by the United States into Cambodia during the Vietnam War. It also marked the first time that students had been killed by the U.S. military during a peaceful demonstration. The incident triggered massive demonstrations involving over four million students at several hundred universities both at home and abroad. President Richard Nixon, whose actions precipitated the demonstration, was rushed to the presidential Camp David retreat for his safety, but he returned to make an unannounced visit on May 10 to the Lincoln Memorial, where he met with two dozen protestors, delivering a monologue that his opponents found "condescending" and that his supporters described as an attempt to "reach out." I had left the Kent State faculty several years earlier, but had stayed in touch with several faculty and students, many of whom described their reactions and those of their colleagues.

Arrival in Kent, Ohio

My life did not change on May 4, 1970; that milepost goes to July 20, 1961, when I held my first conferences with my new colleagues in Kent State University's school of education. I had brief meetings with Clayton Schindler, dean of the school; Marian Van Campen, chair of the department of elementary education; and Walter Barbe, a faculty member who focused on doctoral students and who had also studied under Paul Witty at Northwestern University. I had a longer meeting with Dwight Arnold, founder of the university's counselor preparation program, and we reviewed the courses that I would be teaching. He also introduced me to a new book by Carl Rogers, *On Becoming a Real Person*, a publication that he predicted would have a major impact on the field of counseling and guidance.[1] He was right. Rogers stated that the underlying reason people sought counseling was to "become their real selves," a quest that could be facilitated by what became known as a "person-centered" approach. I immediately ordered the book and it changed my life, introducing me to an important (and essential) aspect of humanistic psychology.

In April of 1957, as a graduate student, I had requested and obtained a short interview with Rogers when he was a visiting professor at the University of Wisconsin. I apologized for intruding on his time but said I would limit my inquiry to one question. "If you could have only one interview with a person in need, would you still take a non-directive approach?" He replied, "I can think of no better use that could be made of that time when we would be together." Decades later, when we became close friends, I recounted this incident, and Rogers remarked that he had given me an appropriate answer.

I integrated Rogers's ideas into my first two courses, Sources of Occupational Information and a counseling practicum in which students role-played with each other and eventually worked with actual clients who had applied for assistance. I also introduced students to the occupational theories of Donald Super and Anne Roe, whose ideas I had incorporated into my doctoral dissertation on the educational and vocational interests of junior high school students. In August, Walter Barbe asked me to give a guest lecture to his class on "New Frontiers in Counseling and Psychotherapy." I started my presentation by discussing Rogerian counseling, but then included Albert Ellis's Rational Therapy, existential psychotherapy, and hypnotically facilitated psychotherapy, all of which were unknown to members of the class.

I also had several meetings with Warren Cutts, director of the Reading Center, a position that I was slated to inherit. Cutts had accepted a position with the U.S. Department of Education as its first reading specialist, a post for which he was uniquely qualified. He showed me his card files of information about reading; whenever he was asked to lecture on the topic, he simply pulled out the appropriate cards and put them in coherent order. My appointment was a disappointment to another faculty member who felt that she was better qualified for the job. Actually, she was right—but she did not have a

---

[1] Rogers, C. R. (1961). *On becoming a person*. Houghton-Mifflin.

PhD, which was required for the appointment. She snidely told her colleagues that I had taken only one course in reading at Northwestern. Again, she was right. But Walter Barbe had taken the same course and had become a recognized authority on the topic. He and I formed the "One Course in Reading Club," prepared certificates, and enrolled several other members. The ridicule was probably responsible for the aggrieved faculty member's several outbreaks of hives; once she recovered, we heard no more complaints.

The Reading Center

When I became director of the Reading Center, my responsibilities expanded. In addition to my courses on counseling and guidance, I was assigned courses on special education as well as the research practicum for students who planned to develop a career in remediating learning disabilities. My approach differed from what had been taught previously because I perceived most problems in learning as due to psychoneurological issues and faulty teaching rather than to emotional problems, which was a popular etiology at the time. I emphasized "body-based" remedial efforts, including tactile–kinesthetic methods and "experience charts," for which boys and girls would write stories about their own lives. I was able to teach students how to administer tests for reading proficiency, vocabulary-based intelligence tests, and interest inventories. My students also were introduced to such terms as "dyslexia" and "dysgraphia," and how to detect these problems by observing their pupils' reading and writing performance. I administered the more "clinical" measures, such as the Stanford-Binet, the Wechsler Scales, and the Bender Visual-Motor Gestalt Test. Much of my time was spent administering these tests, arranging conferences with parents, where they would be apprised of the results of my testing (and testing by my students), and writing specific suggestions for our clients' classroom teachers.

Much to my surprise, the Reading Center attracted considerable attention, due in part to my presentations at meetings of the International Reading Association, the American Educational Research Association, and the National Association for Gifted Children. Visiting psychologists from Argentina and Portugal requested tours of the Reading Center and a discussion of our remedial efforts; the *Kent Courier-Record* ran a full-page article about the center; and the *Cleveland Plain Dealer* did a feature story as well. Prentice-Hall Publishers sent a representative to see me regarding a book on my approach to learning disabilities; I politely turned them down, simply because I did not have enough experience under my belt to qualify as an "expert." When Science Research Associates (SRA) asked me to give a workshop in Cleveland, I was about to turn them down because of a class conflict, but my assistant, Frances "Fran" Dillon, volunteered to fill in for the class, and her generosity launched me on a series of SRA-sponsored workshops on learning disabilities that continued for over a decade. Fran's devotion reminded me of Ann Coomer's work for Paul Witty at Northwestern; Fran, who took all of my courses, was an adroit learner, and I made sure that she was invited to join me at various conferences in the area.

Because of my work with Paul Witty on gifted and talented children, we began to see a few exceptional boys and girls. Based on this expansion of our services, I proposed changing the title to "Child Study Center." The dean approved of the change, but said it would need to be "Educational Child Study Center" to avoid confusion with the Psychological Clinic. I agreed, but never used "Educational" in my professional writings because it was too cumbersome.

During my first year at Kent State, I submitted half a dozen articles to various journals, all of which were published. The dean of men asked if he could send me some university students who were having trouble reading; I accepted his offer, worked with several of them, used hypnosis when requested, and wrote up the results for the *American Journal of Clinical Hypnosis*.[2]

I had studied projective techniques at Northwestern, spending an entire semester learning how to administer and score the Rorschach Inkblot Technique, also known as the Rorschach Inkblot Test. During an annual convention of the American Psychological Association, I learned about a new projective technique, the Holtzman, and received permission to buy a copy and use it for research purposes. Within a few years, I had enough data to write an article on the aspects of the test that were more likely to be linked to improvement in remedial reading instruction. In 1967, the *Journal of Clinical Psychology* published my article on the topic.[3]

In September 1961, I noticed that Horace Page was a newly appointed member of the psychology department. He had been one of

---

[2] Krippner, S. (1967). Review of *The varieties of psychedelic experience* by R. E. L. Masters and J. Houston. *American Journal of Clinical Hypnosis, 9,* 220–221.

[3] Krippner, S. (1967). Relationship of reading improvement to scores on the Holtzman Inkblot Technique. *Journal of Clinical Psychology, 23,* 114–115.

my professors at the University of Wisconsin; I knew he would not remember me, but I greeted him anyway. He invited me to a reception for the Kent State University psychology clinic, which he now directed, and we had several pleasant interactions over the years. However, my closest friend in the department was Charles Winslow. I joined him and his wife at the local Presbyterian church every Sunday when I was in town. Professor Winslow, the former director of Kent State's Psychology Clinic, had a narrow escape from death a few years before I met him and moved with a noticeable limp. He appreciated my patience with him when he could not move quickly, and I speculated that his churchgoing might have tied in with his close brush with death.

Enter Harry Easton

In early August 1961, I made my annual trip to the American Psychological Association convention, this time held in St Louis, Missouri. I attended notable sessions, including one on suicide; I visited with Gardner Murphy and other friends, including Robert Frager, whom I had first met at Harvard University during my psilocybin initiation. Robert introduced me to Harry Easton, a psychologist working for the city's Jewish Employment Services, specializing in deaf clients. Harry and I "clicked" immediately because we had mutual interests, one of which was art, so we went to the St. Louis Art Museum to see a recently discovered Cezanne painting.

A month later, I returned to St. Louis for a longer visit with Harry, who took me on my first outings to lesbian and gay bars, and introduced me to a transvestite friend who did not feel "at home" in either gender. He kept his female garb and cosmetics in a closet in his office, and literally "came out of the closet" when he wanted to engage in external activities as a woman.

During my years in Kent, I visited Harry numerous times; he delighted in "educating" me, taking me to gay and lesbian bars, transgender parties, and visits with "queer" friends of his. Once in a while we would "pick up" young women and go to secluded spots to "make out."

Harry and I shared many interests such as existentialism and existential psychotherapy, which I had first encountered at Northwestern. Drawing on Harry's work with deaf people, we co-authored two articles on existential aspects of deafness.[4,5] We had both read a 1958 book[6] edited by Rollo May and two colleagues, which emphasized clients' self-determination, their search for meaning, and the acceptance of anxiety as a basic part of the human condition. Each year when the ballots were issued, Harry and I voted for Rollo May as the president of the American Psychological Association. He never succeeded, but in 1971 he won the APA Award for Distinguished Contributions and in 1986 the American Psychological Foundation's Award for Lifetime Contributions.

Another mutual interest was sociopathy (later referred to as "antisocial personality disorder"), which usually manifests by the age of ten or eleven. A popular term, *psychopathy*, is rarely used by clinical psychologists, but it sometimes describes more severe cases; both afflictions are marked by a lack of concern for other people's rights and feelings. When I had given the Minnesota Multiphasic Personality Inventory to adults, I always checked for the "Pd Scale" ("psychopathic deviate"), finding that it accurately identified clients who manifested the symptoms, which included manipulation, chronic lying, and attention-seeking behavior. I was able to identify enough cases to write an article on the topic, which was published in *Exceptional Children*, garnering dozens of requests for reprints.[7]

Harry also visited me in Kent, and on August 22, 1964, I was best man at his wedding to Betsy Gasser, another school psychologist. They went to Mexico on their honeymoon and settled in New Mexico, where I continued my visits, with warm feelings resulting from seeing them so happy together.

Harry's first attempt to "educate me" occurred a month after my road trip with Steve Klineberg, who had joined me for the psilocybin experience at Harvard earlier that year. We visited the Grand Canyon, Bryce Canyon, and Zion National Park, marveling at the incredible natural formations. We ended up in Los Angeles where Morgan McNeel

---

[4] Easton, H., & Krippner, S. (1966). Disability, rehabilitation, and existentialism. In C. E. Beck (Ed.), *Guidelines for guidance: Readings in the philosophy of guidance* (pp. 427–433). Wm. C. Brown.
[5] Easton, H., & Krippner, S. (1971). Disability, rehabilitation, and existentialism. In H. A. Moses & C. H. Patterson (Eds.), *Readings in rehabilitation counseling* (2nd ed., pp. 144–149). Stipes.
[6] May, R., Angel, E., & Ellenberger, H. F. (Eds.). (1958). *Existence: A new dimension in psychiatry and psychology*. Basic Books.
[7] Krippner, S. (1963). Sociopathic tendencies and reading retardation in children. *Exceptional Children, 29*, 258–266.

was staying before returning to Hawaii, where I had initially met him. Morgan's attempts to "educate me" included a visit to a male person who engaged in sex work and whose clients included a male television mega-star and a teenage idol. On Sunday, we picked up Frances "Pat" Brose, Humphrey Bogart's sister, for services at the local Christian Science Church. When we entered her apartment, I noticed a huge photograph of Bogart on one wall and one of his wife, Lauren Bacall, on the other wall. I made a point of noting the glamorous photograph of "Betty," knowing that this is what Bacall's friends called her, making an impression on Pat.

Steve made a different impression; Pat was so taken with him that she invited him to join her and her friends on a cruise to Catalina Island. He accepted the invitation with pleasure, and the trip began quite well. But Pat had assumed that Steve was gay, having been in the company of Morgan and his friends. She knew that she had "nymphomania" tendencies, hence preferred the company of gay men who would not put her at risk. But when she noticed that Steve was flirting with comely young women on the cruise, she lost control. That night she came to his door asking to be let in; Steve refused to open the door, and she started screaming and banging on it. She created such a ruckus that other cruise members called for the police, who took her off the ship. It took several weeks of psychotherapy for Pat to retain her equilibrium.

Enter Alex Gildzen

On March 1, 1964, my landlady, Rita Goodman, invited me to watch a television special starring Judy Garland. Her nephew, Alexander "Alex" Gildzen, a journalism student, joined us, and we became good friends. A few weeks later, Alex celebrated his 21st birthday, using the gift money to join me on a trip to New York City, where I introduced him to several of my New York friends. We saw *Anyone Can Whistle*, a musical that lasted only a few weeks. But we both adored Angela Lansbury, the star, and I went on to see her in nine other productions. We also bought standing-room tickets to *Funny Girl* starring Barbara Streisand, and visited several museums. We took a bus to Richmond, where Margaret Hudson prepared a steak dinner for us.

When Margaret arrived in Kent for her summer school stint, we all spent a weekend in Windsor, Canada. Back in Kent, I took Alex and his girlfriend, Betty Jean (who was in training for the Olympics) to several summer stock productions, notably Jayne Mansfield in *Bus Stop* and George Nader in *Mr. Roberts*. Alex had a surprise party for me, asking me to describe my psilocybin experience from earlier that year. He also attended the farewell party that my students arranged for me before I left for New York City. His cousin, Regina Yando, arrived for a visit, and we became close friends; after she won a teaching position at Harvard University, she married one of her students, and I paid them a visit whenever I was in the Boston area.

Alex graduated from Kent State and was appointed publications editor for the university. In 1970, he found himself the center of attention when the news media requested details about the notorious shootings. He was on the site at the time, which gave him a unique first-person perspective. Some people would have thrived, but Alex was extremely uncomfortable with the role. He was never happier than when he was writing poetry and editing his little journal, *Toucan*. In 1984 he was named curator of the library's special collections, a position he held until his retirement in 1993.

Visitors

During my tenure at Kent State, I had several visitors; the space in my apartment was limited, but I booked rooms for them at a nearby hotel or asked Walter Barbe to host them. My parents spent weekends with me at least two times a year, bringing my Aunt Gertrude Munson along for one of them. My Camp Richmond buddies, Wayne Woods and Pete Mowbray, trekked to Kent as well, as did Fred Gros, the college admissions director for Kamehameha Schools in Hawaii. When I inquired about teaching at Kamehameha, he told me there would be a position opening for a director of counseling services. I was quite excited but did a "reality check" with Morgan McNeel, who told me that the position would go to a *kama'aina* (native of the islands) who was already on staff. My Northwestern University friend Dom Raino visited me once or twice a year when he could get time off from his naval air force duties.

Bill Karolus

Early in May, I received a letter from Bill Karolus letting me know that he would be arriving in New York City on the 21st. We had become friends when he was a high school student in Warren, Illinois, followed by a summer at Phantom Lake YMCA Camp, where he supervised the rifle range. We had visited each other's homes several times before he went into the Army, and now his tour of duty was complete. He visited points of interest in Europe for several weeks, hoping that I could join him. This was not a practical proposal, much to my regret. But I did arrange to spend a weekend in New York, followed by welcoming him to Kent State.

When I arrived in New York City, I discovered that there would be a Democratic Party fundraiser on the 19th, thinly disguised as the 45th birthday party for President Kennedy. I went to a ticket agency, discovered that they had two tickets left, and bought one of them, using all of my cash to do so. It was a wise investment because the evening was unforgettable. Some 15,000 people were crammed into Madison Square Garden, where they were entertained by a bevy of luminaries. Toward the end of the evening, the actor Peter Lawford, the President's brother-in-law, introduced "the late Marilyn Monroe," jibing her reputation as coming to movie sets late. Little did he know that she would be dead before the end of the year; singing "Happy Birthday, Mr. President" was her last public appearance.

On the 20th, I went to hear the Rev. Norman Vincent Peale, author of *The Power of Positive Thinking*, speak at the Marble Collegiate Church. I also attended the New York Philharmonic's last concert in the old Carnegie Hall. The next day, I went to the pier to watch Bill disembark, after which we spent the day together. He returned to his parents' home in Dwight, Illinois, and then drove to Kent to spend the weekend with me. Walter Barbe hosted him and joined us for a few meals. Bill was eager to discuss his military service, during which he attained the rank of Private First Class, as well as his "whirlwind" tour of Europe. He was married a few years later and began a successful career in the insurance business. Remembering how shy he was when we first met, I was very happy that he had worked through his timidity to become a salesperson.

Margaret Hudson

On January 24, 1962, I phoned Margaret Hudson with some surprising news. I had been asked to recommend teachers for the 1964 summer session, and my nomination of her met with immediate approval. On May 22, Margaret and Olivia, her African American maid and companion, arrived and were warmly received by the faculty. She made a big hit with the summer session students; she described how she had organized the special education services in Richmond and gave detailed examples of her work with speech- and hearing-challenged pupils as well as those with orthopedic and emotional issues. During her time in Kent, my parents visited, as well as my sister and her husband. They had heard so many stories about Margaret and her flamboyant style that they were delighted to meet her. The feeling was mutual.

Wayne Woods, another Richmond friend, visited me during her tenure; they had already met but never in "northern" territory. I took them all to Pepe's Restaurant, my favorite dining spot because Pepe, the owner and chef, prepared dishes that his customers had requested the previous day. I recall treating them to veal scaloppini, one of his specialties. When Margaret's daughter and two grandsons also visited at various times, we often went swimming in the nearby Joy Lake. We also visited a nearby Montessori School, a system that eschewed planned curricula, basing activities on the interests of the children.

On August 22, Margaret and Olivia hosted a farewell reception, importing a Smithfield ham from Virginia for the occasion. Olivia told me that she had never had a similar experience; not only was there an absence of segregation, but no condescending acceptance of her. Marjorie Snyder, my replacement as the center director, arrived in Kent just in time to attend the reception.

Lola May
Lola May was my debate and forensics coach in high school, and our interactions were unforgettable. She inspired us, gave us practical advice, and traveled to tournaments with our team. I met her again at Northwestern, when she and her girlfriend, Margaret Bendix, were fellow graduate students. She received her doctorate from Northwestern in 1964 and became a mathematics consultant for the Winnetka, Illinois, public schools. We stayed connected by letter, and the trips she and Margaret took to various islands in the West Indies stimulated me to put Puerto Rico, Trinidad, Tobago, and similar destinations on my "wish list."

On June 30, 1964, Lola arrived in Kent, the special guest of the department of mathematics. I attended all her lectures and seminars, and we had a private dinner together. Sadly, her girlfriend, Margaret Bendix, had passed away, but not before she saw Lola achieve national fame as an expert on the so-called "new math," which emphasized the conceptual understanding of mathematics rather than technical memorization. This was my last encounter with Lola, but she wrote a delightful autobiography, *Lola May Who?*[8] In reading it, I discovered that Lola had written a series of books on math education and had lectured in all fifty states. Not too shabby!

---

[8] May, L. J. (1991). *Lola May Who?* Author.

Enter Dorothy DeBoer

On April 16, 1962, Dwight Arnold and I took a train to Chicago for a counseling conference. Also in attendance were Romeo Olivas and Dorothy DeBoer, two of my former classmates from Northwestern, both now university faculty members. Once the conference ended, Dorothy drove me to Evanston so that I could visit Frank Miller and Claude Mathis, two members of my dissertation committee. I also linked up with Charles Marshall, a friend from those days; Charles was now the president of LaSalle Law School, and told me about its at-a-distance learning program, then called a "correspondence school."

Dorothy was an attractive redhead; I have always been partial to "carrot tops." I have had personal encounters with several "ginger" actors such as Agnes Moorhead, Eleanor Parker, Susan Sarandon, and Gwen Verdon, as well as Deborah Kerr, whose framed autographed picture, obtained after her performance in the play *Tea and Symphony*, graced my desk for years.

Dorothy and I hit it off, and I invited her to visit me in Kent. On June 7, she and her son, Daniel, arrived for the weekend and I took them on a tour of the campus, pointing out the wild black squirrels that had been imported from Canada to preserve the species. My secretary, June Sarver, had invited us to join her and her family for an afternoon at their swimming pool and then a steak dinner, which was a culinary highlight of the weekend. I could not top June's cooking, but did prepare blueberry pancakes for brunch one morning; they passed muster, but left blue stains on the DeBoers' teeth for the rest of the day. On Sunday, I took them to mass at the campus's Newman Center, after which they left for their home in Chicago. On the 16th, I received a large box of candy from them, and stayed connected by telephone. Along the way I asked Daniel what he planned to do when he grew up, and he replied, "I will be a priest, I guess," without too much enthusiasm.

A few weeks later, I took the train to Chicago to spend more time with Dorothy; we had dinner with Romeo and Gloria Olivas, and I was impressed by how happy they were. We also had dinner with Larry and Marilyn Levy, two other friends from my Northwestern University days, who had a gloriously intimate marriage. On the 12th of July I proposed marriage, and Dorothy accepted. We set the date for 1963, and on the 25th I flew to Chicago to meet her mother, her grandmother, and Father John Richardson, the vice president of DePaul University, where Dorothy was teaching. Dorothy's first marriage had not worked out and she obtained a divorce. However, she was still married in the eyes of the church, and Father Richardson explained how difficult it would be to get an annulment because her son, Daniel, was proof that the marriage had been "consummated."

At this time, the anti-Catholic statements of my Wisconsin pastor, Carl Bruhn, as well as those by my father resurfaced. Even more important were statements by prominent officials of the Roman Catholic Church stating that "outside of the church there is no salvation." On the 27th, I wrote a long letter to Dorothy stating that it did not look as if her marriage could be annulled.

But we did not give up. The DeBoers came for a visit on September 6; I had arranged to meet them at a summer theater to see Patrice Munsel in *The Merry Widow*. En route, I bumped into another car in the parking lot and was relieved that I was the only passenger. During the performance, Dorothy squeezed my hand when Munsel's character spoke of marriage. On Sunday, they returned to Mass at the Newman Center, while I made my customary trek to the local Presbyterian Church.

In October the three of us met again at a conference in Pittsburgh at Clarion University. Dorothy did not have good news about an annulment, so we decided to put our marriage plans on hold. We met at numerous psychology conferences several times over the years, but our moment had passed. It was ironic because the Second Vatican Council had convened earlier that year, resulting in significant changes to church doctrine. Dorothy remained single, but her son's career plans changed, and she became a grandmother. Twice.

The Empty Teat

On March 28, 1962, I arrived at the office of Robert Weimer, MD, for my first psychotherapy appointment. I had been having stomach pains, but a physician's exam could find no reason; hence I thought they might be psychosomatic. I met with Dr. Weimer every Monday during the time I taught at Kent State. He had a picture of Sigmund Freud on his office wall, and engaged in what I later discovered was "psychodynamic psychotherapy," a less ambitious and less expensive form of psychoanalysis. Dr. Weimer asked me to take the Rorschach Inkblot Test, which I was happy to do with the cooperation of Professor Charles Winslow of the psychology department. Early on, he suggested that I was suffering from a case of "vagina dentata," a fear of being castrated during sexual intercourse; this would explain why my lovemaking over the years had always stopped short of penetration.

He listened attentively as I described my childhood, viewing my relationship with my father as generally positive and consistent. When it came to my mother, he noted several inconsistencies. She rewarded my diligence at the piano, only to take the reward back when I told her I was playing my own compositions. She allowed a neighbor to give me weekly comics so that I could read about Mandrake the Magician, but then canceled the gift when I misbehaved. She scared me by claiming that my sister and I would kill her with our misconduct. Along with my father, she facilitated my attendance at summer camps and membership in church and social groups. But she also insisted that I not take showers following our high school gym classes, while embarrassing me by asking our high school principal why I was not the class valedictorian. Dr. Weimer saw these incidents as evidence of maternal deprivation in infancy, naming it "the empty teat," either an actual withdrawal or a symbolic one. He also concluded that "the empty teat" had left me fixated at the "oral stage" of psychosexual development. Whether or not I recalled the events accurately was not the issue. It was my unconscious reactions to the perceived events that was important.

He linked my fear of harming my mother and the two injuries my maladroit actions had inflicted on my sister with my reluctance to drive an automobile to pick up my date. He urged me to overcome this phobia by driving into Akron, picking up a girl at a bar, and driving back to my apartment for the night. I never was able to pull off that request. When I told him about my summer romance in Hawaii with Grant, he dismissed it as "mutual masturbation"; I never brought up the topic again. I did mention my participation in the Harvard University psilocybin study that had taken place before I started psychotherapy, but Dr. Weimer dismissed this as "a series of hallucinations," and so I did not discuss it during further sessions.

However, I did discuss my romance with Dorothy DeBoer and our short-lived engagement. Dr. Weimer suspected that I did not intend to carry through with the engagement and that I overemphasized her church's complications as an excuse to curtail it. He thought she was too similar to my mother for my liking, and that my actions were an unconscious rebuff to my mother. He also thought that my financial setbacks were an attempt to "keep the teat empty," again as a protest. He might have been right. I had handled various budgets with aplomb, starting in high school when I was co-chair of the junior prom and co-editor of the school yearbook. At the University of Wisconsin, I was chair of the Union Forum Committee and kept our expenses within the budget, as I did when I directed the junior and senior class plays in Warren, Illinois. I handled the Reading Center budget quite well; although we spent more money than either the Psychological Clinic or the Speech and Hearing Clinic; we earned more money than either of them as well. However, my subsequent financial shortcomings could have been avoided with better planning on my part.

We also discussed my many rejections over the years; in high school, I was nominated for several class offices but was never elected. When I was at Badger Boys State, I was defeated; I ran for the presidency of the Wisconsin Student Union, but lost again. My nominations were the ideas of others; hence, I was not upset with the outcomes. However, the picture was much different when I was turned down for a date; Dr. Weimer attributed my over-reaction to these rebuffs as another example of "the empty teat."

Pete Mowbray, a friend from Richmond, spent a week with me at Kent State, and I took him with me to meet Dr. Weimer, noting that he was one of my close male friends, as were Dom Raino, Don Taylor, Harry Easton, and a few others. Dr. Weimer suggested that there was a mutual sexual attraction but one that could not be consummated for a number of reasons. I was aware of my attractions, as they were all exceptionally good-looking men, but would never have instigated sex for fear of losing them. They were not aware of their attraction to me (according to Dr. Weimer,) although I remained skeptical), but sublimated it; further, it gave them the chance to have an extremely intimate relationship with a man but one that was non-threatening to them. I commented that I was more than happy to have done them a favor! And once in a while, I did have a "sexual friendship," as was the case with Finn of Hawaii. But my non-sexual friendships were just as fulfilling to me and usually lasted longer.

I brought several of my dreams to Dr. Weimer and he did an excellent job of interpreting them from a psychoanalytic perspective. One dream was especially puzzling; I was watching a group of hunters shooting four turkeys, but not intending to use them for nourishment. Dr. Weimer saw this as another example of inconsistent nurturance, and he was probably right. But I recalled this dream in 1970, when four students were shot and killed by the Ohio National Guard during the notorious Kent State Killings.

My father was a salesperson for Nutrilite, a popular food supplement "chock full of vitamins," as the sales pitch put it. He kept me supplied, and Dr. Weimer felt that his reliability was in contrast to "the empty teat." This carried over into my significant relationships; I had no problem establishing deep connections with male friends as well as "platonic relationships" with female friends. It was only when the latter became erotic in nature that I was hesitant and unsure of myself. But my mother was successful in motivating me to succeed academically and socially, and this effort outweighed her uneven track record in other areas.

Dr. Weimer prescribed tranquilizers, which stopped my stomach pains. It also cast doubt upon the efficacy of my psychotherapy and my original goal. When I moved to New York City, he gave me the name of a psychoanalyst, recommending that I now needed a female therapist. Shortly after I arrived in New York, I met his colleague at a social gathering and mentioned my work with him. She spoke highly of him but lamented that he was "stuck" in a backwater town that did not deserve his talents. For better or worse, I never requested a session with her, mostly because I found myself too busy with my new professional duties.

A Diva and Two Icons

When the United States entered the Second World War, I followed developments closely, including the efforts of entertainers to boost the morale of our troops. The first "Stage Door Canteen" was opened on Broadway in March 1942; Tallulah Bankhead and Walter Pidgeon were among the first hosts, Helen Hayes served sandwiches, and Alfred Lunt cleaned dishes. Similar canteens were organized elsewhere, the most famous being in Hollywood, where the driving forces were John Garfield and Bette Davis, both of whom had previously worked in the Broadway canteen. A frequent host was Marlene Dietrich, one night appearing fresh off the movie set of *Kismet*," still wearing her gold makeup.

I read several accounts of Dietrich's patriotism and services to her adopted country; in addition to serving food at the Hollywood Canteen, she went on tours to sell war bonds and made recordings of German songs that were dropped behind enemy lines as propaganda. She also made over 500 appearances during war campaigns in Europe, sometimes near the front lines. My father enjoyed Bette Davis, so we went to see many of her films, but neither parent was especially interested in Marlene Dietrich, despite her war efforts. In 1956 I saw her daughter Maria Riva in a touring production of *Tea and Sympathy*, thinking this would be as close as I would get to viewing Dietrich herself.

I was wrong. I read an announcement of her upcoming concert at Chicago's McCormick Place and immediately ordered a ticket. I took a bus from Kent to Chicago, arriving early on December 1, 1961, and checked into a hotel. Dietrich, who faced a sold-out house, performed her first act in the fabled beaded silk gown that gave the illusion of transparency. She wore a tuxedo for her second act, and received a standing ovation. She acknowledged her accompanist, Burt Bacharach, who stood and awkwardly held a few pages of sheet music over his crotch. Dietrich was presented with a huge bouquet of lilies and seemed surprised; I later discovered that she used the same bouquet over and over again until the flowers wilted. As soon as the house lights went on, I dashed to the exit and tried to find my way backstage. I went by Burt Bacharach's dressing room just as he was telling a friend, "When Marlene introduced me tonight, I noticed that my fly was open and grabbed some sheet music to cover it up." Without that serendipitous event, I never would have understood Bacharach's bizarre behavior.

I was one of the first to reach Dietrich's dressing room. When her assistant opened the door, everyone gasped. Why? She looked her ag, but was incredibly glamorous, dressed in a purple shingled dress. The person preceding me in line was an older woman, who said, "Miss Dietrich, when I was a little girl, I went to hear you sing in Berlin, and you autographed this photograph for me. The ink has faded, and so I would like you to sign it again." Many divas would have recoiled at this demonstration of their age, but Dietrich was extremely gracious, even sharing details of her Berlin appearances. When Dietrich autographed my program, I complimented her performance in *Witness for the Prosecution*, and she replied, "Be sure to see *Judgment at Nuremberg* because I think you will like it." I saw the film, liked it, and it won multiple awards.

The next day, I was on my way to a pre-Broadway matinee performance of *Night of the Iguana* when I spotted the author, Tennessee Williams. He gave me his autograph, we chatted amiably for a few minutes, and then I enjoyed the play, Williams's last great critical and commercial success. The play starred Patrick O'Neal, Margaret Leighton, and Bette Davis—who, along with Williams—was one of the two icons I would encounter on December 3. Once the play ended, I went to the stage door, where I had a brief conversation with O'Neal; I would often dine in his Manhattan restaurant decades later. I had no time to wait for the other actors, because I needed to catch a bus back to Kent; but I had met Davis years earlier, so felt no need for further engagement. One diva and two icons in a weekend was not too bad!

Chapter 6

My Uncle Max
9 December 1946. A Day When My Life Changed

One evening my mother returned from her ladies' society meeting with surprising news. A member of the group had reported seeing a desert scene with an oasis. However, she was nowhere near a desert at the time. This was my first report of what became known as "an anomalous experience," an experience that is either rare, unexplainable by mainstream science, or both. Synesthesia (hearing colors or tasting sounds) is rare as well, but there are a number of scientific explanations for the phenomenon. Dreams about future events are not rare, but, if valid, cannot be explained by mainstream science. I never forgot my mother's story, as I later discovered that her friend's experience, if accurate, could have been a mirage, the result of light refraction. Later, I concluded that anomalous phenomena were not necessarily hallucinations, attempts at attention-getting, or "miracles"; they were part of the human condition and worthy of serious study.

Uncle Max Munson

My father's sister, Pearle Harriette Krippner, did not have an easy life. After the death of my paternal grandfather, John Krippner, she moved to a modest house near the downtown area of Fort Atkinson with her mother, Hattie Krippner. For many years, she worked as a receptionist for a local physician—later being terminated because of her age. Her work was more than competent, but the physician wanted a young woman to greet incoming patients. Yes, this would have been grounds for a lawsuit in the 21st century, but it was considered justifiable in the 1940s. Aunt Pearle began to sell the World Book Encyclopedia.

Since I loved to read, especially about historical and scientific topics, I asked my parents to buy me a set. Aunt Pearle was eager to assist the purchase, lowering the price to $100, forgoing her commission. But even that price was more than my parents could afford. Devastated by the news, I retired to my room in tears. But I had an inspiration that came as a flash. I had one relative who was fairly well-to-do, my uncle Max Munson, an executive for a dairy company in Madison, Wisconsin. I resolved to write to him and ask for a loan. But then I had another flash. I could not ask Uncle Max for anything because he was dead. I was puzzled by this revelation because we had just seen him at a family gathering where he seemed to be in robust health.

Suddenly, I heard a scream from downstairs. I ran down to see my mother holding the telephone, visibly shaken. She cried, "Your Uncle Max just died!" This was completely unexpected. The date was December 9, 1946, and it changed my life.

Joseph "The Amazing" Dunninger

From that point on, I read anything that came my way about premonitions, precognitions, intuitive hunches, and the like. I was an avid listener to the radio show featuring Joseph "The Amazing" Dunninger, and for years believed that his "mentalism" acts were genuine instances of "extra-sensory perception" or ESP. This belief was reinforced when Dunninger moved to television and I was able to see him, as well as hear him, in action. It was not until I entered the University of Wisconsin that I learned otherwise.

As a member of the Union Forum Committee of the university's Memorial Union, I suggested inviting Dunninger for an appearance. A member of the Union House Committee heard of my intention and spent some time enlightening me. Mentalists have several skills that they employ, such as reading body language, facial impressions, and vocal clues. They also depend on probabilities and quirks in mathematics. They may sometimes use sleight of hand, for example, when predicting headlines. Only the less skilled mentalists use confederates; Dunninger offered a cash reward to anyone who could demonstrate that partners were involved in creating his effects. Because of my long-standing interest in sleight of hand, everything my friend told me made sense, so I abandoned my efforts to bring Dunninger to the campus.

Decades later, a psychiatrist friend, Berthold Schwarz, invited me to join him and his wife for front row seats at a magic show in New York City. His other guest was Joseph Dunninger! I told him about my fascination with his radio show, and—long since retired—he was delighted with the news. I later discovered a celebrated quotation by Dunninger: "Any child of ten can do this—with forty years of experience." I also found out that Dunninger had a track record of exposing fraudulent mediums and using his skills to reproduce their alleged "contacts with the dead." Berthold Schwarz confided that Dunninger had genuine "psychic gifts," but they were too unpredictable to depend upon when he was performing.

Enter A. Campbell Garnett

In the meantime, my philosophy professor, A. Campbell Garnett, informed me that scientific studies of ESP were being carried out at Duke University by Joseph Banks Rhine and his wife, Louisa E. Rhine. Garnett, born in Australia, suffered a severe attack of poliomyelitis at the age of nine, which left him with a lifelong limp, but he was known for his sunny disposition. A stroke later in life further disabled his movements, but he never complained about either condition. Ordained as a minister in the Church of the Disciples of Christ, he went on to attain graduate degrees in psychology and philosophy. He held university positions in Australia, China, Great Britain, and Germany, beginning his tenure at the University of Wisconsin in 1935. He was serving as department chair when I met him; I had received permission to enroll in his class, typically reserved for juniors and seniors.

I sought out Professor Garnett after hearing that he was the only theist in his department. I had found his book *A Realistic Philosophy of Religion*[1] to be especially meaningful, notably his agreement with William James in calling for an empirical approach to religious studies. He stated that "here we find in the moral nature of man empirical evidence that the human spirit is organic to a larger spiritual reality just as the human body is organic to a larger physical reality."

Garnett discussed the ethical implications of this stance in his book *The Moral Nature of Man*,[2] which had just been published when I enrolled in his course. In that book, he noted that the "variously motivated horrors of Hiroshima and Buchenwald" had led many people to conclude that humanity's moral nature "was an illusion," with little evidence for "rational faith and hope." His inclusion of Confucianism, Hinduism, and other Eastern philosophies was my first introduction to these bodies of thought, laying the groundwork for my interest in the writings of Alan Watts. His assertion that humanity's moral nature draws "the self out of itself," directing its attention to others, was a

---

[1] Garnett, A. C. (1942). *A realistic philosophy of religion.* Harper and Brothers.
[2] Garnett, A. C. (1952). *The moral nature of man: A critical evaluation of ethical principles.* Ronald Press.

theme I would encounter when I began to study transpersonal psychology.

Class discussions were memorable, with many of the upper-class students taking issue with Garnett, especially for his Christian orientation. Others said that if he was such an advocate of empirical research, he should become a logical positivist like most other members of his department, who held that for a statement to be meaningful, logic, observation, and experiment must have demonstrated it to be so. Garnett countered this argument by arguing that it assumed a greater knowledge of reality than what was warranted, and that recent developments in physics and neurology "cut the ground" from under these assumptions. Again, this was the first time that I had heard someone link physics and brain function to philosophical topics. But Garnett could also modify his views as a result of these discussions; When some students questioned his use of the term "disinterested" as a description of a moral stance, he agreed that this was not the best word, suggesting that "impartial" or "equitable" might have been better.

When I chaired the University of Wisconsin Union Forum Committee, we instituted a series of programs featuring illustrious faculty members. Garnett was our first speaker. He spoke on the topic "Science and Religion," criticizing those who said the two disciplines were contradictory. Garnett noted that their spheres of influence were quite different, so they only got into conflict when they invaded each other's territory. This is a topic that I have followed ever since, noting that in 2002 the evolutionary biologist Stephen Jay Gould wrote eloquently on this issue in his book *Rocks of Ages: Science and Religion in the Fullness of Life*.[3] Gould proposed that cultures needed to cultivate both to provide their members a rich and balanced life, and I agreed with those sentiments.

Garnett and I stayed connected over the years; when he retired from the university, he accepted a position at Texas Christian University in Fort Worth. In April 1967, I had a speaking engagement nearby, so I joined him for a memorable luncheon, which was our final encounter.

Enter J. B. Rhine

Having been persuaded to drop negotiations with Dunninger's agent, I sent a letter of inquiry to J. B. Rhine—a direct result of the

---

[3] Gould, S. J. (2002). *Rock of Ages: Science, religion, and the fullness of life.* Random House.

discussion I had with Professor Garnett. On May 23, 1953, I received a positive response from him. Rhine and his wife had studied botany at the University of Chicago, quickly amassing four graduate degrees between the two of them. Earlier, Rhine had served in the Marine Corps, earning a sharpshooter medal for his prowess with rifles. Shortly after receiving their degrees, the Rhines attended a lecture by Sir Arthur Conan Doyle, the author of the Sherlock Holmes mysteries, on the topic of mediumship and the possibility of life after death. Rhine later mused that this was the "most exhilarating thought I had had in years." The Rhines then relocated to Boston for a year of studying psychic phenomena with Walter Franklin Price and the Boston Society of Psychical Research.

In 1927 the Rhines moved to Durham, North Carolina, to work with William McDougall, with whom Rhine had intended to study at Harvard University, only to discover that McDougall had just left for England. A year earlier, Rhine had examined the claims of a prominent medium, concluding that she was fraudulent, and published the results in the *Journal of Abnormal and Social Psychology*. When Conan Doyle read the article, he called Rhine "an ass" and defended his earlier positive appraisal of the medium. Such events led Rhine to bypass mediumship in favor of an experimental approach to the topic; thus he and McDougall laid the groundwork for parapsychology. He and Rhine founded the peer-reviewed *Journal of Parapsychology*. After McDougall died in 1938, Rhine carried on the work by himself, publishing several books on the topic and conducting psychology's first "meta-analysis," a systematic analysis of research in a given field with conclusions and suggestions for further study. One of Rhine's books, *New World of the Mind*,[4] was published in 1953, providing a readable summary of his research at Duke University; after I read the book, I recommended it to other members of the Forum Committee.

Later, I discovered that Rhine had corresponded with Joseph Dunninger, offering to assess his abilities at Duke University. Dunninger turned him down, stating that the outcome might compromise his reputation as a "mentalist." Of course, he was right!

Reaction and Concerns

Perhaps it was naïve of me to expect that the psychology department would welcome our invitation. Nevertheless, when our committee needed extra funds for Rhine's honorarium, I wrote to the department

---

[4] Rhine, J. B. (1953). *New world of the mind*. William Sloane.

chair, Harry Harlow, to ask for help. Not only did he decline, but he stated that if Rhine came to the campus, his appearance would have "unfortunate emotional consequences" for the students. He further stated that if we persisted with the program, the logical next step would be to invite Father Divine (a well-known "faith healer" of the era) to lecture on "Recent Advances in the Art of Healing."

When I suggested that this might be an appropriate topic for one of our Wisconsin Union Debates, Harlow wrote back that such a debate would be similar to having a scientifically trained atheist debate Bishop Fulton Sheen (a prominent cleric of that time), taking the position that "the Immaculate Conception of the Virgin Mary has been experimentally proven." I was pleased that these sarcastic responses did not diminish the support of Forum Committee members for the program. Rather, they seemed to revel in the controversy; many of them were inspired to join the "Stick-Out-Your-Neck Club," which had been founded as a response to the antics of Senator Joseph McCarthy. On September 24, the Forum Committee voted unanimously to bring Rhine to the UW campus from his laboratory at Duke University. When Rhine heard about the controversy, he told us that he had been invited to address the American Chemical Society in Chicago in December, and that he would be happy to decline an honorarium if we could cover his train fare from Chicago and back. We accepted his offer, reserved a room for him at the Wisconsin Union Hotel, and scheduled a welcoming dinner with committee members and Professor Garnett, who had been instrumental in initiating the project.

In the meantime, the anthropology department had scheduled a lecture by John Gillam, a distinguished faculty member from the University of North Carolina. Several of us met with Professor Gillam and were delighted to hear that he and Rhine were friends and that he held Rhine's scholarship in high regard. At the same time, another UW psychologist, Julian Stanley, told his class, "If you are interested in ESP, you might as well hear about it from the horse's mouth from the biggest horse's ass of them all." Earlier, another group at the university had invited Owen Lattimore, a political scientist and a McCarthy target, to speak; Rhine seemed to have become the most controversial speaker since Lattimore's appearance on campus.

Unlike the earlier Lattimore lecture, there were no picket lines on December 9 when Rhine took to the podium. His generosity allowed us to make this a free event, but we were still concerned about attendance. There was a theatrical event scheduled concurrently in the Wisconsin Union Theater, so we held our program in the Union's Great Hall. Exam week was coming up, and there was a snowstorm raging outside; we feared that students would stay close to home and "hit the books." Additional members of the psychology department had denounced Rhine. Indeed, the student who was slated to introduce him withdrew, fearing recrimination from his psychology professor, and I took his place. All our concerns were negated when the Great Hall was filled to capacity, with hundreds of students making it a "standing room only" event.

Rhine did not disappoint his audience. A charismatic speaker, with deep-set eyes and a piercing glance, he placed his work in the context of how new ideas are introduced into science. He discussed why they often raise dissent, and how they need to be judged—basically, on the quality of the evidence garnered to support them. Rhine described how he and his colleagues had developed a stack of twenty-five cards containing equal numbers of five characters—circles, squares, triangles, stars, and wavy lines. By sheer chance, one would guess five of the concealed cards correctly. Consistently higher scores would provide evidence for "psi-hitting" and lower scores for "psi-missing." The Greek letter "psi" was used to describe both "extra-sensory perception" (ESP) and "psychokinesis" (PK). The three forms of ESP that emerged from these studies, and others like them, were "telepathy" (ESP of the mental processes of another person), "clairvoyance" (ESP of events beyond the range of the senses), and "precognition" (ESP of future events). My revelation about Uncle Max's death could have been precognition (knowledge about my mother's phone call before she received it) or telepathy (communication between me and my cousin, or telepathy between me and my mother). But scoffers would say it was coincidence, or that I did not recall the sequence of events correctly.

Rhine used the term "receptive psi" to encompass telepathy, clairvoyance, and precognition. PK, or "expressive psi," was originally suggested when a gambler told Rhine that he was successful when he followed a "hunch" while throwing dice. Rhine created mechanical dice-throwing machines that would test a participant's ability to evoke randomly selected numbers on the dice, again using statistics to evaluate the success of their efforts. He provided examples of each type of psi, both from his experimental studies and from the "spontaneous cases" that had been collected by his wife, Louisa. He concluded by attributing much of the strength of the opposition to him to the social conformity so prevalent in the 1950s, while observing that "Science can be functionally blind when it would shock its complacency to see." He encouraged students to form their convictions through reason and experience, and then stick to them.

A few days later, I received a gracious letter from Rhine telling me that his reception at the university was one of the greatest ovations of his career. He wrote, "I had a good stirring time with the chemists in Chicago, although it was not nearly so exciting as my experience in Madison. In fact, I have not had more fun in years than I had up there with you folks."

The following day, we saved money by driving Rhine to Chicago for his return to North Carolina. We drove by my parents' farm and made a quick stop, fortunately catching both of them at home. I had told my parents about the controversy, and they were happy to meet Rhine and to know how successful his presentation had been. Once I had completed my graduate work, I had the opportunity to interact with both Harry Harlow and Julian Stanley, who had so forcefully opposed having Rhine on campus. Our encounters were positive and pleasant; of course, I did not mention their reactions to Rhine's controversial lecture in 1953.

The Forum Committee sponsored discussions of Rhine's work in the Union Library, featuring Professor Garnett and, later, Professors Herschel Liebowitz, a psychologist, and Julius Weinberg, a philosopher, both of whom took negative positions, while I, as moderator, tried to maintain a neutral stance.

Aftermath

In January 1953, the UW department of philosophy announced a forthcoming lecture by C. D. Broad, an eminent British philosopher. I wrote to him, requesting a meeting with students interested in parapsychology, and he accepted. We all attended his lecture, which incorporated various parapsychological concepts to support his so-called "libertarian" stance regarding "free will." None of the philosophers objected, and the talk was very well received. The informal discussion session was a morale boost for members of our committee, who felt further vindicated regarding our decision to bring Rhine to the campus. Broad served twice as the president of the Society for Psychical Research; even though I did not know it at the time, he was what would later be called a "gay activist," recommending that same-sex activity be decriminalized in a letter also signed by philosophers A. J. Ayer and Bertrand Russell, and writer J. B. Priestley.

Later that year, the department of philosophy invited the Welsh philosopher H. H. Price to speak. Price was best known for his work on the philosophy of perception, and this was the topic of his presentation. But I knew that he was a past president of the British Society for Psychical Research and sent him a request to meet with a group of students who shared his interests. He accepted, and we had a stimulating discussion, focused on his views about "hauntings" and "ghosts," which he proposed were the result of "place memories," thoughts that were disconnected from a person's mind, becoming attached to a particular location. This concept was associated with his views on life after death, which Price envisioned as a "dream world of memories," one that could be shared with other deceased persons by telepathy.

Further vindication occurred on January 11, 1954, when *Life* magazine published an article by Aldous Huxley titled, "The case for ESP, PK and PSI."[5] Years later, I became good friends with Huxley's second wife, Laura, and told her how the timing of the article occurred a month after the Rhine lecture. I also mentioned that the Forum Committee sponsored a lecture on evolution by Aldous Huxley's brother, Julian Huxley, who told us that he was very sympathetic to parapsychology. My other contact with the Huxley family was a book titled *Shamans Through Time*, co-edited by Francis Huxley, Julian's grandson, which I have cited numerous times since its publication in 2000.[6]

Rhine had invited me to visit the Duke University Parapsychology Laboratory, and I was finally able to do so on April 14, 1956. I attended the weekly staff meeting, reviewing Rhine's visit to the University of Wisconsin. A special guest that day was the actor Adrian Booth, who wanted to demonstrate glossolalia, or "speaking in tongues." Rhine and his staff were very attentive to her, thanked her for her visit, and gave her some suggestions for further study. I noted that Ms. Booth was not invited to return, as there seemed to be no direct connection with the topics the laboratory was studying. This was my first opportunity to observe this phenomenon, and I later read the research on the topic, learning that the sounds produced do not qualify as a "language" and that the linguistic centers of the brain are not active during their production. However, it appears to reduce stress, which might explain its frequent occurrence in Pentecostal churches and other religious

---

[5] Huxley, A. (1954, January 11). The case for ESP, PK and PSI. *Life, 36*(2). 96–108.
[6] Narby, J., & Huxley, F. (Eds.). (2000). *Shamans through time: 500 years on the path to knowledge*. Penguin/Random House.

groups. Following the staff meeting, the Rhines took me to their farm for dinner, where I met two of their daughters, one of whom took me to a campfire with several of her friends, where I was introduced to "S'mores," roasted marshmallows dipped in chocolate and placed between two graham crackers. What a memorable event! It was one that was repeated many times over the years.

Assignments

I was flattered when Rhine sent me on several assignments, visiting a number of locations of supposed psychic phenomena.

Lady Wonder

My first assignment was a visit to see "Lady Wonder," an allegedly psychic mare kept by Mrs. Claudia Fonda at her Virginia farm. Rhine had visited the farm in 1927, concluding that the mare's abilities were genuine, but, after a subsequent investigation, he decided that those abilities had dissipated and that Mrs. Fonda's subtle movements were cueing her. When I visited on May 13, 1959, I paid my entrance fee and observed a huge typewriter with padded keys; Lady Wonder pressed her nose against a key, which triggered a metal card containing a letter or a number.

Our session began with a series of computations. When I asked Lady Wonder to add or subtract various digits, she did so correctly. Mrs. Fonda used a whip to prod the mare when she did not answer quickly, and I soon realized that this was a cue to direct her to the correct answer. Then I asked Lady Wonder to predict the Democratic Party's Vice-Presidential nominee for the upcoming elections. I suspected that John F. Kennedy would be the presidential nominee, but did not know who would be the other member on the ticket. Mrs. Fonda asked me who was in contention and I gave her the names of Kefauver, Symington, and Johnson. The filly correctly spelled out "Johnson," presumably because that name was the easiest to spell. But I noticed that Mrs. Fonda was cueing the filly before each of the letters.

I sent my report to Rhine, who then disclosed that his second visit had detected the subterfuge, something I did not know at the time. I suspected that he had given me this "test" to see if I could detect the mechanics of Lady Wonder's abilities. Incidentally, Johnson *was* the vice-presidential nominee. And I thought that the horse was indeed a "wonder" for being able to pick up the clues so adroitly!

Margaret Foos

My second assignment was to examine the claims of Margaret Foos, a young woman who asserted her ability to read printed material even though blindfolded. Rhine and his staff had tested her earlier in the year, and he was eager to get my opinion. On July 26, 1958, I went to her Virginia home, accompanied by John Scherer, my magician friend from my summers at Camp Richmond. Her father blindfolded her securely, asking John and me to assist him. Several wads of cotton were placed under the bandage to assure opacity. We had brought our own material, to avoid any duplicity. Mr. Foos placed the material on a table, and Margaret read it perfectly. We then gave him a newspaper, pointing to the page and column we wanted her to read. Again, she was correct in her reading. I told Mr. Foos that I would be happy to report our impressions should he want a testimonial.

We asked if they had visited the Duke University Parapsychology Laboratory. Mr. Foos reacted angrily, stating that they had thrown a jacket over Margaret's head and this so unnerved her that she was unable to perform. They had left in a huff. Although Rhine's staff could have used a gentler way to check for fraud, we knew why they were suspicious. When John and I returned home, I had him duplicate the bandages. As he was applying the bandages and the cotton, I scrunched my eyes. Once the bandages were affixed, I relaxed my eyes and could see down the corner of my nose and could read anything placed in front of me. When the printed material was placed at eye level, however, I could not read it. I sent our observations to Rhine, who concurred with our judgment.

In 1960, Margaret and her father visited a Veterans Administration Center in the hope that they could get a governmental contract to teach blinded veterans "blind reading." I found a report concerning the visit that stated that the psychiatrists who examined Margaret could find no evidence of cheating, but I doubted that they were experts in sleight of hand or "mentalism." Why didn't they contact Dr. Rhine? Why didn't they contact me? They probably thought it would be below their dignity to ask parapsychologists for their advice, and to do so might lead to censure from their peers. In any event, they did not hire Margaret and her father to teach the classes.

On August 25, 1958, I discussed the Foos case at a staff meeting of the Parapsychology Laboratory, where I met several notable figures in the field. One of them was J. Gaither Pratt, who had worked with Rhine off and on since the mid-1930s. Others were Wadeh Saleh, a volunteer from Egypt; Rhea White, a librarian; and Margaret Anderson, an educator. The latter two had been studying the existence of ESP between schoolteachers and their pupils. Another was Stephen Abrams, a graduate student at the University of Chicago, where he had organized a parapsychology study group. Abrams went to London for further studies and, while there, attained international attention in 1967 for sponsoring a full-page advertisement in *The Times* calling for the legalization of marijuana. The signatories included the psychiatrists R. D. Laing and David Cooper, biologist Francis Crick, anthropologist Julian Huxley, and the Beatles. I conducted my own less ambitious campaign in the United States, but had to wait some seven decades to see our efforts reach fruition.

The Iowa Poltergeist
My most ambitious assignment was to investigate an alleged poltergeist in Gutenberg, Iowa. Poltergeists are alleged "noisy ghosts" that create havoc, usually in someone's home. When Rhine was approached for advice by local authorities, he asked me to visit the site and provide my impressions. I enlisted the aid of a fellow graduate student, Arthur Hastings, who was also a talented magician. The house was located at the end of a country road in a spot marked by steep cliffs and deep gullies, inhabited by flocks of black crows. The local chief of police told us that "the whole hillside looks as if it could be haunted," a comment that laid the groundwork for people's expectations.

An older couple, the Bremers, owned the house, and their son had sent Marvin, their 16-year-old grandson, to live with them and serve as their caretaker after Mr. Bremer became bedridden with a broken hip. The first incident occurred one night when they were awakened by a loud noise, after which Marvin emerged with his face covered with black soot. A few weeks later, a glass of water landed on Mrs. Bremer's head, an egg flew across the room, the refrigerator toppled over, and a flower stand crashed to the floor—all within a few days. These disturbances frightened the Bremers and they left the house, moving in with neighbors in a nearby town. Mr. Bremer told us, "I don't know what would have happened next. If I had stayed, I probably would be dead by now."

Well-meaning visitors reported subsequent occurrences; there were additional noises, a stick flew through a window, and a 265-pound sailor was tossed out of bed by what he described as a "rising mattress." When the county sheriff investigated the site, a bottle crashed at his feet, and he immediately ordered the house closed and locked. He made an exception for two physicists from a local university who arrived with an oscilloscope, a Geiger counter, and an argon radiation counter. They reported normal levels of radiation and no cracks in the bedrock. The foundations of the house appeared to be solid, with no evidence of unusual vibrations or earth tremors. When a group of sociology students spent the night at the house, they reported that nothing aberrant occurred.

Local newscasters, television commentators, several newspapers, and *Newsweek* magazine reported the occurrences, sometimes overly dramatizing them. The publicity resulted in visits from curiosity-seekers breaking into the house to go "spook-hunting," leaving the modest building in shambles. After a few weeks, the publicity died down, and the crowds dwindled. As there seemed to be no ordinary explanation for the events, the "ghostly" hypothesis prevailed. This was the situation when we arrived.

Arthur Hastings and I interviewed the Bremers and discovered that their grandson had been visibly present during each of the incidents that motivated them to leave the premises, with the exception of the fallen refrigerator, at which time his location was unknown. We discovered that Mr. Bremer had done a good bit of "dowsing" for water in his younger years, perhaps disposing him to accept a paranormal explanation for the events. We also learned that Marvin was a high-school dropout, known to race around the countryside in an old Ford that he had acquired. We discovered a family conflict: Mrs. Bremer and her daughter-in-law had not spoken to each other in years.

When we examined the egg incident, Mr. Bremer told us that his son had brought the egg to the premises and balanced it on a lamp chimney to see if the house's vibrations would cause it to fall. When nothing happened, he left, and his son noted that all the other incidents had occurred in the dark. Once the lights were turned off, the egg flew across the room and splattered. Nonetheless, his parents did not suspect his complicity. The original explosion could have been due to a malfunction of the heating system, giving Marvin some ideas. We concluded that he tossed the water at his grandmother and toppled the refrigerator and flower stand. Mr. Bremer told us that the refrigerator had been disconnected for several weeks and could have been toppled "with one hand."

When visitors came to the house, they expected strange events to occur, so any naturally occurring noises would have been given a paranormal explanation. Some of the noises were said to have resembled exploding firecrackers, but nobody suggested that they might indeed have been firecrackers. What about the sailor who had been thrown out of bed? We discovered that he had retired after drinking a few beers, suggesting that the spirits were in the sailor, not in the mattress. When a bottle fell at the sheriff's feet, the nearby newspaper reporters accused each other of tossing it.

When we interviewed Marvin, he arrived sporting black sideburns, a black leather jacket, and a motorcycle cap. After answering a few perfunctory questions, he jumped into his Ford and disappeared for the rest of our visit. When we expressed our suspicions to his grandfather, Mr. Bremer replied, "I had never thought of that. I will have a talk with Marvin." He probably did so—and that explains why coverage of the "ghostly" disturbances dropped out of the media. Hastings and I wrote up our investigation in an article published in *ETC: A Review of General Semantics*, under the title *Poltergeist Phenomena and Expectancy Set*.[7] We opened our article with a quotation from Shakespeare, "In the night, imagining some fear, how easily is a bush supposed a bear." When an expectancy set is created, someone often interprets events in a way that conforms to that expectation. Rhine applauded our efforts; it saved him the trouble of sending a member of his staff to investigate the "poltergeist."

Northwestern University

When I was a graduate student at Northwestern University, I was an active member of Phi Delta Kappa, the honorary educational society. When we made plans for our annual banquet in 1958, I suggested that we invite Rhine to be the guest speaker. My suggestion was approved, Rhine accepted, and—once again—the psychology department raised a furor, with the chair telling his faculty not to support the program or attend the public lecture that was also scheduled. Because Phi Delta Kappa was a male society, I asked Pi Lambda Theta, its all-female counterpart, to co-sponsor the public lecture, and they agreed. Rhine also accepted my invitation to give an informal presentation at Foster House, the dormitory for which I was the counselor.

All three events went well, and the August 18 public lecture drew a crowd of 800 people, about the same number that turned out at the University of Wisconsin. Rhine's talk on the topic "Parapsychology:

---

[7] Hastings, A., & Krippner, S. (1961). Expectancy set and "poltergeist" phenomena. *ETC: A Review of General Semantics, 18*(3), 349–360.

Frontier Science of the Mind"[8] was held in the auditorium of the university's Technological Institute. Rhine covered several newer developments, such as his staff's work with ESP in cats and homing pigeons, and in pupil–teacher relationships. He noted the expression of interest in his work by psychiatrist Carl Gustav Jung, biologist Julian Huxley, and several other luminaries, and fielded post-lecture questions admirably.

The following day, Arthur Hastings and I drove Rhine to Chicago for his return trip to Durham. Noting that we would be passing by my parents' farm, I insisted that we drop by for another visit. My mother was not at home, but my father was working in the yard. Of course, he knew all about my interactions with Rhine and was both surprised and happy to meet him. It has been suggested that I saw Rhine as a "father figure," but I have always disagreed. My relationship with my father had always been positive, despite his earlier disappointment that I showed no interest in staying on a farm and orchard that he had energetically and meticulously cultivated over the decades. The same could be said for my relationships with Gardner Murphy, Paul Witty, and several other prominent men I had known over the years. However, they certainly were my mentors, and I will always be grateful for the role they played in my life.

Once Rhine had returned home, I sent him clippings from several newspapers, some of them based in Chicago. The Associated Press covered the lecture, and friends of mine around the country sent in the articles, which I forwarded to Rhine. CBS noted the event, as did several local radio networks, surpassing the coverage from our Wisconsin lecture. Notably, none of the coverage was negative or insulting, perhaps because of Northwestern's prestige and the status of the sponsors.

In 1959, Rhine and Pratt published *Parapsychology: Frontier Science of the Mind.*[9] Rhine told me that he was quite happy with the book because it was written as a text that could be used for courses on the topic. Over the years, very few such courses were approved by colleges and universities, and, by the time that some of them did develop, the book was outdated. Nonetheless, the book was important historically and garnered a favorable review from Michael Scriven, a celebrated philosopher. In 1968, Scriven received the Donald Campbell Award

---

[8] Rhine, J. B., & Pratt, J. G. (1959). *Parapsychology: Frontier science of the mind.* Duke University Press.
[9] Rhine & Pratt (1959).

from the Policy Studies Association; ironically, Campbell had ignored his department chair's instruction to avoid Rhine, attending the discussion session I had arranged at Foster House, where he presented a thoughtful critique of Rhine's findings. I held Scriven in high regard for many contributions, among them his creation of evaluation studies as a "transdisciplinary field," one that is neither cross-disciplinary nor multidisciplinary because it demands its own domain. Later, I suggested that parapsychology (or "psi research") was transdisciplinary in nature because it cannot be encapsulated by psychology, anthropology, physics, or any other single discipline, even when they work together.

From Duke University to FRNM

In 1964, Rhine reached retirement age and left Duke University, much to the relief of some psychology faculty members, who claimed to have been embarrassed to have been members of a department where research in parapsychology was being conducted. I thought that they might have been jealous that Rhine had received more publicity than they had, and had brought in more funding as well. Rhine and his staff set up the laboratory in a nearby house, naming it the Foundation for Research on the Nature of Man (FRNM). The foundation was envisioned to house several "institutes," the first being the Institute of Parapsychology, but funds were never obtained for the Institute of Healing or anything else.

On March 28, 1966, Montague Ullman and I spoke at FRNM, describing our research on dreams and ESP at Maimonides Medical Center in Brooklyn, New York. Earlier in 1966, Rhine had hinted that he might have a position for me at FRNM, but I finessed his suggestion, not only because I had planned to accept the Maimonides post, but because I had noted that many of his young assistants had left after a few years, citing irreconcilable conflicts. I did not want anything to interfere with the long-standing relationship that we had nurtured over the years. I had also developed a close relationship with Louisa Rhine, and recall a lecture that I heard Rhine deliver on June 11, 1971, in New Jersey. When a member of the audience asked Rhine about his wife's work, he replied, "It is equally important as mine. Other people have repeated what I have done but nobody has come close to matching her work." He was referring to Louisa's careful collection of what are called "spontaneous cases" in parapsychology—real-life instances of putative psi.

I have cited one of these cases in several of my articles because it is one of many that apparently saved someone's life. A young woman in the state of Washington woke up at 2:30 AM, having had a nightmare. She dreamed that the large chandelier over their daughter's bed in the next room had collapsed, crushing the baby. The clock on the infant's dresser read 4:45, and she could hear tumultuous wind and rain outside. She awakened her husband, who told her it was "just a silly dream"; furthermore, the weather was calm. But she could not get back to sleep and brought the baby into their own bed. Some two hours later, the couple was awakened by a loud crash. They rushed to the nursery to find the fallen chandelier on the crushed crib. In addition, the weather had changed, the wind was howling outside, and rain was beating against the windowpane.

Louisa Rhine published three books on these cases,[10,11,12] and their daughter, Sally Rhine Feather, continued the tradition with her book, *The Gift*, published in 2005. One of the many memorable cases she mentioned involved a woman who was planning to take her own life. Suddenly, she heard the voice of a close friend saying, "Don't do that, Marian!" This stopped the suicidal ideation, and the next day her friend contacted her, saying that she had awakened in the middle of the night sensing that Marian needed help. She began to pray, and kept on praying until dawn. In retrospect, Marian observed, "It was one of the most beautiful and mysterious experiences I have ever had."

Both mother and daughter cautioned that unlike laboratory psi spontaneous cases cannot rule out the possibility of coincidence, faulty memory, or fraud. J. B. Rhine added that spontaneous cases can point the way to innovations in laboratory research, and this was certainly the case with the work that Montague Ullman and I did with ESP and dreams. Louisa Rhine's initial work revealed that the majority of spontaneous cases involved dream reports, and I have credited her work in my own publications. In addition, some people become obsessed with or terrified by ESP after a personal experience. Neither outcome reflects a helpful balance between gullibility and undue skepticism. A better outcome combines open-mindedness and critical judgment.

---

[10] Rhine, L. E. (1961). *Hidden channels of the mind.* Time–Life Books.
[11] Rhine, L. E. (1969). *ESP in life and lab.* McMillan.
[12] Rhine, L. E. (1981). *The invisible picture: A study of psychic experiences.* McFarland.

On September 5, 1967, Rhine spoke on the history of parapsychology for one of the divisions of the American Psychological Association; I was present for his talk and was pleased that it was well attended and that the reception was very favorable. Earlier that year, I had been the program chair for the annual meeting of the Parapsychological Association; moreover, in 1982 I was elected president of the Parapsychological Association, and in 1983, I received the Dr. J. B. Rhine Award for Lifetime Achievement in Parapsychology from Andhra University in India. And to think it all started with the tragic news of my Uncle Max's death.

Chapter 7

Mandrake Gestures Hypnotically
15 February 1961. A Day When My Life Changed

On June 11, 1934, a new comic strip character, Mandrake the Magician, was introduced. Ostensibly a stage entertainer, Mandrake's real passion was fighting crime, aided by his African sidekick, Lothar and often by his girlfriend, Narda. For several decades, Mandrake showed up in comic books, movies, and television shows; he has been called the "First Superhero" of U.S. comics. He outwitted his adversaries by "gesturing hypnotically," producing illusions, engendering confusion, and sometimes making himself invisible. Mandrake's enemies included not only gangsters and "mad scientists," but also extraterrestrial villains.

From Comics to Parties

My parents subscribed to two local newspapers: the *Cambridge News* and the *Daily Jefferson County Union*. Neither publication featured comic strips, which I enjoyed, so a friend of the family dropped by every week with a collection of issues of a newspaper published in Madison, Wisconsin's state capital. I eagerly awaited this treat and devoured all the comics, especially Mandrake the Magician. I enjoyed reading about how he would utilize his hat, wand, and cape—accoutrements with magical properties passed down from his father. I was intrigued by accounts of his home, Xanadu, located on a hilltop in New York State, and the site of an international crime-fighting movement, Inter-Intel, overseen by Mandrake's cook, Hojo.

My weekly treat was brought to an abrupt end when my mother decided to punish my misbehavior by telling her friend not to bring over any more newspapers. I was crushed. I do not recall what my misdemeanor was, but I did not think that the punishment fit the crime. However, I kept reading about hypnosis, mainly in "popular psychology" columns. Sometimes directions for inducing hypnosis were provided, and I practiced with friends who had given their consent.

During my high school years, I was a member of a social group that enjoyed travelling together and hosting weekend parties. When newcomers joined our party, we welcomed them with a ritual called "Hypnosis by Candlelight." For example, when my neighbor Dorothy Dingledine joined us for one of these festivities, I requested her permission to have her participate in an "initiation hypnosis ceremony." She agreed. After we darkened the room, we asked her to stare at a candle while holding a kitchen plate in one hand and rubbing the bottom of the plate with the other hand. I provided the directions, stating that hypnosis would deepen with each successfully executed command:

> Rub the bottom of the plate very slowly in a counterclockwise manner. If it took you a moment to decide which direction was counterclockwise, you must be going very deeply into hypnosis. Now rub the plate in a clockwise direction, making sure that all five fingers are touching the bottom of the plate. Now quickly bring your fingers up to your forehead. Move them from left to right across your forehead. Again, if you had some trouble identifying left and right, your mind must be behaving in a very unusual manner, and the hypnosis must be working very well. Now touch your chin with your hand and bring your fingers up to your left cheek and across your nose and over to your right cheek. Now hold out your hand and I will place a mirror in it. You are now so deeply hypnotized that you will see whatever I tell you to see. As you look into the mirror, you will see that your face looks like that of a zebra, with dark black stripes alternating with flesh-colored stripes.

Needless to say, the plate had been held over the candle earlier that evening, so it had been covered with soot. Once Dorothy looked into the mirror, members of our group started to laugh, and so did she once the lights had been turned on. But every now and then, newcomers would take a minute or so to regain their composure, and I sensed that they had actually experienced something akin to hypnosis. However, I made sure that they were wide awake and alert before the merriment continued.

When I was a dormitory counselor at Northwestern University, some of the students, knowing I was studying psychology, asked me to hypnotize them; I complied, but with great care and caution. One student wanted me to take him back in time to a "former life." This was a novel request. I made sure that there were other students in the room, so that I could not be blamed if something untoward were to occur. Once hypnotized, he related his experience in the U.S. Army, where he eventually attained the rank of general. He also told of his escape from advancing Japanese troops in the Philippines, including how he rebounded and retook the ground he had lost. I asked him for his name, and he proclaimed, "I am General Douglas MacArthur!" His fellow students and I chuckled because MacArthur was alive and well at the time.

I also demonstrated post-hypnotic suggestion whenever I found a student who was especially suggestible. I refrained from implanting a behavior that could have been embarrassing, instead telling the hypnotized student that he would arise whenever I used the word "rise" in a sentence. This worked quite well, whether that word was used in a usual context, such as "Rise and shine," or in a context that was unusual, such as "Did you see the sunrise?" The student left campus for the summer, but, when he returned, I casually mentioned that I had been reading a book, *The Sun Also Rises*. Immediately, the student stood up, much to the puzzlement of his friends, until we explained what was going on, thanks to such principles as conditioned responses and role-playing.

When I was teaching at Kent State University, the Dean of Men asked me to work with college students who were having academic problems. With their permission, I used hypnosis to help them improve their academic achievement and published my results in 1963. At the same time, I used hypnosis with pupils attending a summer reading clinic that I directed at Kent State, with parental permission, and published the results in 1966.[1] Years later, I was asked to provide an overview of this work for two anthologies published in 1976 and 1977.[2] These articles, which were widely cited,

---

[1] Krippner, S. (1966). The use of hypnosis with elementary and secondary school children in a summer reading clinic. *American Journal of Clinical Hypnosis, 8*, 261–266.

[2] Krippner, S. (1976). Hypnosis as verbal programming in educational therapy. In E. Dengrove (Ed.), *Hypnosis and behavioral therapy* (pp. 235–243). Charles C. Thomas.

stimulated better controlled and more extensive research in subsequent decades.

One of my students at Kent State, whom I will call Marvin, was doing so poorly on examinations that he was about to withdraw from school. After an initial interview, I concluded that he had the capacity to do well in his courses but suffered from what is often called "examination anxiety." When he was hypnotized, I reinforced his self-image as a competent student with enough intelligence to do well in his courses. I had him repeat those statements, but in the first person, for example, "I have the mental capacity and the verbal skills to do well in school." I then had him rephrase it to, "I have the mental capacity and the verbal skills to do well on my examinations." I asked Marvin what physical object he could bring with him to remind him of those statements, and he mentioned that his parents had given him a good luck charm, a pendant that he never wore. I told Marvin he did not need to wear the pendant but simply bring it with him to examinations as a reminder of his resolve. After the hypnosis session ended, I told him to bring the pendant along for our next session, which he was happy to do. I said, "In my opinion, there is no inherent magic in good luck charms, because we make our own luck—at least as much as circumstances permit." Marvin went into his next examination with resolve, as well as the pendant, and felt no anxiety, nothing but confidence. He ended up with a "B" average in his courses at the end of the semester. Marvin, who was an excellent photographer, took some pictures of me for the university yearbook, photos showing me in the psychology laboratory manipulating an apparatus—one that I had never learned how to use in any of my courses. My aplomb gave Marvin's self-confidence a boost; if I could pull off a stunt for which I was unprepared, he could answer examination questions for which he had been preparing for months.

Much to my surprise, when I asked parents for permission to hypnotize their children, they tended to agree, often enthusiastically. My work with Marvin utilized a very direct form of hypnosis, with arm levitation suggestions (e.g., "Your arm is getting heavier and heavier; as it drops to the arm of the chair, you will go deeply into hypnosis"). For children, I did not even mention the word "hypnosis," although they all knew this was what we would be doing. Our work did not focus on examinations but on developing better study habits, for example, "Imagine that you are doing your homework. What would help you do the best possible job?" Many of them responded that they would turn off the television or radio, and work in a space where their siblings would not interfere, among other suggestions. I reinforced each image by repeating it, adding a few details such as having them imagine the time of day and the room in which they would be working. At the end of the semester, I had no complaints from parents and several reports of academic success.

Because I am not a clinical psychologist, I never used hypnosis for any type of psychotherapy. However, I wrote up my work with students for several books and journals, including the *American Journal of Clinical Hypnosis*, which, in 1968, also published my article on a simple telepathy test I had conducted at Kent State: Students attending a summer school session attempted to identify a picture in a collection that a graduate student in another room had been focusing upon.[3] The overall results were highly successful; the correct picture was chosen more often than chance or coincidence would have provided.

Enter Milton Erickson

On February 15, 1961, the American Psychiatric Association gave its official approval to the use of hypnosis in treating a variety of conditions. The APA had made the same recommendation in February 1960, while the American Medical Association had initiated a training program in hypnosis in September 1958. When I heard about the APA's decision, I decided it was time for me to take hypnosis seriously and to undergo formal training.

By this time, I was in the final stages of my doctoral work, so I was able to attend training sessions sponsored by the American Society of Clinical Hypnosis (ASCH), founded in 1957. I later attended additional training sessions sponsored by the Society of Clinical and Experimental Hypnosis (SCEH), founded in 1949. Both societies attempt to regulate the field and are open to qualified psychologists, psychiatrists, physicians, dentists, social workers, and other healthcare practitioners.

Originally, SCEH was designed to foster research in hypnosis and to bestow awards for excellence in the field, while ASCH's mission was to provide training in hypnosis for healthcare professionals and to uncover clinical applications for the research findings. Initial membership was limited to practitioners with graduate degrees in

---

[3] Krippner, S. (1968). An experimental study in hypnosis and telepathy. *American Journal of Clinical Hypnosis, 11*, 45–54.

either research or clinical work, but over time the two groups' memberships began to overlap; people (like me) ended up paying dues to both societies and attempting to attend both annual conventions.

In 1971, I was able to attend the joint conference of ASCH and SCEH, and recall Milton Erickson being carried to the speakers' table in a wheelchair, a striking figure in his bright purple jumpsuit. A friend told me that Erickson was color blind for every hue except purple, so he wore it as often as possible. Erickson had contracted polio when he was 17 and was so profoundly paralyzed that his recovery was in doubt. While recuperating in bed and being unable to speak, he became aware of the significance of nonverbal communication, body language, and body memories. By focusing on these memories, he was able to speak again, subsequently attending college and medical school and undergoing psychiatric training. In 1949, he established a private practice in his Phoenix, Arizona, home and began to provide training programs in hypnosis. His many contributions to the field were cited in a 2005 book by Ronald Havens, *The Wisdom of Milton Erickson*.[4]

Erickson co-founded the *American Journal of Clinical Hypnosis,* and I was delighted when he accepted one of my articles for publication in 1963.[5] This was a description of how I had used hypnosis to facilitate study habits and improve examination performance among the university students in my dormitory. He also accepted my articles on a variety of topics, including hypnosis and creativity in 1965, hypnosis and attention in 1974, and, in 2014, a proposed mind–body–spirit paradigm.[6,7,8] The journal called on me to review several books, notably those with a psychedelic theme such as *The Varieties of Psychedelic Experience* by my friends Robert Masters and Jean Houston. Once I became a member of the Society of Clinical and Experimental Hypnosis, I began to publish in its journal, notably an article, "Trance and the Trickster," which connected the placebo

---

[4] Havens, R. (2005). *The Wisdom of Milton H. Erickson.* Crown House.
[5] Krippner, S. (1963). Hypnosis and reading improvement among university students. *American Journal of Clinical Hypnosis, 5,* 187–193.
[6] Krippner, S. (1965). Hypnosis and creativity. *American Journal of Clinical Hypnosis, 8,* 94–99.
[7] Krippner, S., & Bindler, P. R. (1974). Hypnosis and attention: A review. *American Journal of Clinical Hypnosis, 16,* 166–177.
[8] Krippner, S. (2014). The mind-body-spirit paradigm: Crisis or opportunity? *American Journal of Clinical Hypnosis, 56,* 210–215.

response, shamanism, and suggestibility.[9] If early humans were suggestible, they would have been more likely to benefit from shamanic concoctions and rituals, making suggestibility an adaptive trait. Those who were not suggestible did not benefit from shamanic intervention; thus, they would succumb to their maladies, and their genes would drop out of the gene pool. This was hardly an original hypothesis, but I was able to make the connection with hypnosis clearer than previous authors had.

Some writers have referred to Erickson as a modern-day shaman. I am very circumspect regarding how I use the term, but the case could be made that Erickson performed many shamanic-like functions for his clients and students, notably in initiating procedures that were consciousness-altering in nature. Before Erickson arrived on the scene, most hypnotic practitioners provided a set of instructions for a client or patient to follow. Erickson, however, used formal procedures in only about 20 percent of his cases, preferring to interact with individuals, couples, and families. Quite often, he did not even use the word *hypnosis*, instead using storytelling and imagination to stimulate their inner resources. After Erickson's death in 1980, the Milton H. Erickson Foundation continued to conduct training programs and host international psychotherapy conferences.

I considered myself fortunate to have learned so much from Erickson earlier in my career. I used his storytelling procedures with the children I was attempting to assist at Kent State University; one of my articles for his journal described an experiment I conducted in which hypnotized students improved their reading skills significantly more than those who had the same instructions but without hypnosis. Many years later, I became friends with two of his daughters, one of whom gave me a small Milton Erickson puppet, which looked dapper in a bright purple suit.

Enter T. X. Barber

Theodore Xenophon "Ted" Barber was the son of Greek immigrants, who gave him the middle name of an ancient Greek philosopher and military hero. He spent his career conducting research in hypnosis and writing acclaimed articles and books on the topic. When I heard his presentation at an annual convention of the American

---

[9] Krippner, S. (2004). Trance and the trickster: Hypnosis as a liminal phenomenon. *Journal of Clinical and Experimental Hypnosis, 53*, 97–118.

Psychological Association, I was struck by his iconoclasm, as he insisted that hypnosis was not an "altered state of consciousness" but a phenomenon that could be explained by known psychological principles. Ted's research demonstrated that he could produce all the major hypnotic phenomena, such as anesthesia, without using a formal hypnotic induction and even without mentioning the word *hypnosis*. Instead, he utilized research participants' suggestibility, expectations, imagination, motivation, and related traits to shift their cognitive and behavioral responses. He was also able to produce these phenomena by putting participants in a social situation that they would perceive as "hypnosis," but without using a formal induction. I found this of interest, as I had always used a number of inductions after discovering what my participants expected. If they expected their eyes to close as a result of my instructions, I provided that framework. If they expected me to use a candle flame, a moving pendulum, or a spot on the wall, I would oblige. Sometimes I preceded induction with a few "suggestibility tests," such as one in which I would have them stand with their eyes closed and imagine that a strong wind was blowing their body forward—or backward.

Ted would often infuriate other people in the field by placing the word "hypnosis" in quotation marks when he wrote about it. He maintained that he wanted to de-mythologize the term and to demonstrate that it was a social construct, not a special mental state. After his presentation at the American Psychological Association, I gave him my address and asked for some of his articles. Much to my surprise, he sent me a dozen of them, along with a personal letter. I soon discovered his interest in parapsychology and sent him some of my articles about my experiments with telepathic effects in dreams. It was not long before I was able to introduce him to Virginia Glenn and my other friends in New York City, who arranged for him to present an all-day seminar that won him a new bevy of admirers. Eventually, he proposed a typology of hypnotic participants: those who were "fantasy-prone," those who were highly motivated, and those who dissociated easily and were prone to amnesia.

In 1969, Ted published his classic book, *Hypnosis: A Scientific Approach*,[10] and edited *Advances in Altered States of Consciousness &*

---

[10] Barber, T. X. (1969). *Hypnosis: A scientific approach.* Van Nostrand Reinhold.

Human Potentialities[11] in 1976. By that time, we had become friends, and he included my article about A. H. Maslow and the "plateau experiences" in this anthology.[12] I was able to get him invited to an annual meeting of a conference sponsored by the Menninger Foundation, where he spoke on an evolving interest of his, the presence of consciousness in nature, ranging from subatomic particles to galaxies. He developed this theme further when he was invited to give the banquet address for the Parapsychological Association, and—before his sudden death—in a book, *The Human Nature of Birds*.[13]

The Physical-Mental Universe

Ted took early retirement as director of research for the Medford Foundation and our contacts continued, both at meetings of hypnosis societies and whenever I was in the Boston area. I also met his companion, Sheryl Wilson, who wrote her doctoral dissertation on the topic of "fantasy-prone" individuals, a study soon replicated by other researchers. Ted once told her, "If I die before my book is completed, Stan Krippner is the only one who will be able to finish it." Following his death, Sheryl sent me his incomplete manuscript, some of it resurrected from handwritten notes. I patiently pieced them all together; instead of the projected forty chapters, I was able to create twenty chapters.

Ted stated that the basic assumption of "official science" is that the universe is non-mental, non-purposive, and without meaning. He disagreed totally, maintaining that people live in a wondrous cosmos of "mindful matter," and that all entities of the universe, "from quanta to molecules, to organisms to galaxies, share the same physical–mental substance, the same mind–matter that is the essence of you and me." The implication was that this realization would lead to an "ecstatic consciousness and joyous life."

For example, Ted maintained that the physical–mental subatomic particles of the sun are organized into plasma that "acts as if it is alive,

---

[11] Krippner, S. (1976). The plateau experience: A. H. Maslow and others. In T. X. Barber (Ed.), *Advances in altered states of consciousness and human potentialities* (Vol. 1, pp. 651–664). Psychological Dimensions.

[12] Krippner, S. (1976). The plateau experience: A. H. Maslow and others. In T. X. Barber (Ed.), *Advances in altered states of consciousness and human potentialities* (Vol. 1, pp. 651–664). Psychological Dimensions.

[13] Barber, T. X. (1993). *The human nature of birds: A scientific discovery with startling implications*. Penguin.

and manifests intelligent organization, ingenuity, memory, and ability to regenerate." In addition, the movement of the solar system "is comprehensible if each kind of celestial object is comprised of mental-matter, self-organized to act purposefully and intelligently within its own cosmic niche." Furthermore,

> At every level of the hierarchy of galaxies and at every standard part of each kind of galaxy, we see purposive, mindful structures such as the great jets of plasma (shot out symmetrically from opposite sides of incredibly immense radio galaxies) that maintain their collimated, straight-line, linear trajectories for tens of millions of light years and finally terminate by forming two immense lobes of plasma (separated by tens of millions of light years) that are astonishingly symmetric as if the plasma matter that formed them had mindfully implemented a symmetric blueprint.

I sent my truncated version of Ted's book to an agent who found it very exciting, perhaps groundbreaking, and was sure he could find a major publisher. Ted's Japanese publisher heard about the book and was eager to begin a Japanese translation. But then everything fell apart. Sheryl Wilson discovered that Ted had not changed his will, having named his ex-wife as the person who controlled his future publications. Sheryl was not on good terms with the former Mrs. Barber and feared an expensive lawsuit. The book was aborted, which was one of the major disappointments of my life.

All was not lost, however. Another friend of mine, Jeremy Narby, a cultural anthropologist, had produced related ideas that he presented in his 2005 book, *Intelligence in Nature*. Although not as comprehensive, it took a similar perspective, and I did what I could to get the book reviewed and publicized.

Definitions

It is noteworthy that neither Milton Erickson nor Ted Barber thought that a formal hypnotic induction was necessary for someone to be hypnotized, although their definitions of hypnosis were radically different. Erickson defined it as "a state of consciousness in which there is a marked awareness to shared ideas and understandings, and an increased willingness to respond either positively or negatively to those ideas." For Barber, being hypnotized was a role people played;

they acted "as if" they were hypnotized, "thinking and feeling" along with the hypnotist. He spelled out this perspective in his 1969 classic, *Hypnosis: A Scientific Approach*.

The *APA Dictionary of Psychology*[14] defines hypnosis *as* "the procedure, or the state induced by the procedure, whereby a hypnotist suggests that a subject experiences various changes in sensation, perception, cognition, emotion, or control over motor behavior. Subjects appear to be receptive, to various degrees, to suggestions to act, feel, and behave differently than in a normal waking state." It defines suggestibility as "a state in which the ideas, beliefs, attitudes, or actions are readily and uncritically accepted," and hypnotic susceptibility as "the degree to which an individual can enter into hypnosis." I am in accord with most of those terms, but would prefer the word *domain* for *state*, because, in my opinion, there are many states that can be referred to as hypnosis.

The Society for Psychological Hypnosis also uses the state paradigm, defining hypnosis as "A state of consciousness involving focused attention and reduced peripheral awareness characterized by an enhanced capacity for response to suggestion." Hypnotizability is defined as "an individual's capacity to experience suggested alterations in physiology, sensations, thoughts, or behavior during hypnosis." This Society is the former Division 30 of the American Psychological Association, for which I served as president from 1978 to 1980. I attained fellow status in that society, as well as in the ASCH and SCEH; the latter gave me its Human Treasure Award in 2013, and five years later created the Stanley Krippner Award, given annually to newcomers to the field. I had been a newcomer myself in 1962,when my application for membership in the American Society for Clinical Hypnosis was approved; a few years later my membership application for membership in the Society for Clinical and Experimental Hypnosis was approved. I often mention that fact when I write congratulatory emails to the annual winners of the award.

Enter Frank Shames

Frank and Dorothy Shames were frequent participants in the various "happenings" and workshops that Virginia Glenn organized. Frank

---

[14] American Psychological Association (2007). *APA Dictionary of Psychology*, (pp. 436. 457, 907). American Psychological Association.

was a successful business executive in Manhattan, and his wife delighted in throwing small dinner parties for friends. Few of their business associates and houseguests would have been aware of Frank's interest in hypnosis and a project that he helped initiate in 1964. In November of that year, Frank contacted me and discussed the program. The treatment site was an office suite at a Roman Catholic Church, where Father James Pitcanthley had initiated the program after taking courses on hypnosis from a lay "hypnotherapy" association. The program had one focus: the treatment of heroin addiction among young people.

I had avoided official contact with the various hypnotherapy associations, although many of my friends, such as Frank Shames, had been members. I am aware of the positive results some "hypnotherapists" have obtained when working with their clients, but I have a fundamental issue with the term. Hypnotherapy implies that hypnosis is a "therapy," but I maintain that, at best, it facilitates therapy. Hence, there can be "hypnotically facilitated cognitive therapy," "hypnotically facilitated psychodynamic therapy," "hypnotically facilitated humanistic therapy," among others. Each of those therapies can be practiced with or without hypnosis, but include hypnosis when it seems to facilitate the therapeutic process. Moreover, each of those therapies is supported by decades of theory and research that delineate their perspectives, providing a depth that the single word *hypnotherapy* lacks.

When I observed hypnotherapy being practiced in Frank Shames's program, it was apparent to me that its claims of success were probably justified. The clients only recently had become persons with a substance use disorder and were not long-term, "hardcore" addicts. I recall two well-dressed teenage males who visited the church for the first time when I was there. They had "shot up" out of curiosity, then were shocked to find themselves coming back for more, even stealing and selling household goods to support their habit. Their hypnotherapist used basic hypnotherapeutic suggestions, focusing on the desired end goal, not on hypothetical unconscious motives or conflicts that might have been underlying causes. For example, they had their clients imagine that they were drug free and were enjoying the feelings of liberation. Or they had them imagine that each attempt to "shoot up" would engender severe pain, feelings of disgust, or unpleasant images. Even so, withdrawal from heroin addiction is not easy and underlines the advice, "It's so good, don't even try it once," which is a mantra for prevention.[15]

Frank Shames and his associates appeared to have helped many young people break free of heroin addiction, but the group did very little record-keeping, much less follow-up studies. When assessments of hypnotherapy are made, the results show little or no improvement in such areas as tobacco cessation, weight loss, or pain during childbirth. Clinicians who practice hypnotically facilitated therapy have higher rates of success because hypnosis is used in combination with an established psychotherapeutic approach. Notable was Irving Kirsch's use of hypnosis with moderately depressed clients, for whom he found hypnotically facilitated therapy was as effective as medication, if not more so, and without the risk of side-effects. In 2009, Kirsch published his results in the book, *The Emperor's New Drugs,* which is a landmark study of hypnosis, the placebo effect, and psychotherapy.[16] Kirsch made the case that people often experience what they expect to experience, and this is especially true of both hypnosis and placebos. Kirsch's book evoked considerable controversy, notably from psychiatrists who accused him of selective reporting; in response, Kirsch countered that people's "expectancy response" enables them to experience what they expect to experience, a principle underlying both placebo effects and reactions to hypnosis, as well as their reactions to most anti-depressants. Kirsch and two co-authors subsequently conducted a new analysis that reiterated his previous stance.

Exit Jerry Garcia

In 1995, Jerry Garcia contacted me, requesting that I use hypnosis to help him stop smoking tobacco. We made an appointment for me to see him in my office at Saybrook University. I suspected that Jerry was hoping that hypnosis would assist his recovery from his other addictions (to cocaine and heroin), but I did not voice my hunch; further, I knew Jerry's schedule of the Grateful Dead's concerts would keep him from engaging in more than one session, and I had never been able to work that quickly. The overall success rate for tobacco

---

[15] Smith, D. E., & Gay, G. R. (Eds.) *It's so good, don't even try it once: Heroin in perspective.* Basic Books.
[16] Kirsch, I. (2009). *The emperor's new drugs: Exploding the anti-depressant myth.* Random House.

cessation was not impressive, but I had been able to stop a dozen friends and students from smoking either over periodic sessions or a weekend "marathon." I pulled out all the stops, using a "multi-sensory" approach in which I suggested that the smell and taste of tobacco would make them nauseated, that looking at a cigarette would trigger repulsion, and that they should find a temporary substitute, such as sniffing perfume, shaving lotion, or some other pleasant odor. I warned them that even if my treatment was ineffective, they would never enjoy smoking tobacco again. This approach was based on Albert Ellis's "Rational Emotive Behavior Therapy," which used cognition and affect to bring about changes in one's activities that are self-harmful.

At the time, I had little energy because I was recovering from a near-fatal accident in Spain, where I had been hit by a moving vehicle while jogging and had few expectations for the success of our time together. I had asked Stuart Fischer, a former assistant at the Dream Laboratory, to create a menu of healthy vegetarian foods for Jerry, as I intended to use that list as a post-hypnotic suggestion. Stuart had requested no fee, simply an autograph—and Jerry obliged by drawing his own caricature and signing it. The session went well, and Jerry left my office on an optimistic note. I was told that he adhered to Stuart's dietary suggestions, which may have given him a few extra days of life. On August 9, 1995, I received the sad news that Jerry had had a fatal heart attack while in residence at a drug treatment center. Perhaps his earlier reaching out to me had indicated that he was finally ready to confront his addictions, but the resolution had come too late.

Jerry and I had known each other for two and one-half decades, and our encounters, albeit rare, were always memorable. On one occasion, he told me that some practitioners of yoga had identified musical tones that they believed were associated with each of the so-called "spinal chakras," and that he was trying to track down details so that he could produce a musical composition based on the tones. During another visit, we discussed high voltage "Kirlian" photography, and he asked if it could record an impression of his missing right middle finger, given that there were several Kirlian photographs that claimed to have recorded a "phantom leaf" following the removal of a portion of that leaf. Ronny Mastrion, a Dream Lab volunteer, was eager to give it a try, but time simply ran out. Jerry left an incredible legacy, including recorded sessions (many of them "bootlegged"): over 2,500 with the Grateful Dead and another 1,000 with smaller ensembles. *Rolling Stone* magazine in 2015 listed

Garcia as number 46 on its list of "The Greatest Guitarists of All Time." The Grateful Dead performed before an estimated 25 million people during its three-decade run, an all-time record.

Chapter 8

It Started with Disney
6 February 1943. A Day When My Life Changed

My earliest memory was sitting on my mother's lap while she was singing a song. It was improvised, citing the flavors of candy I enjoyed. I recall interjecting, "I like lime, too!" Without missing a beat, my mother sang, "And he also likes lime-flavored candy." Some years later, she wanted to know what kind of cake she should make for my birthday. I responded that I wanted the cake in three colors, and she dutifully prepared a cake with layers of pink, yellow, and green. Of course, all the layers tasted the same; because food colors had provided the hues without changing the taste, but it was a delicious cake, nonetheless.

Technicolor Krippner

Much later, I discovered how central color was in biological evolution, serving as an enticement, a disguise, and a warning. Many other animals can see ultraviolet hues, which are not available to humans. Still others have fewer, or more, than the three basic colors of the human spectrum. And there are human populations that make no differentiation between such colors as blue and green; but that is due to culture, not to biology. I learned that color is more of a subjective than an objective phenomenon. When light hits an object, it is absorbed or reflected—but the resulting color experience depends upon the viewer's biology and, in humans, the cultural context. My biology professor at the University of Wisconsin called me "Technicolor Krippner," because I used different colors of ink on exams involving depictions of various specimens.

One of the university's most distinguished faculty members, Helen White, was known as "The Purple Goddess" because of her apparel and her exceptional height. I never took a course from Professor White, but I did attend her lectures whenever I could because of her expertise in English literature. She was the first female president of the American Association of University Professors, and after I left Madison a new building housing the English department was named in her honor. The director of the Wisconsin Memorial Union, Porter Butts, with whom I worked for three years, was known for signing his documents with green ink. As a member of the Union Forum Committee, I brought Frank Lloyd Wright to the campus and discovered that his logo, appearing in most of his buildings, was cast in a spectrum of earthy red colors that Wright referred to as "Cherokee Red."

Much earlier, my fascination with color was apparent when I read about the forthcoming Walt Disney film, *Fantasia*. The film was released in 1940, and I begged my parents to take me to Madison, as it was not playing in smaller cities. The film is memorable for many reasons, among them Mickey Mouse enacting a role in Paul Dukas's orchestra piece *The Sorcerer's Apprentice*, and the abstract art that accompanied J. S. Bach's *Toccata and Fugue in D Minor*. I was so delighted with each of the eight segments that I went to see it each time it was re-released; it remains one of my favorite movies.

However, my enthusiasm was not shared by the movie-going public, and *Fantasia* was a box-office bomb. The Walt Disney Studios laid off hundreds of animators and was on the verge of financial collapse when the Japanese attacked Pearl Harbor in December 1941. The studios were occupied by 500 U.S. troops to protect the nearby Lockheed aircraft production plant. The U.S. government approached Disney, asking him to produce propaganda films to enhance the war effort. Disney agreed, receiving about $5,000 for each of the 20 films he and his staff created. In retrospect, it is likely that the studios would have closed without this government contract.

I recall seeing *Victory through Air Power*, which extolled the ability of the U.S. Air Force to win the war, and *Der Fuehrer's Face*, which parodied life under Adolf Hitler and won the Academy Award for best animated short subject. I also remember a film encouraging people to buy U.S. Savings Bonds, for which I used every available penny during the war years, and which I did not cash in for twenty years. Later I discovered that there were films that encouraged people to pay their income taxes, and others requested by every branch of the U.S. Military.

The U.S. State Department sent Walt Disney and twenty members of his staff on a tour of Latin America as part of the war effort's "Good Neighbor Policy." Since several of those countries had close ties with Nazi Germany, the policy was designed to counteract its influence. Upon his return, Disney launched plans to cooperate with the newly formed U.S. Office of Inter-American Affairs, headed by Nelson Rockefeller. In addition to producing a short documentary about the Amazon Valley, Disney created a full-length film, *Saludos Amigos*, which premiered in

Rio de Janeiro in 1942 and was released in the United States on February 6, 1943. That movie changed my life.

Saludos Amigos

The film introduced its audiences to scenes in Argentina, Bolivia, Brazil, and Chile, combining real-life photography and animation. The animated characters included Mickey Mouse, Goofy, and José Carioca, a wise-cracking Brazilian parrot. J. B. Kaufman, a film historian, claimed that the movie did more to cement a community of interest among peoples of the Americas in a few months than the State Department had done in fifty years.

I found the Brazilian segment especially memorable, with its colorful depiction of Carnival activities and such samba-infused songs as *Tico-Tico* and *Brazil*, the latter being the first Brazilian song to be played more than one million times on U.S. radio. I also did some research on Carnival, as I was enchanted by the festive music, the costumes, and the dances that were portrayed. I discovered that Carnival (*O Carnaval do Brasil*, in Portuguese) is a six-day celebration preceding Lent, a period of some 40 days with its accompanying austerities. It is celebrated differently in various parts of the country, but all are characterized by spectacular costumes, as well as the dance music typical of that area. Carnival crosses class lines; indeed, many poor Brazilians save money for an entire year in order to purchase flamboyant garb in which they may revel. I promised myself that someday I would visit Brazil and experience the festivities first-hand.

The popularity of *Saludos Amigos* prompted Disney to make another film about Latin America, *The Three Caballeros*, in which Donald Duck and José Carioca were joined by a Mexican rooster, Panchito. Once again, there was an effusiveness of celebratory clothing and music. As a result of seeing the two films, I began to follow the careers of Getúlio Vargas, Brazil's president (and dictator) during the war years, and Carmen Miranda, the Portuguese-born Brazilian singer and film star, who in 1945 was the top female wage earner in the United States. Miranda was invited to appear in a Broadway musical, but she insisted on bringing her Brazilian band; the producers agreed, but refused to pay for their transportation. President Vargas produced the money, realizing the diplomatic advantages to Brazil of her appearance.

Portuguese Classes

In 1950, I graduated from high school and entered the University of Wisconsin, discovering that two years of studying a non-English language were required. Knowing my limitations, I thought I would be overwhelmed by the huge class enrollment in French, German, or Spanish, even though I had taken two years of Spanish in high school. I opted for Portuguese, finding that my classmates were all Hispanic majors; I was perfectly content to be the only member of the class who received a "B" every semester instead of an "A," the grade my classmates received.

Professor Alberto Rosa had us read such Brazilian classics as *Dom Casmurro* in the original Portuguese. Every Friday would be a *festa,* or celebration, replete with Brazilian and Portuguese snacks, as well as Portuguese songs. He also gave philosophy lessons in Portuguese, and I recall him comparing philosophers with people who had been given a large mound of beans. It would be impossible for them to consume all the beans, so they needed to be selective; indeed, that is what happens when philosophers present their way of understanding the world, each perspective being limited by each philosopher's culture and personality. It was Professor Rosa who introduced me to existentialism, a philosophical perspective that he found especially appealing and one that had a major influence on my life. I liked its emphasis upon freedom of choice and its insistence that "existence precedes essence." Rather than focusing on innate "forms," existentialists deny that humans have inborn identities. Instead, humans create their own identities and forge values that provide meaning to their lives. Later, I referred to this as the "backpack" model of identity, given that the backpack symbolizes one's genetic and cultural possibilities and limitations as contrasted to the "seed" model that postulates an innate identity that flourishes or ossifies as a result of one's milieu.

Professor Rosa introduced us to contemporary Brazilian popular and classical music. I spent hours in the university "listening room" playing recordings of classical music by Hector Villa-Lobos and also hacked out the popular song "Brazil" on the piano, eventually coming up with a version that I could perform for friends without making too many mistakes. The piano classes I had taken with Grace Snell much earlier in my life not only enhanced my enjoyment of music but enabled me to construct a small repertoire that I could perform in informal settings.

A young colleague of Rosa's, Professor Don Robinson, who had lived for several years in Brazil, took over the class from time to time. He also staged a production of *Vestido de Noiva* (*The Bridal Gown*), a 1943 play by Nelson Rodrigues that ushered in the modern era of Brazilian theater. Members of our class were invited to audition for the play, and I ended up playing a newsboy. Professor Robinson had translated the play into English, and the production won positive reviews, notably from members of the university's department of Spanish and Portuguese.

Professor Robinson recruited me to serve as a tutor for two brothers from Brazil who had just moved to Madison. My assignment was to acquaint them with the English-language words that described love, sex, and romantic activities. Apparently, my tutoring helped, as they became wildly popular in both of their high schools.

A few years later, I began my graduate studies at Northwestern University, which then required competence in a non-English language. I told my advisor, Professor Paul Witty, that I wanted to take my exam in Portuguese. He made an appointment for me to see the dean of the college to ask for permission. I came well prepared with a list of landmark psychological texts from Portugal, chief among them the work of Antonio Muñoz, who made significant contributions to the understanding of the Babinski Reflex in infants. After listening attentively, the dean told me that the reason I wanted to take the exam in Portuguese was that I didn't know any other foreign language. I told him that I had studied Spanish in high school, but wanted to avoid the huge classes in Spanish at my previous university. The dean then told me that I would gain great satisfaction in reading pioneering psychological treatises in the original German or French, to which I replied that I would gain even more satisfaction by reading the works in English. Finally, the dean told me that I should let my conscience be my guide, and that he would approve my request, albeit reluctantly.

A few days later, as the beloved Disney character Jiminy Cricket reminds us, I informed the dean that I had "let my conscience be my guide," upon which I was told to file for the exam. After doing considerable homework, I reported to the hall where the tests were given. Not surprisingly, I was the only one taking the exam in Portuguese. When I received the two items that I was to translate, I was surprised. One was a section of a catalogue from a Portuguese university. The other was a selection from a Portuguese novel—one written in the archaic style that was employed before a team of scholars reconciled Portuguese and Brazilian Portuguese. I wrote a preface to my translation of the latter work, pointing out the dated nature of the selection, and observing that I would provide an exact translation (in one color of ink) and then a less literal translation (in another color). My strategy must have worked because I passed the exam.

Flying Down to Rio

I did not want to lose what little fluency I had in Portuguese, so I watched Brazilian films and memorized lyrics to such popular Brazilian songs as "Chiquita Banana" and "Brazil." A 1933 Hollywood film, *Flying Down to Rio*, which I saw much later, featured the song "Carioca," a term used to describe inhabitants of Rio de Janeiro. (Incidentally, none of the music from the movie was composed by Brazilians.)

I made my first trip to Rio in 1973, following a stop in São Paulo, where my paper had been accepted for presentation at the InterAmerican Psychological Association's annual convention. Alberto Villoldo, who had earned his doctorate under my tutelage, came with me to São Paulo, where we contacted Carmen and Jarbas Marinho, with whom I had been in correspondence. They regaled us with delicious Brazilian food and took us to one of the classes where they were introducing neophytes to mediumship. They were members of the Spiritist Federation, whose practices follow the teachings of the French author Allen Kardec. In the mid-1880s, Kardec (a pen name) became interested in mediumship and conducted long interviews with ten mediums, finding similarities in their beliefs and practices. He distilled their statements in *The Book of Spirits*, published in 1847, and four additional volumes. These books became popular with many highly educated Brazilians, and soon spread to all social classes, making it the third most popular religion in Brazil, following Catholicism and the various denominations of Protestantism.

Alberto and I were told that Spiritists maintain cordial relationships with the African-based religions, so we asked the Marinhos where we could attend a Candomblé session. They gave us an address, and the following night we hired a taxicab to take us there. Our taxi driver told us that the address was in one of the most dangerous sections of São Paulo and dropped us off as quickly as he could, so we had to ask for directions, finding the townspeople friendly and cordial. The session had already started, but we were welcomed and observed a remarkable ceremony in which a "spirit guide" known as "Blue Feather" was "incorporated" by one of the mediums, following the ingestion of strong tobacco. The medium then embraced members of the group, including

Alberto and me, passing on "healing energy." Following the session, we were invited to socialize with the group and enjoy the homemade coconut delicacies that were quickly served. A group member took us to a bus stop, which eventually brought us close to our hotel, bringing our foray to a safe and successful closure.

Later, I visited several Spiritist and Candomblé sessions, as well as those associated with Umbanda, the other major African–Brazilian religion. Umbanda, which originated in the 1930s, is quite eclectic. Its doctrines and ceremonies contain several aspects of Catholicism and Spiritism a well as its African heritage. I was able to put my Portuguese to good use, and Alberto's fluency in Spanish also facilitated communication. Years later, my interest was rewarded, as I received a certificate naming me an honorary member of both Candomblé and Umbanda.

In Rio, as well as São Paulo, we were introduced to the popular dish *feijoada*, whose origins go back to the days of slavery. Enslaved people concocted a hearty dish from black beans, rice, meat scraps, orange slices, kale or a similar green, and farofa, a flour made from the roots of the mandioca plant. When the dish passed into the cuisine of slave masters, roast beef or pork substituted for the pig's ears, pig's tails, and other scraps that enslaved people had at their disposal. Many variations ensued; if black beans were not available, red beans were used, collards sometimes replaced kale, and pasta was used instead of rice by the Italian colonists who soon arrived in significant numbers.

Alberto and I also discovered *Guaraná*, a soft drink made from the red guaraná berries found in the Brazilian rainforests. Indigenous people ate the berries for energy, because of their high caffeine content. But in the early 1900s, a way was found to decrease the caffeine and enhance the flavor by adding other ingredients, although one variation is known as *Guaraná Plus*, which retains its caffeine. I found this drink invaluable when I attended an all-night celebration at the end of Carnival. The parade of the prize-winning samba bands was so spectacular, I did not want to miss a thing!

Enter Alberto Villoldo

Alberto and his family left Cuba in 1959, just as Fidel Castro and his troops were entering Havana. Ten years later, Alberto and I met when I was lecturing at the Inter-American University in Puerto Rico; later, once he arrived in New York City, he visited me at Maimonides Medical

Center, where I was directing our Dream/ESP Project. We stayed connected, and once I began to work for an at-a-distance graduate school, Alberto became one of my students and I served on his dissertation committee.

In 1976, Alberto created the Four Winds Society, taking its name from the four cardinal directions, a motif probably first used by the ancient Babylonians in about 4000 BCE. The society sponsored correspondence courses, in-person workshops, and trips to Peru, where Alberto introduced his groups to the Q'ero practitioners with whom he enjoyed a collegial relationship. The Quechua-speaking Q'ero tribes live in the Cuzco area of Peru and are renowned for their textiles, using designs and materials that date back centuries.

Alberto drew upon his background as both a psychologist and a medical anthropologist, as well as his knowledge of neuroscience, to design a number of programs. Some of my friends have been among his most avid students, several of them joining his expeditions to South America. Even more have read his books on the topic. Although English is his second language, his books are reader friendly and engrossing. One of them, *One Spirit Medicine*,[1] was on the *Wall Street Journal's* best-seller list, and I was flattered to learn that Albert had dedicated another one of them, *The Heart of the Shaman*,[2] to me. Given that Alberto had spent considerable time with the Q'ero people of Peru, in this book, he applies what he had learned to contemporary life issues, along with exercises to allow his readers to implement those teachings.

Alberto and I have seen each other frequently over the years, notably when we both attended the same international conferences. He and I wrote two books together; I contributed a chapter to another of his books, *Millennium: Glimpses into the 21st Century*,[3] and he did the same for one of mine, *The Shamanic Powers of Rolling Thunder*.[4] Alberto and I also wrote a few articles together, including one in which we applied insights from quantum physics to understand how

---

[1] Villoldo, A. (2015). *One spirit medicine: Ancient ways to ultimate well-being.* Hay House.

[2] Villoldo, A. (2018). *The heart of the shaman: Stories and practices of the luminous warrior.* Hay House.

[3] Krippner, S., & Hastings, A. (1981). Parapsychology. In A. Villoldo & K. Dychtwald (Eds.), *Millennium: Glimpses into the 21st century* (pp. 104–119). Jeremy P. Tarcher.

[4] Jones, S. M. S., & Krippner, S. (Eds.). (2016). *The shamanic powers of Rolling Thunder.* Bear.

parapsychological phenomena may operate. We were not physicists, of course, so we cited and discussed the work of Evan Harris Walker, a physicist who wrote an entire book on this topic.[5]

The IONS Tours

In February 1983, I led a tour group to Brazil organized by the Institute of Noetic Sciences (IONS) in California. Our itinerary was planned to include a celebration of Carnival in Salvador, the capital city of the state of Bahia, where members of our group had reserved seats in the balcony but were also invited to march with townspeople in a special segment of the parade.

In São Paulo, our group met with the Marinhos, whose daughter demonstrated how she "incorporated" various spirits, notably for a woman who was grieving the loss of one of her children and wanted to make contact. We also spent time with Hernani Andrade, an engineer who had taken a keen interest in reincarnation and wrote detailed case histories of people who claimed to have recalled their "former lives." Several of his cases found their way into the English language parapsychological literature. Andrade was a prolific author who frequently discussed his concept of a "biological organizing model" (BOM) that he felt surrounds all living things. An organism's initial cells "flow" in this framework, but with enough irregularities to permit individual differences.

Years later, Gordon & Breech Publishers sent me a manuscript by an English biologist, Rupert Sheldrake, whose concept of "morphogenetic fields" bore a striking resemblance to Andrade's BOM. I recommended publication, but the publishers rejected the manuscript. Later, his book *A New Science of Life*[6] was published by Park Street Press and became one of its most popular publications. When I sent Sheldrake an English-language summary of Andrade's BOM, he was struck by the similarity and wrote Andrade a very complimentary letter, one that Andrade cherished.

We met Marta Gallego, who directed a group of mediums and their friends that organized a series of social outreach projects for poor people. Dona Marta was one of several Spiritists devoted to charitable

---

[5] Walker, E. H. (2000). *The physics of consciousness.* Perseus Books.
[6] Sheldrake, R. (1981). *A new science of life: The hypothesis of formative causation.* J.P. Tarcher.

work; indeed, we were told that their number exceeds that of projects initiated by the two major religions. But we were quite impressed by the health care system started by a Roman Catholic nun, Irmã (Sister) Dulce. Her concern for the ailing poor led her to open a makeshift hospital for 70 people in a chicken coop, but her determination, and her ability to inspire others, soon expanded her Charitable Works Foundation into a nationwide network. She was canonized as Saint Dulce of the Poor by Pope Francis in 2017.

Mãe Stella de Oxóssi was trained as a nurse but became interested in Candomblé, visited West Africa to explore the origins of the religion, and established an orphanage and other charitable projects. Her guiding *orixá*, or deity, was Oxóssi, the lord of the forests, and she added his name to hers in his honor. When we visited Mãe Stella at her orphanage, we were impressed by its size, its organization, and its cleanliness. She had a knack for using donations and was able to buy a hotel, the profits from which financed many of her charitable projects.

We also visited the compound of Divaldo Pereira Franco, a Spiritist medium and a prolific author. Years later, I had the opportunity to meet him again when we both appeared at a conference sponsored by the Spiritual Frontiers Fellowship in Toronto, Canada.

Our group was quite impressed by our interview with Elsie Dubragas, who was in her 90s at the time of our visit and did not pass until she reached the age of 102. Elsie was a talented journalist who wrote articles on a variety of topics. She introduced our group to Luis Gasparetto, who claimed that he was able to "channel" such deceased artists as Van Gogh and Matisse, producing a great variety of paintings.

I co-led the IONS tours with Margarida de Carvalho, a psychotherapist from São Paulo. We made a formidable team, given that she was able to provide perspectives that I would have missed. The city of Belo Horizonte was one of our frequent stops, and I always took our group to the Church of Saint Francis of Assisi, designed by the world-class architect Oscar Niemeyer. I told the group that I identified with Saint Francis because of his love of animals and because the day of his death, October 4, was also my birthday. On one trip, two members of our group also had October 4 birthdays, so we had our photograph taken together in front of the church's façade.

Spoon Bending in Brazil

Each time I led an IONS tour group to Brazil, I scheduled an evening "spoon-bending session." These sessions were quite popular, always ending with a display of spoons that had been bent, supposedly without participants exerting any force upon the metal. I told group members that there were three strategies that had seemed to work in the past and gave them their choice. One method was to "merge" with the spoon, and work from the inside out, imagining a union with the metal molecules that would enable bending to occur. Two other strategies employed an outside-in procedure, whereby participants could focus on the spoon, commanding it to bend with as much vocal power as they could summon. Or a participant could take a milder approach, persuading the spoon to bend by offering encouragement and praise. There did not seem to be any clear-cut superiority of one method over the other. I always made sure that there was at least one Brazilian in the spoon-bending sessions because their spoons bent more quickly and more dramatically than anyone else's.

Because participants had some degree of physical contact with their spoons, it was quite possible that they exerted more pressure than they had intended. Hence, I always placed a spoon in the middle of the table, covered by a transparent cover of glass or plastic. After participants' own spoons had been bent, many of them attempted to bend the enclosed spoon without touching it, but they never succeeded. Nor did I succeed in bending the spoon that I had been using for demonstration purposes. On one occasion, the champion spoon-benders were an elderly husband and wife from Canada. On our return flight, they attempted to bend the cutlery the airline served with their meals. They succeeded all too well, not only with their spoons but with their forks as well. Before we landed, they desperately tried to unbend the spoons and forks less they be charged for their feats. Of course, those were the days before airlines opted to use plastic cutlery rather than the more elegant metal versions.

Enter André Percia de Carvalho

In 1991, the Parapsychological Association held its annual convention in Heidelberg, West Germany, and I booked a hotel room near the conference venue. I was accompanied by Shin Aoki, the son of Hiro Aoki, a martial arts practitioner and teacher whom I had met on an earlier trip to Japan. Once we arrived, a German friend, Rolf Taube, asked me if he could sleep on our floor, and I agreed, because Rolf lived far from Heidelberg and lacked the funds for his own room. Much to my delight, a Brazilian participant, André Percia de Carvalho, arrived. I was the only conference participant who spoke Portuguese, so I wasted no time in getting to know him. When I discovered that André also did not have a hotel room, I offered him the floor, and he was happy to accept, turning the room into a miniature United Nations.

I met with André again when I lectured in Brazil the following year, discovering that he was a psychologist with a private practice in his hometown of Niterói, a city near Rio de Janeiro. Knowing of my interest in architecture, André took me to the Museum of Contemporary Art in Niteroi, a striking edifice designed by Oscar Niemeyer, the architect who had designed most of the buildings in Brasilia, the country's capital city. He also took me to an island resort and other sites I would never have thought of visiting if left to my own devices.

André and I were both invited to speak at a parapsychology conference in Valencia, Spain, in 1993. I was looking forward to doing some sightseeing and was assured that this would be part of the program. Indeed, it was; after dinner, André and I joined the other speakers for a bus tour of Valencia, one with no narration and no stops; moreover, we could barely discern the city's features because of the darkness. I had to wait two decades until a lecture engagement enabled me to visit the cultural centers I had missed on my previous visit.

André and I arranged to meet during most of my subsequent trips to Brazil. Then in 2001, he and his friend Marcia Brito arrived in New York City. André had always been an Elton John fan, and I joined him for the Elton John/Tim Rice musical *Aida*. Marcia missed *Aida*, but not before she and André told me about an upcoming contest in which she was playing a pivotal role. To foster tourism to the Mardi Gras in New Orleans, Marcia's friends had arranged a lottery; the winner would receive a roundtrip ticket from Rio to "The Big Easy," a nickname often applied to the city. When André vowed that he would win the lottery, I told him that if he won, I would join him and Marcia. I had enjoyed Carnival in a dozen Brazilian and other Latin American cities, but had never been to a U.S. version.

Once André began to use all his "psychic skills," his ticket was chosen from several thousand entries. I booked my flight and reserved my hotel room, and we had an incredible time. Marcia stayed with her friends Rick and Barbara Tolsen, jazz musicians who performed several times during Mardi Gras. Marcia herself, who teaches English classes in Brazil, is an accomplished vocalist and joined the Tolsens when they and their band performed U.S. popular music from the 1930s and 1940s, her specialty being Cole Porter's songs such as "Night and Day." The Tolsens lived in the French Quarter, which was the scene of much of the merriment. One afternoon, we went for a stroll and passed the balconies where folks were tossing down beaded necklaces—for a price. They called out, "Show us your teats!" and several female revelers were happy to comply. When they screamed, "Show us your cocks!" André, a very handsome young man, lowered his shorts, and the necklaces came showering down. I went around picking them up and put them to good use at various events back in the U.S.

We enjoyed the Cajun and Creole food, the gumbo, jambalaya, beignets, and other "Big Easy" specialties. The daily parade afforded more colorful events, and I spotted the film director Spike Lee in the crowd. Apparently, he was gathering impressions for his later tenure as the Mardi Gras Grand Marshall.

André and I collaborated on a book, *Sonhos Exotics* (Exotic Dreams), that we later expanded into an English-language book, *Extraordinary Dreams and How to Work with Them,* co-authored by my longtime friend Fariba Bogzaran.[7] In 2003, André paid his first visit to San Francisco, where the three of us gave several lectures and workshops that featured our book. André returned to San Francisco with his boyfriend Yago for several sightseeing expeditions and joined me in China in 2017. By that time, André was a skilled practitioner of Neurolinguistic Programming (NLP). I had attended early seminars by NLP's founders, Richard Bandler and John Grinder, and was intrigued by their proposed connections among "neuro" (neurological), "linguistic" (language), and "programming" (acquired behavior). NLP has never become a mainstream psychotherapeutic technique but, like some other methods of dubious validity, it can serve as a useful framework for a skilled therapist to evoke positive changes. André's Chinese audiences enjoyed his presentations and enthusiastically practiced NLP on one another.

Each of my sessions in China was followed by a dinner in an excellent restaurant, where it was the custom for the guest of honor to sing before the food was served. I had my own repertoire of songs, such as *I'll Be Seeing You*, *As Time Goes By*, and *Yesterday*, which I noted had come to its composer, Paul McCartney, in a dream. André and I sang a Brazilian standard, *Paguei um Ita do Norte* (I Took a Trip to the North) that I had learned in my Portuguese classes at the University of Wisconsin in the 1950s. Obrigado (thank you), Paul Witty, for allowing me to take my language exam in Portuguese at Northwestern University!

---

[7] Krippner, S., Bogzaran, F., & de Carvalho, A. P. (2002). *Extraordinary dreams and how to work with them.* SUNY Press.

Enter Pierre Weil

Brazil's capital city, Brasilia, was a "planned city," literally created out of nothing by city planner Lucio Costa and architect Oscar Niemeyer in the 1950s. In 1985, Brazil emerged from two decades of a so-called "benevolent" military dictatorship, whereupon the civilian governor of Brasilia wanted to turn the army post into an outpost of peace. He established the *Fundação Cidade da Paz*, which soon sponsored the International University of Peace (UNIPAZ). The governor participated in the opening of the first Brazilian Holistic Congress in 1987, fulfilling his desire to establish an ecumenical space that would serve all citizens in the capital of Brazil. He turned the project over to Pierre Weil, a French naturalized Brazilian, who was its first president and also the first rector of the International University of Peace.

I had met Pierre earlier, when he was a guest professor at the University of Minas Gerais, where he initiated what he called the "didactics of the culture of peace"—namely, peace with oneself, peace in one's relationship with others, and peace with the environment and the cosmos. This resembled what I had learned earlier when I studied Rational Emotive Behavior Therapy (REBT) and its emphasis on accepting oneself, accepting others, and accepting one's world as the first steps in psychotherapy, going on from there to make desired changes. For his didactics programs, Pierre received the UNESCO Prize for Peace Education in 2000.

Pierre invited me to give workshops and courses at UNIPAZ, and I returned about two dozen times. Noteworthy was my trip in 1987 for a special ringing of the "Peace Bell," a temple bell or *bonsho* from the United Nations (UN) Association of Japan. In 1952, the first bell had been given to the UN Secretary General and installed in the Japanese Garden of the UN headquarters in New York City. A one-ton replica was sent to two dozen other locations, the metal being composed of coins collected from peace initiatives in various countries. The bell had been given to UNIPAZ earlier in 1987, honoring its status as one of the world's three "peace universities," along with those in Japan and Costa Rica. A Brazilian shaman and I were given the honor of striking the bell, which was inscribed, in Japanese, "Long Live World Peace" and placed in an outdoor shrine, visible to all who entered the City of Peace.

I returned to UNIPAZ several times, giving lectures and workshops to Pierre's students. Especially memorable was my participation in the 20th anniversary celebration of UNIPAZ. I was rushed from the airport to the dining hall, where local dignitaries had gathered for the event, and, suffering from jet lag, tripped over the cord connecting a microphone to the dais. Not only did the microphone fall to the floor, but so did the entire array of floral bouquets that had so artfully decorated the speakers' stand. It was a catastrophe, and quick repair work never restored the flowers to their earlier glory. When it was my turn to speak, I apologized—in the best Portuguese I could muster—saying that I was in such a hurry to join the celebration that I had not noticed the errant cord. The crowd was very forgiving, and the rest of the celebration proceeded without a mishap.

Sometimes I visited the UNIPAZ day school for young children and sang, "A Arca de Noe" (Noah's Ark), a Carnival song from the 1930s that I had learned in my Portuguese classes. I sang it through once, making all the proper animal noises ("o gato faz meow, meow, meow"), and then had the children join me during the reprise. The Brazilian rooster does not sing "cock-a-doodle-doo," but, rather, "que que que que que que."

A Tale of Three Cities

In 2019, I spoke at three Brazilian conferences. My niece, Laura Peck, and her husband, Brad Snyder, had timed the vacation of their daughter, Ella Snyder-Peck, so that they could join me for the first of conference. One of my former students, Henny Kupferstein, and a New York friend of mine, Steve Speer, joined us in Curitiba for a gala birthday party on October 4 and stayed with me for the duration of the trip. I had told all of them that Curitiba was my favorite Brazilian city, and they soon discovered the reason.

Curitiba

Under the direction of a pioneering mayor Jaime Lerner, Curitiba developed the Bus Rapid Transit System, which eliminated stairs and levels, allowing people to step directly from the platform into a bus. The junction was seamless, enabling passengers to keep dry even in a rainstorm. Lerner installed a large number of parks containing aviaries and recycling procedures, making Curitiba the "greenest" city in the country. Joe Garcia, a Brazilian educator who accompanied me on many of my IONS tours, had first introduced me to Curitiba, taking me to areas ignored by most tourists such as a short railroad in the surrounding hills where passengers could take a train ride amidst spectacular scenery. Joe also took me to "A Cidade Antiga" (The Old City), a collection of natural stone formations that has an uncanny resemblance to human-made buildings.

When I met Joe, he was teaching at Brazil's only Spiritist University, but it had closed by the time of my 2019 visit, which I regretted. I had been friends with its president and several other faculty members, such as Fabio da Silva, who hosted an annual convention of the Parapsychological Association, an event that gave many of my colleagues their first exposure to Brazilian culture. Joe had also introduced me to Pai (Father) Ely, whose Candomblé temple in Recife had been a popular stop on most of my IONS tours.

My niece and her family are vegans, so they were delighted to see the large number of vegetarian restaurants, where one's food is weighed and priced accordingly. I especially enjoyed the tangy green cress, which reminded me of the watercress I had collected from the creek that ran near my Volenberg grandparents' home, providing a healthy vegetable that was not easily found in U.S. supermarkets.

I took my friends to see Curitiba's two pyramids, one the headquarters of the local Rosicrucian study group, an organization that promulgates "traditional wisdom" from such sources as Egypt, Greece, and the Middle East. I had previously visited the group's international headquarters in San José, California, also housed in a pyramid and featuring a museum that holds an admirable collection of artifacts from ancient Egypt. One of our "star participants" in the Maimonides ESP/Dream Project had taken a correspondence class from the San José headquarters, learning such skills as lucid dreaming and "out of body experience," which were put to the test in our laboratory. On the fourth night of his time with us, the participant's brain waves changed dramatically. Upon awakening, he told us that he had been "out of the body" and accurately described a picture that had been placed on a ledge above his bed before he retired.

I also took the family to the Pythagorean headquarters housed in the other pyramid, which also hosted correspondence classes in which the teachings of Pythagoras were disseminated. Pythagoras made many contributions to philosophy, astronomy, musical theory, and mathematics. He traveled to Egypt and Italy, and founded a school that was so secretive that none of his original writings remain; hence the Curitiba-based classes rely on secondary sources. Nonetheless, we saw dozens of assignments from students, some of them overseas, indicating that many people found the classes of value.

I then took my friends to see the spectacular glass opera house as well as the "Hansel and Gretel Trail," which contains edifices in which visitors could retrace every step of the young siblings' journey to the famed "gingerbread house." The original folk tale depicts a wicked witch who lures children to the house and then devours them, but the Brazilian version presents a benign and hospitable witch who greets visitors at the end of their journey, offering them treats and good cheer.

Joe Garcia told me that in the 1970s Curitiba's mayor led a delegation of townspeople to visit Oscar Niemeyer, requesting him to design a new city hall and educational center. They had a limited amount of money, but Niemeyer graciously offered them designs for a building that had been commissioned by the Iraqi government before it was overturned in a revolution. The Curitiba group was more than happy to accept them, even though the building had been designed for a desert, not the rain forest. When I saw it, I was struck by its low ceilings, small windows, and white façade—perfect for Iraq, but far from the "organic architecture" envisioned by Frank Lloyd Wright, who insisted a building should seem to "grow out of its surroundings." Nonetheless, the mayor and his staff moved out of their modest quarters into the new building, and it soon garnered favorable notices and international attention. When Niemeyer died in 2012, his supporters wanted to create a museum in his honor. They persuaded the Curitiba group to allow them to build a stunning second floor on their city hall, and I took my family to visit it and the Brazilian artwork it featured. The city staff moved back to humbler quarters but reveled in the attention the new museum brought to their city.

On October 7, I spoke at the second conference on Anomalistic Psychology and the Study of Religion. Following my talk, I received an elegant plaque that was a "Career Tribute" for my work in studying anomalous phenomena. A few days later, when I spoke to a group of educators, I brought my nephew-in-law, Brad Snyder, given his years of work as an advocate for children, especially those who had been bullied. Joe Garcia had arranged the event, and his son served as translator. Joe's son was the result of his short-lived marriage to Mae East, a social activist who had left Brazil to design programs for the Findhorn spiritual community in Scotland. I had been on a panel with Eileen and Peter Caddy, Findhorn's founders, and have followed news of the community, including its 60th birthday celebration in 2022.

Brasilia

On October 12, I spoke at a UNIPAZ conference in Brasilia. Pierre Weil had passed, but Roberto Crema had taken his place as the rector of the International Holistic University. Steve Speer, Henny Kupferstein, and I stayed in the UNIPAZ lodge, and André Percia de Carvalho joined us there. I was able to visit with Mãe East, Joe Garcia's ex-wife, who had returned to Brazil from Findhorn for a short visit, and Naira Tatsu, who had been arranging the event and who later solicited at-a-distance lectures from me for UNIPAZ events. Naira was able to schedule a talk by Henny, who is autistic and who enjoys opportunities to discuss autism with people who know little about it.

While in Brasilia, I was able to spend a day with Theresa and Greg McCasky at their home, and the next day I talked to Theresa's Joseph Campbell Society group. I first met Theresa at a meeting of the International Association for the Study of Dreams, and we became instant friends. Theresa's work with sand play therapy intrigued me, and I brought her a few small figurines that she could add to her collection. Her work as a therapist draws from her study of dreams, her acquaintance with Joseph Campbell's insights on cultural myths, and her own insights, making her a formidable figure in the Brasilia psychotherapy scene.

On October 13, I took our group to the local market, a unique experience for Henny and Steve. They were fascinated by the variety of food, clothing, craft items, and souvenirs that existed in profusion. I introduced them to Brazilian "snack foods," including my favorite, *Pão de Queijo* (cheese bread). These crispy balls are made of tapioca flour and cheese; ordinarily, I am repulsed by anything cheesy, but the exceptions are cheesecake and *Pão de Queijo*. Most of my Brazilian friends are aware of my liking and try to have some cheese bread available for my visits.

Goiana

Since my first visit in 1973, I have been all over Brazil, even giving a seminar at the Federal University of Juiz da Fora in the state of Minas Gerais. Established by President Juscelino Kubitschek in 1960, the university has several strong departments and an imposing campus. My seminar was sponsored by Alexander Almeida-Moreira, a psychiatrist who has become internationally renowned for his research in spirituality and parapsychology, as well as for his use of Brazilian Spiritism in various theoretical works. We co-authored an analysis of supposedly diseased tissue from the alleged "psychic surgeon" João Teixeira de Faria (known as "John of God"), finding a variety of tissues, both from humans and other animals but nothing pathological.[8] Shortly

---

[8] Moreira-Almeida, A., Moreira de Almeida, T., Gollner, A. M., & Krippner, S. (2009). A study of the mediumistic surgery of John of God. *Journal of Shamanic Practice, 2*(1), 21–31.

after we published the article, Teixeira de Faria was arrested and jailed for inappropriate sexual conduct with his female patients.

I have been to the Amazon rainforest several times, eaten *churrasco* prepared by the *gauchos* (or "cowboys") in southern Brazil, visited the spectacular Iguassu Falls and the *grutas* (caves) of Minas Gerais, and finally made it to Goiânia, the city with the most amount of "greenery" and the smallest number of *favelas*, or slums.

I was to speak at a major transpersonal psychology conference held in Goiania from October 18 to 20, 2019. Everton Maraldi and Lika Queiroz, two close Brazilian friends, were there, along with over 2,000 other participants not only from Brazil but from neighboring countries as well. I had been asked to speak about how transpersonal experiences had altered history, and I gave several examples, not only in the birth of various religions but in contemporary times. I used the example of Maria Sabina, whose disclosure of her use of the "sacred mushrooms" had not only initiated the discipline of ethnomycology but also impacted the entire psychedelic movement. When I quoted one of her lyrical chants, I spoke in Spanish rather than the expected English, and it brought down the house. I switched to Portuguese for the latter part of my presentation and received an unforgettable ovation. And then it was time for an intermission. I could not get up from my seat because there was a line of conference participants waiting to take "selfies" with me. I was happy to oblige them for an hour or more. What a glorious ending to my sojourn in Brazil! And it all started with Disney and his cartoon character José Carioca, an example of chaos theory's postulate that small shifts in an initial condition can produce unpredictable results. I revisited the movie years later, and the music, color, and festivities still resonated with me, but this time with a greater appreciation of the subsequent, and salubrious, events.

Chapter 9

Seeking the Magic Mushroom
13 May 1957. A Day When My Life Changed

My interest in psychedelics dates from May 1957, when I read an article about María Sabina that had just been published in *Life* magazine. The article, "Seeking the Magic Mushroom,[1]" was written by R. Gordon Wasson, a banker, who, with his wife, Valentina, had a special interest in mushrooms. The ceremonial use of psychedelic mushrooms in Mexico had been banned by the Spanish invaders centuries before, but there were rumors that a few communities had escaped the edict and continued the tradition. The botanist Richard Evans Schultes suggested that the pre-Columbian word *teonanacatl*—flesh of the gods—referred to the mind-altering mushrooms. Wasson followed up on this suggestion; indeed, in 1955, he and his photographer, Allan Richardson, were the first recorded outsiders to ingest the mushrooms in a native ceremony. I read Wasson's article, tore it out of the magazine, and filed it away. In 1960, my interest was reinforced by a panel that I attended at the American Psychological Association, and in 1963, by a television documentary that I watched. I resolved that I would have a first-and experience with the fungi but had no idea how this would happen.

Enter Maria Sabina

María Sabina, the Mazatec shaman who conducted the ceremony, or *velada*, claimed to have had a premonition during one of her *veladas*, about Wasson's arrival. She consulted with a municipal authority in her township, Huatula de Jiménez, who gave his permission for the *gringos* to participate in a *velada*. She later claimed that she would have shared the knowledge even without his permission because the mushrooms were the blood of Jesus, freely available to sincere seekers. Wasson returned later with his wife and daughter, who wanted to share the

---

[1] Wasson, R. G. (1957, May 13). Seeking the magic mushroom. *Life magazine*, pp. 100–120.

experience. In writing about the "magic mushrooms" for *Life*, he disguised María Sabina's name.

A mushroom *velada* is thought to allow the mushroom deities to speak through the voice of the practitioner who leads the ceremony. Typically, it is held at the request of people who need healing, or their family members. The mushroom was thought to advise them on what herbs to take, what saints to pray to, or what pilgrimage to make. It did not take long for readers of the magazine article to discover María Sabina's actual identity, and Huatula de Jiménez became a magnet for people who were on spiritual quests, notably so-called "hippies," whose unsanitary habits brought a variety of diseases into the poor but clean village. As a result, a group of irate villagers burned down María Sabina's store and home and murdered one of her sons.

María Sabina, born in 1894, originally ate the mushrooms to stave off hunger. Some of her relatives conducted *veladas*, and she had been observing the sacred ceremonies since childhood. However, she could not lead them herself because of prohibitions that barred sexually active women from becoming *sabias*, or "wise ones." Once her second husband died, she devoted herself to the *veladas*, and her reputation spread to other villages, bringing to her people of all ages in need of healing. But she felt that her sudden notoriety and the onrush of foreign visitors had deprived the mushrooms of their "purity" and healing power. Once the Mexican army expelled the young foreigners in 1967, María Sabina did her best to resume her practice. Her remarkable life story has been chronicled by Alvaro Estrada in his masterful 1981 biography, *María Sabina: Her Life and Chants*.[2]

Enter Salvador Roquet

In 1969, I received a letter from Salvador Roquet, a psychiatrist, telling me about his work with psychedelic-facilitated psychotherapy and inviting me to visit him in Mexico City. In March 1970, I served as one of several chaperones for a high school science class that was heading to Michuatlan to view a total eclipse of the sun. Our first stop was Mexico City, and I wrote Roquet to see if we could meet. I had no response, but, upon my return, I found a letter from him informing me that he had been in Santa María Asunción de Matamoros, Oaxaca, laying the groundwork for a medical clinic that would serve the local

---

[2] Estrada, A. (1981). *María Sabina: Her life and chants*. Ross-Erikson.

populace. However, he reiterated his desire to meet me and discuss his work, as well as allow me to see him in action.

This opportunity presented itself in 1971, when I was invited to speak at the Fifth World Psychiatry Congress in Mexico City. My presentation focused on the famed statue of the Aztec mother goddess Coatlique, which I had seen the previous year in the National Museum of Anthropology. Coatlique, in Nahuatl, means "serpent skirt," a term that describes the goddess's apparel. Indeed, her head is composed of two serpents, using a juxtaposition similar to a technique Picasso, centuries later, employed in some of his paintings. The two serpent heads probably represented Coatlique's roles as both creator and destroyer, a paradox too subtle for the Spanish invaders to appreciate; instead, they branded the goddess as evil and buried the statue. It was rediscovered in 1790 and put on display in the hope of persuading the native people that the dethroned pagan deities were demonic. However, the Indians were not persuaded; they bedecked the statue with flowers and adoration, prompting a reburial by the Spaniards. The statue was unearthed at the request of the 19th century Prussian geographer Alexander von Humboldt, but was reburied after his departure from Mexico. Eventually, the Coatlique statue was unearthed and became one of Mexico's cultural treasures.

Following the congress, my wife and I visited Salvador Roquet; my secretary, Irene Lozano, served as interpreter for our discussion of his psychotherapeutic procedures. We accepted his invitation to observe a group therapy session and were cordially received by Salvador's patients, even though we did not ingest any of the several mind-altering substances that he administered that evening. As his patients began to feel the effects of the drugs, Salvador's staff projected a violent film on one wall of the room, and an erotic movie on the other wall. I thought that this was very much in the tradition of Coatlique, whose seemingly contradictory roles had not been appreciated by the Spanish invaders, who failed to fathom their underlying unity. Salvador's goal was to assure his patients that a discussion of either their aggressive or sexual impulses was acceptable in this milieu. There were some 20 patients seated on the carpet and cushions of the room. Some began to dance, while others cried or sobbed, turning to each other for support and consolation, as they revealed intimate details about their life conflicts and traumas. Salvador moved among his patients, orchestrating their responses and deftly forming small groups of patients with similar issues. Irene did her best to translate salient snatches of the conversations, but even without her help it was apparent that the group had bonded in a way that facilitated individual insights.

The three of us were sitting near one male patient, an artist, who told his group how his father had rejected him because of his sexual orientation. He stated, "In fact, I can see my father coming toward me right now, even though I know it is a hallucination." In actuality, Salvador had persuaded the young man's father to attend the session and to confront his son. Once his son realized that he was not hallucinating, he wasted no time in telling his father how much the rejection had hurt him. At this point, the father apologized, adding that he loved his son regardless of his sexual orientation, and the two of them embraced and wept. They continued their conversation for the duration of the all-night session. The three of us returned to our hotel, realizing that we had seen a master psychotherapist at work.

Upon my return to the United States, I notified my colleagues at the Maryland Psychiatric Research Center about Salvador's work. They immediately invited him to Baltimore, where he gave a number of well-received lectures about his approach to psychotherapy. He was allowed to participate in one of their "psychedelics for professionals" sessions, during which he ingested LSD under the staff's supervision. This allowed Salvador to have a first-hand view of how the Maryland psychotherapists utilized psychedelics. In December 1972, John Rhead, a research psychologist at the center, wrote me, "I just put Salvador Roquet on a train for New York after his second visit here at the Center. He had a session with Bill Richards and Rich Yensen, and we all had a nice visit. Thank you once again for getting us all together." Subsequently, I discovered that Stanislav Grof was also present during the session, and that Yensen, who spoke fluent Spanish, did most of the facilitation. Yensen also facilitated two additional sessions for Salvador at the center during subsequent visits.

Salvador, who knew of my long-standing interest in María Sabina, arranged for me to join him and his patients on an expedition to Huatula de Jiménez in January 1980. Our caravan consisted of two automobiles and three vans; I had invited a few friends to join us, including Walter Houston Clark, Michael Winkelman, and Erik Peper. Clark was a scholar of religious traditions, Winkelman was an anthropologist specializing in shamanic states of consciousness, and Peper was a leader in the newly developing field of biofeedback and "mind–body medicine."

We spent the night of January 8 in a modest hotel in Oaxaca de Juárez, the capital city of the state of Oaxaca, where Huatula was located. We arrived in Huatula the following day, located a hotel, and paid our initial visit to Doña María ("Doña" being a term of respect). Nicolás Echevarria, creator of a 1978 documentary about Doña María, had built a small house for her, affording a splendid view of the mountainous landscape.

On our way to this house, we observed datura flowers in full bloom. I remembered that Roquet often used datura seeds in his work, usually in combination with ketamine, an animal tranquilizer found to have potentially therapeutic effects when administered to humans in a therapy session.

Bonnie Colodzin, a Hollywood-based photographer and the sister of Ben Colodzin, one of my former students, asked permission to take photographs; María Sabina responded affirmatively and excused herself to change into a traditional gown, a *huipil* that she had used to conduct *veladas*.

Richard Yensen, a psychiatrist who had been working with Roquet, not only translated for us but lent Bonnie Colodzin his camera, which was a more advanced model than the one she had brought with her. María Sabina did not speak Spanish, so Yensen's translation had to be preceded by another version from a townsperson who was fluent in both Mazatec and Spanish. But there were parts of our visit that needed no translation. When Doña María emerged in her *huipil*, Bonnie Colodzin became enraptured, and, crying uncontrollably, was unable to operate Yensen's camera. Immediately, Doña María took her aside, called for fresh flowers, and began to pray as she passed the flowers around Colodzin's body. Colodzin's resulting photographs were stunning, as well as probably the last professional photographs taken of Doña María and the house that had been built for her.

In response to our inquiry, Doña María told us that the mushrooms were the blood of Jesus. I was aware of the version that attributed the mushrooms to Quetzalcoatl, the mythological emperor who had left his throne in disgrace, having been seduced by a sorcerer. Quetzalcoatl then wandered through the countryside, preaching the message of universal love. When rocks and thorns cut into his bare feet, the blood turned into sacred mushrooms. After the Spanish invasion, Quetzalcoatl was merged with Jesus, as both of them were marked by their compassion and, according to legend, were able to heal the sick.

Doña María's daughters, María Apolonia and María Aurora, began to solicit donations, even though I had given Doña María some money shortly after our arrival. Later I was told that Doña María had told her daughters that they did not have the *don* or gift that would enable them to follow the tradition. Before leaving, I gave Doña María a necklace that

I had received from a shaman I had met in Moscow, as well as my sports jacket, thinking she might need it in cold weather.

Roquet joined us the following day. Doña María was wearing the sports jacket and the Russian necklace I had given her. Her daughters showed signs of intoxication, and I was told that they had spent our donation on beer and other alcoholic beverages. Nonetheless, Roquet attempted to arrange for a *velada* that evening. Doña María explained that she was too frail to officiate, but Roquet located another *sabia*, Doña Cleotilde Nova. Upon our arrival, Doña Cleotilde informed us that she did not have enough *hongitos,* or "little mushrooms," for our entourage, which consisted of a dozen of Roquet's patients and a few of my friends. I informed her that I would abstain, having already partaken of the "flesh of the gods," to which she replied that I could be her assistant. I learned much more as her assistant than I would have learned as a participant.

Doña Cleotilde's sanctuary adjoined her house. It was a small room with a concrete floor, one covered with pine boughs that emitted a pleasant odor. My first act was to help Doña Cleotilde adhere the candles to the floor. She deftly let a small amount of melting candle wax drop to the floor, and then placed the candle in the wax until it cooled. I tried to do the same, but my candles kept falling down. But then I noticed that Doña Cleotilde had given me candles with a rough bottom, while keeping the smooth bottomed candles for her own use. I realized that this made her look adept, while her assistant looked clumsy. I was only too willing to enhance her image, so I simply let a larger amount of wax drip from the candles before trying to affix them. It worked quite well.

But I made my own contribution to the *velada*. Doña Cleotilde had trouble lighting her matches, which had been stored in a container that was not waterproof. I had brought along a package of waterproof matches, which lit the candles very easily. I left the remainder of the matches with Doña Cleotilde, knowing that she would now have some "magic" not available to other practitioners.

Once the *hongitos* began to take effect, there was the usual laughing and crying, smiling and wailing. Two of Roquet's patients, who were having an especially difficult time, were vomiting profusely. One was a concert pianist who had become overcome with stage fright and could not continue performing. Another was a former Miss Kentucky, whose looks were fading. Thrown back on using her inner, rather than her outer, resources to make her way in the world, she panicked, because she had few inner assets to draw on. I went to their corner of the room and asked them to tell me what was going on. First one and then the other spoke about their messages from the *hongitos*, positive messages of encouragement and hope. The advice was quite specific and very meaningful. They were so delighted with my help that they began to hug me and kiss me, one on my left cheek and one on my right.

Ordinarily, this would have been a pleasant experience, but the stench of the vomit was so severe that I had a hard time keeping from becoming nauseated. And then I realized the function of the pine boughs. I knelt close to them and inhaled their fresh scent. This strategy allowed me to keep focusing on the revelations, doing my best to reinforce the ones that made sense.

Walter Houston Clark appeared to be having a rough time as well, and Doña Cleotilde asked me to help him out. Clark, the veteran of several positive psychedelic trips and an esteemed guide for others, was puzzled by the negative imagery that came into his field of vision. Clark described a stream of vampire bats hovering over him. I told him that vampire bats are actually admirable creatures, piercing their skin so that their babies could suck their blood for nourishment. Clark was astonished; he had not appreciated that what often seems negative can be quite positive once the larger picture is envisioned. He remarked, "I should have realized that." I responded that even the most capable among us sometimes needs a little help from friends. At the end of the night, it was apparent that I had learned a great deal from being Doña Cleotilde's assistant.

Salvador joined us early in the morning. Most of us were fatigued, but he was cheerful and energetic. Salvador led a group therapy session so that participants could share and process their experiences. We expressed our gratitude to both Salvador and Doña Cleotilde for providing this unforgettable experience. Later that day, most of us returned to Mexico City, but a few stayed with Salvador, who had promised to introduce them to another Mazatec practitioner who also used mushrooms in his healing practice.

Shortly after returning to the United States, I was informed that Doña María had remarried and was finally living an enjoyable and peaceful life. But there are those who claim that her *gringo* friends from the 1950s could have done more for her after she was chastised by many of the villagers. One person who stood by her was Doña María's priest, who saw no conflict with her church membership and her work as a *sabia*. She had helped found the Sisterhood of the Sacred Heart of Jesus, a society of local women who were church members.

Indeed, the spontaneous chants that characterize Doña María's *veladas* display an overlay of Roman Catholic imagery as well as Mazatec mythology. She referred to herself as a "Lord clown woman," and a "Lord eagle woman," as a "woman who investigates," concluding "that's the way it looks when I go to Heaven." María Sabina passed in 1985, her historic role as the inadvertent co-founder of "ethnomycology," the study of the ethnology of mushrooms, secure. I was left with a sense of wonder.

In 1957, when I read the *Life* magazine article by R. Gordon Wasson, the co-founder (along with Maria Sabina) of ethnomycology. I never would have thought that I would someday encounter Doña María. I never would have imagined that I would write dozens of articles about psychedelics and give presentations on the topic at various venues from high schools and colleges to major conferences.

Nor would I have imagined that I would be invited to give three presentations at Albert Hofmann's 100th birthday celebration in Basel, Switzerland. Nor would I have seen myself giving two presentations at the 2019 Psychedelic Science conference in Oakland, California. I never would have suspected that I would get to know most of the major players in this cutting-edge field of study and practice.

Life has often taken me by surprise, sometimes for the better and sometimes for the worse. The spinoffs of that *Life* magazine article about María Sabina were, with few exceptions, for the better.

In 1973, I received a letter from Salvador stating, "We are happy to have you officially on our team as honorary vice president and advisor to the *Instituto de Psicosíntesis*. He also sent me a long description of the Institute's work, affirming that its incorporation of psychedelic substances into psychotherapy began in 1967. The report also noted that expeditions to remote Indian villages had been organized to study the ritual use of natural psychedelic substances. Salvador and his team observed that a frequent focus of the session was the recovery of the client's "lost soul." This term refers to the loss of one's "vital essence." I have seen Indigenous shamans "search and recover" the "lost soul," often with the assistance of psychedelic substances. The team also observed that dosage was carefully measured, and the size of the group was monitored as well.

Salvador had decided to name his psychotherapy "psychosynthesis" (in Spanish, *psicosintesis*), because it interlaced conventional psychoanalysis with psychedelic drugs. He knew nothing about the transpersonal psychotherapy, also named "psychosynthesis," formulated by the Italian psychiatrist Roberto Assagioli, which continues to be practiced several decades after its founder's death. Richard Yensen summarized Salvador's report and his own observations in a presentation he gave at the 1973 convention of the Association for Humanistic Psychology in Montreal, Canada. The presentation was well received and stimulated further interest in Salvador and his work.

Salvador continued to run his controversial sessions under an informal agreement with the Mexican government that overlooked the country's laws against ingesting psychedelics. But then the political power shifted, and Salvador was sent to jail. When I found out about his imprisonment, I wrote letters and articles on his behalf. Several other letters were written by distinguished physicians and psychotherapists, some of whom had never met Roquet but who admired his work. In June 1975, Salvador wrote me that he had been released in April, expressing his gratitude for my support. In July 1975, I received another letter from Salvador that stated:

> I thank you very much for the article you wrote about my imprisonment and the problems we are facing presently to work with psychodysleptics [his term] in psychosynthesis. I feel it is only with such attitude and these kinds of articles that we will be able to produce concern and interest for our colleagues to [reconsider their] use …. Throughout my professional work … I can see with more clarity all the time the benefits that the psychosynthesis therapy provides to the patients. And this certainty gives me strength to keep my standpoint and face the absurdly conservative and reactionary attitude of our colleagues.

In 1976, Salvador was imprisoned again, this time in the United States following a "psychosynthesis" session arranged by his friend Walter Houston Clark. One of my friends, who was a member of this group, described to me the pandemonium that resulted when the police broke into the room where the session was being held, right at the time when the drug effects were at their peak. The case went to trial, and Salvador admitted to a misdemeanor—namely, practicing medicine without a U.S. license. All the other charges against him and his American hosts were dropped.

A year later, Salvador spoke at the annual convention of the Association for Humanistic Psychology in Berkeley, California. In a 1977 interview for the *San Francisco Examiner*, he told a reporter that political pressure elicited his release from the Mexican jail, and that "to this day, I don't know how I got in or how I got out." The help that I, and others of his friends, gave was probably among several gambits that procured his release. Despite the intensity of the drug experience, Salvador claimed that none of his patients had been hurt. "We have 2,000 case histories and recordings of over 900 group sessions. I can say that 85 percent of them had positive results.... The 15 percent who were not helped had at worst 'indifferent' reactions. There were no cases of people failing to make the return trip to sanity."

Salvador told the reporter that he had curtailed his use of mind-altering substances during his "psychosynthesis" sessions, replacing them with *vivencias,* "festivals of life." He noted,

> After I left jail, I began to travel, giving workshops and lectures. We started doing simulated sessions, with the lights and sounds without the drugs.... We found that 90 percent of the participants had reactions similar to those of people who had taken the drugs.... We found that the psychedelics were nothing more than the launching pad, as the nature of the sessions was conditioned by the other techniques we used.

Referring to the common themes evoked in these *vivencias*—madness, death, chaos, birth, and mystical union—he remarked, "They are all terrible and all extraordinary. In death you can feel love, and when you feel love, death is conquered and ceases to exist."

The last time I saw Salvador Roquet was at the San Francisco's Kabuki Hot Springs Spa, where both of us were enjoying the hot tubs. We discussed María Sabina, and he again thanked me for my efforts to release him from jail. He passed in 1995, leaving a legacy of pioneering work in psychedelic psychotherapy and numerous people whose lives had been changed by both his psychedelic sessions and his later "festivals of life." Salvador had made great contributions to my own life and knowledge, but it is possible that none of it would have occurred had I not read the dramatic *Life* magazine article that was published on May 13, 1957.

Chapter 10

Gifted Children
2 December 1957. A Day When My Life Changed

The American Psychological Association's *Dictionary of Psychology* defines *giftedness* as "the state of possessing a great amount of natural ability, talent, or intelligence, which usually becomes evident at a very young age." It can be detected by intelligence tests, academic achievement scores, or "real world" accomplishments in such fields as the physical sciences, the social sciences, the creative arts, the performing arts, athletics, leadership, fashion, cooking, and many more.

Paul Witty Again

I had the good fortune to have Paul Witty as the chair of my dissertation committee at Northwestern University. In 1957, Paul introduced me and other members of his class to the concept of "giftedness." He had edited a book on gifted children in 1950, one that brought the topic to international attention among educators. His articles on gifted children dated back to the 1930s and 1940s, when he was one of the first scholars to identify gifted African American children and to expand the concept of "giftedness" beyond scores on intelligence tests. Even earlier, he and H. C. Lehman had authored an article about children's play that utilized an innovative measure of play activities.[1] Later, he created the Witty Diagnostic Inventory, which I utilized when I directed the Kent State University Child Study Center. In his classes, Paul discussed several ways in which gifted children could be helped to develop their talents, ranging from special schools and special classes to enrichment activities within the regular classroom. His 1976 obituary noted that he dispelled the harmful notion that gifted children were "unattractive, unhealthy, and antisocial."

---

[1] Lehman, H. C., & Witty, P. A. (1927). Play activity and school progress. *Journal of Educational Psychology, 18*, 318–326.

In 1963, the *Exceptional Children* journal published my article "The Boy Who Read at Eighteen Months."[2] Larry Wilson (not his actual name) was brought to the Kent State University Child Study Center by his parents for consultation when he was four years and two months of age. I interviewed both Larry and his parents, and over the course of subsequent meetings administered to him the Witty Diagnostic Inventory, the Stanford-Binet Intelligence Scale, the Weschler Intelligence Scale for Children, the Peabody Picture Vocabulary Test, the Machover Figure Drawing Test, the Keystone Visual Survey, the Vineland Social Maturity Scale, and the Purcell Incomplete Sentences; the latter instrument was authored by Wallace Purcell, a fellow graduate student in Paul Witty's classes. Larry demonstrated an ardent desire for autonomy and completions. His social maturity score placed him above average for his age, and his intelligence test scores placed him in the top two percent of the population.

According to Larry's parents, when he was 18 months of age, he picked up a carton of Vicks cough drops and told his parents, "V.I.C.K.S. spells Vicks." He proceeded to add other words to his reading vocabulary, and soon was memorizing sections of "The Night Before Christmas." At the age of three he was reading a book of children's stories written by Carl Sandburg. The Wilsons noted that they had neither encouraged nor discouraged his interests, which of course was the proper stance to take. In follow-up, they told me that Larry was now teaching his 18-month-old sister how to read!

Paul's impact was apparent among later advocates of the gifted, especially his emphasis on the scientifically gifted. In 1958, John Curtis Gowan, another psychologist, was alarmed by the Soviet Union's successful launch of Sputnik, the first earth satellite. In an attempt to counter this advantage, he founded the National Association for Gifted Children (NAGC). I joined the group once Paul had assured me that it was a worthwhile organization. I began to attend NAGC meetings, publishing several articles in its professional journal, the *Gifted Child*

---

[2] Krippner, S. (1963). The boy who read at eighteen months. *Exceptional Children, 30*, 105–109.

Quarterly.[3,4,5,6] At the 1967 NAGC convention, Paul gave the banquet address, his first as an emeritus professor.

E. Paul Torrance, the Father of Creativity

On April 30, 1969, I left for Chicago and the 15th anniversary of NAGC. It was attended by many leaders in the field, including John Curtis Gowan and Paul Witty, as well as Ann Isaacs, the organization's founder and long-time editor of the *Gifted Child Quarterly*[7]; Walter Barbe, another of Paul's students and my former colleague at Kent State University; Calvin Taylor, the current NAGC president; and E. Paul Torrance, often called "the Father of Creativity." Taylor was a pioneer who helped expand the giftedness concept beyond what could be measured by IQ tests. Torrance had devised the *Torrance Tests of Creative Thinking* to measure such elements of creativity as *frequency* (the number of ideas cited), *flexibility* (the number of categories those ideas fell into), and *originality* (the uniqueness of the ideas). When asked to provide uses for a brick, someone might make a high score on *frequency,* listing "a brick house," "a brick chimney," and "a brick patio," but a low score on the other uses. But someone else might receive a higher score by citing "a doghouse," "a chimney," and "a weapon." To score for originality, one would need to produce a rarely cited use, such as "a door stop."

The *Torrance Tests* tapped into capacities other than those measured by intelligence or achievement tests, the two standard measures of giftedness at the time. Since Paul Witty was one of the first psychologists who attempted to expand the concept of giftedness, he was a precursor to Torrance's work. The *Torrance Tests*, which are both verbal and figural (or non-verbal), can be given to both young children and adults. Paul and I became friends; I admired his insistence that to foster creativity one had to find a way to measure it rather than leave it

---

[3] Krippner, S. (1961). The vocational preferences of high-achieving and low-achieving junior high school students. *Gifted Child Quarterly, 5*, 88–90.

[4] Krippner, S., & Herald, C. (1964). Reading disabilities among the academically talented. *Gifted Child Quarterly, 8*, 12–20.

[5] Krippner, S. (1967). The Ten Commandments that block creativity. *Gifted Child Quarterly, 11*, 144–156.

[6] Krippner, S., & Blickenstaff, R. (1970). The development of self-concept as part of an art workshop for the gifted. *Gifted Child Quarterly, 14*, 163–166.

[7] *Gifted Child Quarterly*. (n.d.). https://journals.sagepub.com/home/gcq

shrouded in mystery. After the University of Georgia created the Torrance Center for Creativity and Talent Development, I had several occasions to visit the university and Paul himself, when he was available.

I had persuaded the NAGC officers to give my old friend Gardner Murphy a special citation for his work in creativity. I knew that there was nothing in the budget to cover expenses, so I paid for his hotel room and train ticket from Wichita, Kansas, the home of the Menninger Foundation, where he worked. Well worth the effort, it came as a welcome surprise to the conference participants, especially John Curtis Gowan, a long-time admirer of Murphy's book *Human Potentialities*. My presentation on "psychedelic art" was attended by friends of mine living in Chicago, notably Nina Graboi, whose book *One Foot in the Future* chronicles the impact of psychedelics on her own life, and George Peters, who was running a "rescue service" for those who had taken psychedelics on their own, without a guide, and were experiencing distress.[8]

Nina and George took a special interest in my presentation on creativity in altered states, as evoked by dreaming, hypnosis, and psychedelics. I cited several examples, such as Elias Howe's invention of the lockstitch sewing machine. The 19th century inventor had tried to do so without success until his attempts were reproduced in a dream, one in which he was told by a savage chief that he only had 24 hours to perfect the device. When he failed, the chief told his warriors to execute Howe, whereupon they threw their spears at him. Howe noticed that the spears had a hole near the tip, which inspired him to realize that he had drilled the hole in the wrong place in his sewing machine; understandably, he thought his insight had come too late. But he woke up, resumed his attempts, placed the hole near the tip rather than at the end, and it worked perfectly, spurring the growth of the textile industry.

I also discussed creativity that had been linked to psychedelics, such as the case of Canadian architect Kyo Izumi, who took LSD before visiting an institution for emotionally challenged persons, where he realized that the sharp edges in the rooms cast shadows that increased their anxiety. He redesigned the facility, using round and circular entrances and exits, which promoted better treatment outcomes. One of the most dramatic instances of creativity stimulated by hypnosis is the celebrated case of Sergei Rachmaninoff's treatment by the

---

[8] Graboi, N. (1991). *One foot in the future: A woman's spiritual quest.* Aerial Press.

physician Nicolai Dahl, who was a musician himself. After Rachmaninoff's *Symphony Number One* was poorly reviewed, he developed a creative block: He could conduct, he could perform at the piano, but he could not create. Dahl collaborated with the composer virtually every day for three months, and Rachmaninoff's next composition, the 1901 *Second Piano Concerto*, was an immense success. Years later, Dahl moved to Lebanon, where he often played viola in a Lebanese orchestra; when they performed the Rachmaninoff concerto, the audience was informed that the work had been dedicated to him.

A Remarkable Convention

April 30, 1969, when I arrived in Chicago for the NAGC convention, gave me an opportunity to renew my friendship with Paul Torrance. It was an event where many of the esteemed leaders of the field (Paul Witty, John Curtis Gowan, Ann Isaacs, Walter Barbe, Calvin Taylor, and Katherine Bruch, among them) were together at the same time.

Katherine Bruch, who had introduced me to Paul Torrance, chaired many of the NAGC meetings, and I was impressed by the way she managed the issue of tobacco smoking during meetings. She referred to "our smoking friends," asking them to sit together at their own table. Later, of course, smoking was banned at meetings, much to my relief because I have always been extremely sensitive to tobacco smoke. She and John Gowan co-authored an influential book about gifted education with the provocative title *The Doubtful Gift*, a reference to how giftedness is often a mixed blessing.[9]

One More Convention

The 1977 NAGC convention was held in San Diego, California. I was on the program, along with Paul Torrance, John Curtis Gowan, Katherine Bruch, and other advocates for the education of gifted children, including Julian Stanley of Johns Hopkins University. We had both been nominated for the NAGC presidency and, when he won, he graciously invited me to an officers' meeting to make future plans.

In 2000, I was invited to write the introduction to the book *Spiritual Intelligence*, written by Paul Torrance and Dorothy Sisk.[10] They defined

---

[9] Gowan, J. C., & Bruch, C. B. (1971). *The doubtful gift: Strategies for educating gifted children in the regular classroom.* Houghton Mifflin.

[10] Krippner, S. (2001). Introduction. In D. A. Sisk & E. P. Torrance, *Spiritual intelligence: Developing higher consciousness* (pp. ix–xii). Creative Education Foundation Press.

the term as the capacity to use a multidisciplinary approach—including intuition, mediation, and visualization—to tap inner knowledge and solve problems of a global nature. Several other psychologists used the same term, including another friend of mine, Frances Vaughan, who defined it as "one's inner life and its relationship to being in the world.[11]" Others have noted that "rational intelligence" tells people what they think, "social intelligence" tells them what they feel, and "spiritual intelligence" tells them what they are. Howard Gardner, who did not include the term in his list of "multiple intelligences," wrote that he preferred the term "existential intelligence"; others have developed ways to measure the concept, no matter how it is defined.[12]

In 2022 I had a surprise invitation, namely, to give a keynote address at a conference in 2023 commemorating the 20th anniversary of Paul Torrance's death. I accepted with pleasure, as this was the very least I could do to honor the contributions of a dear friend.

Enter John Curtis Gowan

John Curtis Gowan started at Harvard University at the age of 17, earning his undergraduate degree four years later. He then earned a master's degree in mathematics, after which he taught at Culver Military Academy for ten years; earned a doctorate at the University of California, Los Angeles; and was a member of the founding faculty at the California State University, Northridge, where he taught until 1975, when he retired with emeritus status. Before he retired, John had been a Fulbright lecturer and a visiting professor at the University of Singapore and several other schools.

Once we met, I discovered that John's concepts had been influenced by Abraham Maslow, Aldous Huxley, and Carl Gustav Jung, an interest reflected in his books *Trance, Art, and Creativity* and *Development of the Psychedelic Individual*.[13,14] He often said that these books, and others that explored unconventional topics, were written for 21st century readers. For example, John traced connections between creativity and the *numinous*, a term coined by Rudolf Otto in 1917 to describe places

---

[11] Vaughan, F. (2002). What is spiritual intelligence? *Journal of Humanistic Psychology, 42* (2), 16–33.
[12] Gardner, H. (1983). *Multiple intelligences: New horizons*. Basic Books.
[13] Gowan, J. C. (1975). *Trance, art, and creativity*. Creative Education Foundation.
[14] Gowan, J. C. (1974). *Development of the psychedelic individual*. Author.

and experiences marked by intense spiritual and sacred qualities. Jung used the term in a somewhat unique way, as a requirement for *individuation*, the ultimate developmental level.

Most of John's massive output focused on bringing creativity into classroom settings. While at Northridge, John developed a program to train campus counselors, and designed the Northridge Developmental Scale, an extension of Erik Erickson's and Jean Piaget's developmental models, one that included mystical states. When discussing psychedelic experiences, John took care to point out that any insights obtained from those experiences (whether evoked by psychedelic substances or occurring naturally) were of no practical importance unless they were put to practical use. This was John's way of merging his more conventional work and his unconventional interests. John felt that his book titled *Development of the Psychedelic Individual* was extremely important, published it himself, and handed out free copies to participants at various conferences. I recommended the book to several of my students and was delighted when they cited it in their doctoral dissertations.

The NACCA and the FGCC

It turned out that John and Ann Isaacs had different perspectives on gifted education. On Valentine's Day, 1974, I attempted to reconcile their differences. John wanted to emphasize the academic aspect of NAGC, while Ann saw it more as a "grass roots" movement; I thought that both perspectives were important. The reconciliation did not last, and Ann initiated her own organization, the National Association for Creative Children and Adults (NACCA).

In 1974, I flew to Cincinnati for the inauguration of NACCA. I joined a panel that explored both scientific creativity and artistic creativity, as well as their interface. I continued to support Ann and attend NACCA conventions until her daughter informed me of her passing. I was gratified when NAGC established the Ann F. Isaacs Founder's Memorial Award, which is awarded annually. Ann deserved all the credit she could get, expending time and energy on behalf of children who in previous decades had been ignored or misdiagnosed as "unruly," "lazy," or even "disturbed."

Marie Friedel was a member of NAGC, taking an interest in giftedness when her adopted son, Lance, exhibited signs of talent. He was bored with school, so she and her husband, Jack, withdrew him and began a program of "home schooling." She discovered several other parents in the neighborhood who also were dissatisfied with the public schools. Marie urged them to withdraw their children and begin to teach them at home.

This led to Marie's establishment of the Foundation for Gifted and Creative Children (FGCC). I was invited to Warwick, Rhode Island in February 1970for the first of several consultations. During my visits, I interviewed both parents and children, giving what sensible advice I could. Some of the children had been diagnosed as "dyslexic," a diagnosis that Marie rejected, insisting that their learning problems were the result of boredom, due to their "giftedness."

Marie had a point. The film director Joe Write once told an interviewer, "I'm dyslexic, and that wasn't diagnosed until I was about 18. Before that, I was just told that I was stupid and lazy." However, I doubted that this applied to every one of the children in whom Marie had taken an interest.

I had hoped to do some diagnostic testing of my own, but hesitated to embark on such a potentially controversial topic without the proper credentials. When I contacted the Rhode Island Psychological Association, I discovered that their membership included Ben Feather (the ex-husband of Sally Feather, the daughter of J. B. Rhine, my old friend and mentor). Having spoken highly of me, he asked the Association to arrange for a licensing test. The dates were sent to me a week or so before the examination, but I had previous commitments for that time. This imbroglio occurred twice, and then I moved to California and gave up trying.

If I had become a licensed psychologist in Rhode Island, I could have administered diagnostic tests to make accurate diagnoses. Furthermore, I might have discovered children who were both gifted *and* dyslexic, as I had previously written about when I was working at Kent State University. Jack Friedel shared my disappointment, thinking that with a psychological license I could charge money for the examinations. He had been paying all of his wife's bills, and the financial drain on the family was apparent to me as well. From my perspective, Marie did not appreciate Jack's situation and all too often criticized him and even ridiculed him in public.

Jack appreciated my visits, as they were a respite from his wife's belittlement. We had a chance to speak about other topics, principally in the realm of politics. When Jack informed me of the 1978 assassination of Mayor George Moscone and Council Member Harvey Milk in their San Francisco offices, I told him how much I had admired both of them. Before he retired, Jack was working for a firm that required federal permission to conduct a line of their endeavors; he was sent to Washington, DC, as a "bagman" who would ensure the support of a leading U.S. senator, one who would later become a presidential nominee. (A "bagman" is an intermediary in a financial interaction involving unethical activities.)

I was not surprised because as director of the Maimonides Dream/ESP Project, I had drafted a research proposal that would have financed an examination of the sleep patterns of dyslexic students. The density of their rapid eye movement sleep (REMs) would have been measured both before (to avoid the "regression to the mean effect" that muddies the waters) and after remediation. There had been some pilot studies that noted less REM sleep on the part of brain-injured participants, and I wanted to obtain more definitive data. One of my colleagues at the New York Institute of Child Development had been told that we could enhance our chances if we sought Congressional assistance, so we sent a "bagman" to the office of a different senator who was also a presidential nominee. Jack's "bag" seems to have paid off; our "bag" was a waste of money, and the study was never done.

Flying to Rhode Island

On various occasions, Ralph Blickenstaff, Michael Healey, Brian Washburn, and Chris Praeger flew to Warwick with me for weekend workshops. Ralph was a student at Queens College, Brian was a volunteer at the Maimonides Dream/ESP Project, Michael was one of my students at New York University, and Chris was studying photography. We took several dozen children through a series of writing, drawing, and dramatic exercises that differed from anything they had encountered in their schools. Ralph and I described these workshops in an article we wrote in 1970 for the *Gifted Child Quarterly*.[15]

Chris's photos were excellent and were used for public relations by the FGCC. Chris had been sent my way by my New York friends Robert Masters and Jean Houston, who had been counseling his father following Chris's attack on his stepmother, leaving her face scarred and ruining her career as a model. Chris's birth mother had died of an overdose of opioids, and he needed a change of venue. He stayed in my Brooklyn apartment for several months and seemed to be doing well. But when he returned home, his "inner demons" re-emerged, and he

---

[15] Krippner, S., & Blickenstaff, R. (1970). The development of self-concept as part of an art workshop for the gifted. *Gifted Child Quarterly, 14*, 163–166.

told his father that he could hear his mother calling him. One evening, he obeyed her call and walked into Lake Michigan. His body was never found.

Wayne Champlain's story had a happier ending. In 1971, the Friedels and the Champlains sent him to live in my Brooklyn apartment in order to attend a high school in Brooklyn for a semester. By good fortune, Wayne's arrival coincided with the opening of the Museum of Contemporary Crafts in Manhattan. He throve in this change of venue and returned to Warwick with a more positive outlook. Over the years, I have discovered that some disturbed teenagers, especially if they are bright, do well in an unfamiliar environment, as the challenge opens up novel coping mechanisms.

Creativity Workshops
These workshops were held in the local Unitarian Church, and I organized the events myself, drawing upon a successful workshop I had conducted in 1970 at the School for Visual Arts in Manhattan for two dozen pre-teenagers. I was assisted by my then-stepdaughter, Carie Harris, and a Dream Laboratory volunteer, Ronny Mastrion. Carie taught the group spontaneous painting, which was enjoyed by everyone, even those who maintained that they had never been "artistic." Ronny held a filmmaking class that succeeded in creating a short but innovative movie. Since we could not bring his filmmaking equipment to Rhode Island, we used psychodrama instead to evoke a spontaneous story. Most of the participants were boys; there were probably just as many gifted girls in Warwick's schools, but they seemed to be able to comply with the classroom direction, or lack of it.

Marie Friedel opened an informal "school" for those children, and I was able to visit it during one of my trips to Rhode Island. Jack, of course, financed it, but he could not sustain it indefinitely. No other benefactors stepped forward, so the school was short-lived. Lance Friedel told me that when he left home to attend Boston University, his father was in tears, begging him not to go. But Lance graduated *magna cum laude* and went on to study in several music schools, both in the United States and in Europe. He became a celebrated orchestra conductor, renowned for his interpretations of Carl Nielsen and the symphonies of several little-known U.S. composers. He was so bright he could have prospered in numerous occupations, but chose to study conducting, even while knowing that this was a difficult field in which to succeed.

Without Lance to serve as a buffer, Jack became despondent and soon passed on. Marie lived long enough to enjoy her son's success— one that she had meticulously crafted since she became aware of his talents. However, she became institutionalized following her diagnosis of Alzheimer's Disease. Lance told me that people in her facility asked her what type of work she had done, and she answered, "I think I used to work with children."

Ten Commandments
One of my most frequently cited articles on the topic was titled "The Ten Commandments that Block Creativity."[16] In it, I spoofed the stereotypes that held parents and teachers back from fostering creative behavior.

1. Everything thou doest must be useful.
2. Everything thou doest must be successful.
3. Everything thou doest must be perfect.
4. Everyone thou knowest must like thee.
5. Thou shalt not prefer solitude to togetherness.
6. Remember concentrated attention and keep it holy.
7. Thou shalt not diverge from culturally approved sex norms.
8. Thou shalt not express excessive emotional feelings.
9. Thou shalt not be ambiguous.
10. Thou shalt not rock the cultural boat.

In 1972, I received the Citation of Merit from the NAGC; in 1981, I was given its Membership Service Award, and in 1985, its Distinguished Service Award. The NACCA's Citation of Merit came my way in 1974. I was named "Colleague" by the Creative Problem-Solving Institute, Buffalo, New York, in 1980. I had attended several of their annual creativity programs and befriended its founder, Sidney Parnes, who chaired Jean Houston's doctoral dissertation when she decided she needed a PhD in psychology as well as the one in philosophy she had earned previously.

I was given the Certificate of Recognition by the Office of the Gifted and Talented, U.S. Department of Health and Human Services, in 1976. This was a short-lived office directed by Harold "Hal" Lyon, the husband of Edith Lyon, one of my students at the Humanistic Psychology

---

[16] Krippner, S. (1967). The Ten Commandments that block creativity. *Gifted Child Quarterly, 11*, 144–156.

Institute. With a change of administrations, the office was abolished, and Hal went on to co-author a remarkable text with Carl Rogers, *On Becoming an Effective Teacher*.[17]

Perhaps my greatest recognition came in 2022, when I was listed as one of the "giants and trailblazers in creativity" in a book by the same title. The chapter about me was written by my former student Glenn Graves, who was working as a clinical psychologist in Singapore. His list of my contributions paled by comparison with such pioneers as Paul Torrance, Steven Pritzker, and Marc Runco, whose *Encyclopedia of Creativity* included two entries by me;[18,19] J.P. Guilford, who emphasized multiple approaches to problem solving as the key to creativity; Graham Wallas, whose model of creativity spanned "preparation," "incubation," "illumination," and "verification"; and Ruth Richards, whose concept of "everyday creativity" made the concept more accessible. In retrospect, it all started on December 2, 1957, the last day of Professor Witty's class on gifted children, a class that changed my life.

Some Personal Insights

I have often been called "gifted" and "creative," most notably in 2021 when I was included in that "giants and trailblazers" book.[20] This accolade prompted me to look into my own background to determine its antecedents. Regarding genetics, my parents were both intelligent and creative; my father managed to run a successful farm and orchard, a complicated task that I could never equal. My mother's intelligence was apparent in her excellent handwriting and her well-worded letters to me, many of which I saved.

In elementary school, I was often called upon to make class presentations, such as an illustrated presentation of Brazil as a hoped-for honeymoon spot. When I graduated from high school, one of my teachers wrote in my yearbook that I would be "going places." I was a bit puzzled, because I was not the class valedictorian or even the salutatorian, simply the "honor roll representative." At the University

---

[17] Rogers, C. R., Lyon, H. C., & Tausch, R. (2013). *On becoming an effective teacher*. Routledge.
[18] Krippner, S. (2020). Dreams. In M. A. Runco & S. R. Pritzker (Eds.), *Encyclopedia of creativity* (3rd ed., Vol. 1, pp. 383–389). Academic Press.
[19] Krippner, S. (2020). Altered and transitional states. In M. A. Runco & S. R. Pritzker (Eds.), *Encyclopedia of creativity* (3rd ed., Vol. 1, pp. 29–36.) Academic Press.
[20] Reisman, F. R. et al. (Eds.). (2021). *Giants and trailblazers in creativity research and related fields*. KIE Book Series.

of Wisconsin, I graduated with "honors," not "high honors," as did some of my classmates. I suspect that a reason was that I never attempted to hide my intelligence, as did some of the male students in both high school and university. One of my university classmates was an extremely gifted artist; I admired his ability to relate to his peers by giving them caricatures. My tested intelligence quotient centered at 135, not too shabby—but in the "moderately gifted," not the "highly gifted," category.

The Ingenuity of Family Members
My grandfather, John Krippner, was described in his obituary as "gentle in his ways, kind in his judgment, and gracious in his disposition." He forged a 32-acre fruit farm, a remarkable feat of creativity, and passed it on to my father, who was popular in his professional circles, serving as an officer in the local fruit growers' association and the Township of Oakland. I never saw my father commit an act of physical violence to my mother or anyone else. I knew that he was disappointed that I would not devote myself to continuing the orchard that he and my grandfather had brought to fruition, attracting customers from miles around.

During my childhood, my father's barn housed a horse and a few cows; he dispensed with the horse when he was able to afford a tractor. Not only did the cows supply our family with milk, but some of it was sold to a distributor. Both my parents worked part-time at the neighboring mink ranch, where I spent several summers earning my own spending money. When I needed to cite his income for a scholarship application, I was surprised to learn that his annual income was a little over $3,000. He certainly made effective use of every dollar, another example of his creativity.

He also sold Nutrilite, a highly regarded vitamin and mineral supplement that became the bestseller in its field. Since I felt that one of my father's greatest gifts to me was my monthly supply of Nutrilite, I was happy one day to accompany him to a sales meeting. I was surprised to hear that no benefits of the supplement were mentioned, only tips on how to sell the product. My father's genial manner and knowledgeable sales pitch made him a successful salesperson. Given that I had severe health problems as a child, I suspect that my daily dose of Nutrilite helped me compensate. Decades later, when he retired, my former stepdaughter, Carie Harris, began selling Nutrilite, and I was her best customer.

My sister, Donna, and I helped pick apples, pears, cherries, strawberries, and raspberries to sell at our roadside stand as well as to neighborhood grocery stores. I was very enthusiastic about fostering sales; when a potential customer asked the name of the apples on display, I was able to provide the appropriate answer, be it Macintosh, Granny, or Red Delicious. When I did not know the answer, I simply made one up. I painted a colorful placard for posting on the roadside sign; it was never used, but it prompted my parents to hire a professional artist to design one. We sold our berries in small wooden containers, and I topped each of them with a strawberry or raspberry leaf. My mother quickly took them off, saying that they distracted from the fruit—and our orchard's reputation. Of course, she was right, but it took me a while to understand her rationale.

Our father fostered a love of nature and the outdoors that was a wonderful gift for us both. Once he no longer had to pay our tuition bills, he created what we called "Lake Krippner" in the marsh that was part of our territory. He enjoyed getting into his boat and going fishing, having stocked the "lake" with minnows shortly after its completion. This was an incredible feat, and one that received compliments from both of us. In retrospect, I wish I had visited the "lake" more often and had taken photographs to document this endeavor. However, his affinity for the out-of-doors stayed with me, and decades later I discovered that there are health benefits to spending time in nature. Many children raised in urban environments rarely venture out, even to visit city parks—and both their physical and mental health suffer as a result.

But our father dispensed with kindness when the occasion demanded it. He had been a trustee of the bank in Cambridge, Wisconsin, that he had helped to found. When the other trustees deemed that he was too old for the job and dismissed him, he promptly withdrew all of our bank accounts and put them into the competing bank, with our approval, of course. He never made a racial or ethnic slur but sometimes was a bit hostile to Roman Catholics, echoing the sentiments of our Presbyterian Church pastor. When John F. Kennedy was assassinated, I recall him saying, "Well, that's the end of our only Catholic President." I recall a conversation he had with my Aunt Gertrude Munson, who had just returned from a visit with a friend she had not seen for years. Her friend was now the mother of three children, and she told Aunt Gertrude that one boy was very special because "he is my priest's son." At the time, this surprised me, but later I was to encounter comparable stories.

Our mother's ingenuity took several forms, notably in the "patchwork" quilts she worked on intermittently, eventually giving them to my sister and me as wedding presents. Her handwriting was beautiful, and I never was able to match it. Like many creative people, she was often unpredictable, notably in terms of her punishments, such as taking away "rewards" when I had misbehaved. The psychiatrist I had consulted during my time at Kent State University referred to this as the "empty teat syndrome," suspecting that breastfeeding was somehow difficult for her. She never criticized our father behind his back, but during a church dinner she made fun of him for spilling some food on his necktie. He took it in stride, but I never forgot it. To fathom my mother's behavior, I grew to realize that she was the youngest of three children; I could imagine that in her childhood she tried to get a bit of attention from her parents and to keep from being overshadowed by her two dynamic siblings.

At an early age, I was dismayed when my parents fought and argued. One day I simply could not take it anymore and decided to "run away from home." I did not get far. Our next-door neighbors, Archie and Evelyn Derlien, saw me walking down the road, picked me up, and delivered me back home, explaining to my parents what had transpired. My parents never fought again, at least not in front of me.

Sometimes I was puzzled by their seemingly incompatible temperaments, even asking myself how they could have stayed married. I suspected that they had a great sex life, and that this is what kept them together. When my sister was quite young, she told me to look into their bedroom because "Mother and Dad are sleeping so close together." I recognized that this was the "primal act" and told her, "Isn't that beautiful that they love each other so much?" Indeed, it was.

My mother's judgmental remarks often focused on people who remarried once their spouses had passed on, or whom she perceived as breaking their marriage vows. More than once, she announced that the worst thing people could do was to be "unfaithful" to their spouses. I thought to myself, "Worse than murder?" Our neighbor, Catherine Dingledine, died before her husband (who had been the family dentist), and our mother was upset when he remarried and moved out of state. Her comment was, "I hope she takes him for every penny." In actuality, he and his second wife produced several children and, from what I understood, had a fulfilling life together.

Our mother was somewhat of a "drama queen." When my sister and I misbehaved, she lamented that we would be the "death" of her, and we took it literally. On a more benign note, she returned from a dinner at an ethnic Norwegian restaurant with some blood sausage, biting into it and telling us, "I am eating blood!" When my parents visited me at the

Maimonides Medical Center in Brooklyn, I invited them to sit in on one of our sessions at the Dream Laboratory. She made a trip to the bathroom and returned in alarm, saying that she had encountered a dark-skinned janitor en route and thought, "Well, this is the end of me."

Her longest-standing prejudice involved people who were "well-to-do," and I traced it back to the fact that she may have "married up," finding a husband who was from a distinguished line of Krippners and Porters. Her sister-in-law, my Aunt Ethel Gleichman, and her husband had two children, both of whom married partners "of substance." When our father died, Aunt Ethel's daughter and son-in-law (my cousins) sent a floral wreath to the church that outclassed all the other tributes put together. My mother was loath to thank them, wanting her sister-in-law to write the thank-you note. My sister and I would not let her do this, as it would have been incredibly impolite.

When her "drama queen" persona took over, she would stand erect to make her statement. I recall several times when she announced, "I used to be soft, but now I am hard." As I think back, I assume that marriage and motherhood had presented her with challenges that she had trouble facing, but becoming "hard" was her way of coping with them. I also recall receiving a handmade Easter card from her when I was a kid, a collage of cut-out pieces that had been so well designed I could not bear to discard it.

Some of her creative insights came out in surprising ways. In October 1974, I was invited to give three lectures at the University of Wisconsin Hospital. One of my talks highlighted observations of the controversial Filipino folk healers; I described how they seemed to extract diseased tissue from a sick person's body by sticking their hands into the problematic area, pulling out toxic tissue. After the lecture, she told me that this was probably due to sleight of hand, and I admired her critical thinking. I probably owe my "skeptical" persona to her, and it has served me well.

My sister, Donna, and I were fortunate to have escaped the dogmatic religious upbringing that befell many of our peers. Both of our parents were regular churchgoers and made sure we attended the weekly Sunday School classes. Our mother could be somewhat hard on herself, and, when she made what she considered a grievous error, she chortled, "Well, I guess I am going to the other place when I die." Never fear. She was never a candidate for doom and perdition.

But our mother often complimented us on our creative and scholarly accomplishments. My sister's creativity was manifested in her theatrical work, her vegetable and flower gardens, and her execution of well-designed clothing, including a Hawaiian shirt that she made for me, which I wear as often as possible. Our mother frequently "pushed" me to join local youth groups and to compete with others, something hard for me to do because I have never been overly competitive. I certainly did not feel I had to "compete" with my sister because our mother never gave any hint of favoritism. She did not have to "push" Donna to join social groups, as she was less introverted and less shy than I was.

My First Scrapbook
At an early age, my mother gave me a scrapbook, making sure it was filled with such memorabilia as birth records, report cards, and greeting cards. Those scrapbooks have had a life of their own; I still have a few dozen of them—and they were invaluable when it came time to write my memoirs. They also demonstrate some modest creativity on my part, as I would group photographs, newspaper clippings, school mementos, and other memorabilia into well-organized categories. She never did the same for my sister, saying that I had all the important documents in my scrapbooks, in case they were needed.

In reviewing the scrapbooks, I had many surprises. I found a notepaper addressed to my mother just after my sister was born. It featured the image of Bashful, one of the 12 Disney dwarfs, and the caption, "Dear Mama, you have a baby girl named Donna." This note, which welcomed my sister into the world, indicates that I did not feel "displaced" or "competitive" with the new family member. But it also suggests that I identified with the reticent Bashful, rather than with one of the more dynamic dwarfs.

The scrapbooks contained newspaper clippings, as well as notable letters from family and friends. When I was quite young, J. Leon Buchen, a magician who went by the stage name of "The Great Oscar," sent me a newspaper from Australia with the headline, "Great Oscar Teaches Stanley Krippner." Even though I knew it was ersatz, it was the first time I had seen my name in a newspaper. Every summer, he and his wife, Florence, would stay at a lakeside cottage at nearby Lake Ripley, and he would take me along when he visited other friends in the area. I was delighted to be treated so royally and looked forward to those summer visits.

Both my grandmother and my father had exhibited fruit at the local Jefferson County Fair and several other venues, my father for over half a century. Their exhibits were always arranged artistically in a way that would attract the favorable attention of the judges. Both of my parents encouraged me to take produce from my vegetable garden to the Jefferson County fairs, where I won a bevy of first-, second-, and third-place awards. For example, at the Jefferson County Fair in 1947, I exhibited 14 vegetables from my "victory garden," including beets, cabbage, carrots, kohlrabi, onions, peppers, and tomatoes. I recall being happy with any of the awards, one time telling a friend, "There is nothing wrong in being second place." I made the same statement decades later, when I missed the Presidency but was elected vice president of the National Association for Gifted Children.

To quote a line from the Andrew Lloyd Weber/Tim Rice musical "Evita," "As for fortune, as for fame, I never invited them in." In retrospect, I might have paid more attention to "fortune." As for "fame," the only time I recall inviting it in was when I asked a friend to nominate me in 2000 for the annual American Psychological Association's Award for Distinguished Contributions to the International Development of Psychology. His nomination was turned down, but with encouragement to try again the following year; I did receive the award in 2002. But my motivation was not immediately apparent, as I had received enough awards by that time to satisfy any urge for recognition I might have had. However, some family members had been extremely critical of me for being absent from home so often, and I felt that receiving the award might have justified my absence. To continue with a few more words from the Weber and Rice lyric, "All you need to do is look at me to know that every word is true." In retrospect, I suspect that it was my creativity, rather than my intellectual brilliance, that instigated that bevy of awards, as well as the plethora of invitations to speak at conventions and conferences.

Chapter 11

Activism and Activists
28 August 1958. A Day When My Life Changed

An *activist* is a person who campaigns to bring about political or social change. Activism can be employed by individuals, groups, movements, or policies. In 1973, Daniel Ellsberg, who had leaked *The Pentagon Papers* to the press, held a joint briefing with Ruth Gage Colby, an investigative journalist who had covered the founding of the United Nations in 1945 and was a long-time peace advocate. Both were well-known activists.

Activism in Action

Since I had been acquainted with both Ellsberg and Colby, I hardly thought I would be called an "activist" as well. But I was first described as an "activist" when I spoke at the International Conference on the Education of Gifted and Highly Creative Children, held in New York City on May 26 and 27, 1972. There were about two dozen speakers, some of them friends of mine, but I was the only one given that sobriquet. My assigned topic was "How Communications Can Be Improved between Educators of the Gifted, Emotionally Disturbed, and Physically and Mentally Handicapped." Apparently, I was the only speaker who had worked with all of those groups, and sometimes I had taken a controversial stance. I objected to the popular notion that autistic children were the victims of poor mothering, insisting that the condition had a neurological basis. I had also emphasized the neurological role played in learning disabilities at a time when parents and teachers were unjustifiably held accountable for them. I was an early advocate of expanding the concept of giftedness beyond what could be measured by intelligence tests. I had pushed for the inclusion of physically challenged youngsters in school activities at a time when numerous parents were told to keep their children at home, where they would be guarded against teasing, bullying, and playground accidents. I had insisted that hyperactive children be given Ritalin and other medication only as a last resort, if psychoeducational and other non-drug interventions had not been effective.

I had been prepared for this role by Paul Witty and Helmer Myklebust, my professors at Northwestern University, and by my time with Margaret Hudson, director of special education for the Richmond, Virginia, public schools, where I had worked with a variety of children with special needs. Eventually, my positions became mainstream, but at that time they were often considered to be radical.

I continued to give lectures and workshops for decades on the topic of learning disabilities and their treatment. In 1970, I recorded ten cassettes on specific learning disabilities and attended the College Reading Association, where I was a member of the Board of Directors. This work with disabilities eventually morphed into my work with people with the diagnosis of post-traumatic stress disorder (PTSD). Again, I championed psychotherapeutic treatment rather than (or, at least, in combination with) drugs, most notably in dealing with PTSD nightmares, for this I advocated such approaches as *imagery rehearsal*, during which someone rehearses a different outcome to the nightmare during waking hours, a practice that usually impacts and changes the content of nighttime dreams.

I have always taken an interest in newsworthy events; one of my childhood scrapbooks contained a six-page history of World War II, with my hand-drawn maps, my own caricatures of the major leaders on both sides, and captions that I had laboriously typed. My years with the University of Wisconsin Memorial Student Union's Forum Committee had given me the opportunity to interact with many opinion shapers of that era, ranging from such progressives as Arthur Schlesinger, Jr., to such conservatives as William F. Buckley, Jr. Along with others in the university's "Stick Out Your Neck Club" (SOYNC), I opposed the actions of Wisconsin Senator Joseph McCarthy and watched the televised so-called "Army-McCarthy Hearings," which led to his demise. (Decades later, I met John Searle, a philosophy professor who also recalled the SOYNC; he had been secretary of the Students Against Joseph McCarthy organization, so we had probably met at that time.)

Once I graduated, I spent one year as a speech therapist in a rural community in Illinois before I went to Richmond, Virginia, where I spent one day a week giving audiometric examinations to public school students. Our speech and hearing clinic was completely desegregated, at a time when the state was adamant about maintaining segregated facilities. From there I went to Northwestern University to work on my doctorate, after which I spent three years at Kent State University and then a decade at the Maimonides Medical Center in Brooklyn. I wrote a chapter for the book *White Racism*, and in 1983 joined Psychologists for Social Responsibility, noting that many humanistic psychologists were members of the advisory board.[1] Their number included Albert Ellis, Jerome Frank, Rollo May, and Carl Rogers, all of whom were to become close friends of mine.

In 1967, I marched in New York City's first demonstration against U.S. military actions in Vietnam, a war that many of us felt was unnecessary and the result of policy blunders. The 1956 peace accords ended France's involvement in Vietnam and called for nationwide elections, a mandate ignored by both the United States and South Vietnam, who suspected that Ho Chi Minh, the communist leader, would win. If the mandate had been honored, thousands of American military lives and millions of Vietnamese lives would have been spared. Martin Luther King, Jr., whom I had met when he lectured at Northwestern University, foresaw the forthcoming calamity quite well, as did champion boxer Muhammed Ali, formerly Cassius Clay, whom I had seen on stage in the short-lived musical, "Buck White."

In 1971, the Brooklyn Psychological Association invited me to speak at its annual conference. I discussed the use of illegal drugs by combat soldiers in Vietnam, predicting the end of the Vietnam War and the legalization of marijuana. The former prediction was simply stating what was obvious, but it took several decades for the second to take place. I had formed a committee to hasten the process through such activism as public events and interactions with public officials. Committee members included Alan Watts, Joel Fort, and Joe Oteri, the attorney whose legal efforts dated back to 1967.

In November 1969, I met with Ed Arrow from "To Right a Wrong," an organization fostering changes in marijuana legislation, and he brought me to Albany as an "expert witness" for the Intercollegiate Debate Conference that was focusing on drug laws. During the same year, I spoke on the topic at a Brooklyn Psychological Association award event for high school students, and in December I testified on marijuana legislation for a New York State legislature subcommittee hearing. I brought a brochure with me in which I had summarized the research that supported my position, and one legislator, Ed Koch, later a long-serving mayor of New York City, vowed to read it.

---

[1] Krippner, S. (1970). Race, intelligence, and segregation: The misuse of scientific data. In B. N. Schwartz & R. Disch (Eds.), *White Racism* (pp. 452–464). Dell/Laurel.

In 1974, the Association for Humanistic Psychology newsletter published my article "Is Psychology Part of the Problem?" based on my AHP presidential address. I pointed out that some of the most eminent "authorities" on intelligence had claimed that Blacks typically made lower scores on intelligence tests. I disputed the claim that autism, schizophrenia, and other maladies were triggered by inept mothering. And I pointed out that Ritalin and similar medications were routinely prescribed for unruly "hyperactive" school children in lieu of educational alternatives. In that same year, I argued about marijuana legalization with an official from the U.S. Department of Narcotics and Dangerous Drugs on a volatile panel during the APA's annual convention.

Early on, I fathomed the therapeutic potential of LSD and other psychedelics, writing and speaking on the topic and rejoicing when restrictions were finally relaxed at the beginning of the 21st century. In 2017, I was invited to speak on two panels at the Psychedelic Science conference, an event held in Oakland, California, attended by over 3,000 people. I remember telling Amanda Feilding, founder of the Beckley Foundation, which co-sponsored the event, that I was overjoyed I had lived long enough to see the potential of psychedelics finally being recognized.

My interest in newsworthy events triggered two streams of activism. In the late 1970s, I began to get invitations to serve as an advisor to so-called "LSD Rescue Centers," and worked with half a dozen of them, noting that they were student organized and student run, which probably helped explain their effectiveness. I also was invited to advise two programs for service veterans dealing with PTSD and other sequelae to their combat service. Once again, these initiatives were organized and run by young people, some of them veterans themselves. I was well aware of the litigious hazards potentially involved had there been a suicide or other untoward incident.

I became involved in other newsworthy events, specifically the anti-Semitism that surfaced in colleges and universities, and the murder of working Mexican women by vigilantes who felt that women needed to stay at home and become good wives and mothers. My activism gained me a few death threats from the assassins, many of whom were men whose "machismo" was threatened by the activities of women trying to obtain a modicum of power.

My work with the Maimonides Dream/ESP Project was a long-term manifestation of activism. When the Maimonides Community Mental Health Center opened in November 1968, it was intended to service the over 100,000 people living in the "catchment area." It included 24-hour-a-day emergency services, and both out-patient and in-patient services; I felt very much "at home" in this milieu.

I was invited to make any number of presentations regarding our work, one of the most memorable being my 1980 discussion in the congressional offices of Charles Rose, a long-time representative from North Carolina. Several other members of Congress attended the event, along with Barbara Honniger, who later joined President Reagan's staff, and John Alexander, a retired colonel who had participated in military parapsychological research. Congressman Rose gave me a pass to attend Reagan's inauguration on January 20, 1981, apologizing that it was in the standing room section because his candidate, Jimmy Carter, had lost the election. I did not mind standing, as I could see Charlton Heston and other celebrities on the far side of our fenced-off section, and I stayed to enjoy a spectacular fireworks display at night. Years later, Barbara Honniger alleged that Reagan's team had conspired with Iranian officials to delay releasing U.S. hostages until after the election, an event often called the "October Surprise."

In February 2023, I received an email from a group named "Edges," Ukrainian psychotherapists who told me that they had conducted "market research" and found my books and articles about PTSD to be especially helpful. They asked for permission to translate them, which I was happy to give to them. The Russian invasion had traumatized both Ukrainian soldiers and civilians, but there was very little material in Ukrainian that was both accurate and useful. I not only gave them permission to do the translations, but I also offered specific advice on treating PTSD and its manifestations.

My work with military veterans with a diagnosis of PTSD came to the attention of Laura and Brandon Millet, who invited me to attend their annual GI Film Festival, usually held in the Washington, DC, area, which I was happy to do until it was canceled as the pandemic struck. I enjoyed watching a variety of new feature films and documentaries, as well as interacting with various celebrities such as the former presidential candidate Ross Perot and actors Gary Sinese, Joe Mantegna, and Lou Diamond Philips.

The 2011 GI Film Festival was especially noteworthy because I brought my stepgrandson, Maurice Harris, with me. I introduced him to one of the honorees, the actor Rick Schroeder, whom he remembered from the TV series "Lonesome Dove." I reminded Schroeder that my friend Chris Ryan had met him on an airplane, while Chris was scanning the page proofs for his book *Sex at Dawn*. Schroeder had taken an interest in the book, suggesting it would make a fine documentary. Chris gave him the page proofs, but never heard from him again. Schroeder told me, "You know, a strange thing happened when I brought that book home." He went on to say that his wife had spotted the book, was shocked at the contents, and burned it. That answered Chris's question, but we were both amused at the coincidence that finally brought closure to the incident. Moreover, we were not surprised when the couple's marriage fell apart a few years later.

Over the years, my paths have crossed with a number of activists, for example: Richard Farson (children's rights); Jacquie Lewis and Linda Riebel (animal activism); Kay Bruch, Steven Pritzker, Ruth Richards, and Tobi Zausner (creative persons activism); Anne Isaacs and Marie Friedel (rights for creative children); Ingrid Kepler-May and Ilene Serlin (women's rights); William Domhoff, Harris Friedman, Lois Holzman, David McReynolds, Marc Pilisuk, Steve Speer, and Don Taylor (political activism); and Harry Easton (ecology activism). George Berticevich has been an activist for Burmese people who had been imprisoned or exiled. Henny Kupferstein has been an activist for people diagnosed as "autistic," seeing autism as an alternate way of knowing rather than as a disease; her controversial approach set off a chain of reactions that improved the lives of many children and adults with the autism diagnosis. Philip Zimbardo, a former president of the American Psychological Association, has been an activist in many ways, notably for recognizing people who carry out heroic acts, and by constructing guidelines for people to become "heroes" in their daily lives.

Robert Freling has been an activist on behalf of solar power, a development I first heard about from Professor Farrington Daniels when I was studying at the University of Wisconsin. Robert's organization has installed solar power technology in schools, enterprises, and private homes in Benin, Bhutan, and 20 other countries, and for the Arhuaco ethnic group in Colombia.

Dennis Carpenter has been an activist on behalf of contemporary pagan religions, such as Wicca. I supervised his doctoral dissertation, where he discovered a link between self-identified pagans' mystical experiences and both ecological awareness and positive life changes.

My fellow parapsychologists are automatically activists, because our work departs from dominant paradigms, and—to a lesser extent—so are my psychotherapist colleagues who use biofeedback, hypnosis, and psychedelics in their therapies, knowing that they work outside the orientations of mainstream therapists. I have known far too many activists for me to discuss them even briefly, but here are just a few more of them.

The Activism of Rollo May

Rollo May, one of the most influential American psychologists of the 20th century and a founder of humanistic psychology, developed and popularized European existential psychoanalysis in America. He incorporated both perspectives into his books about human suffering and crises, notably his best-selling *Love and Will*.[2] I had met Rollo May when I lived in New York City, thanks to my old friend Virginia Glenn, who had faithfully attended most of his public lectures. Rollo and I became friends and colleagues, especially in the years after we both moved to California.

In 1994, Rollo's third wife, Georgia, asked me to give one of the five eulogies at his funeral, and later made me a present of his blue velvet sports jacket, which I wore with great pride for years. I had also befriended Rollo's second wife, Ingrid, who joined me in Salvador, Brazil, for a lecture on family mediation, as she had inaugurated the first such service in the San Francisco Bay area.

I worked with Rollo at Saybrook University for decades, often attending salons at his Tiburon home, sometimes to discuss such topics as transpersonal psychology, at other times featuring a guest, such as the Jesuit priest Daniel Berrigan, who had become a passionate anti-war activist. I was asked to write book reviews for both Rollo's 1991 book, *The Cry for Myth,* and Robert Abzug's masterful 2021 biography, *Psyche and Symbol in America: The Spiritual Odyssey of Rollo May*[3]. In April 1975, I flew to Tucson for a seminar on humanistic psychology attended by Rollo, Gregory Bateson, Carl Rogers, Jonas Salk, Nora Weckler, Stanislav Grof, and Joan Halifax, among others. Rollo's biographer noted that Rollo was especially impressed by Gregory Bateson's presentation, but that Carl Rogers had confused the term "demonic" (being possessed by a demon) with "daemonic," a term used by Plato, Goethe, and Jung (among others) to describe one's inner voice. Rollo had been an activist for most of his life, beginning with his brief stint in the ministry during which he vowed to change organized religion, to his opposition to the Vietnam War, but mainly to his

---

[2] May, R. (1969). *Love and will.* W. W. Norton.
[3] Abzug, R. H. (2021). *Psyche and soul in America: The spiritual odyssey of Rollo May.* Oxford University Press.

embrace of European existentialism, which he brought into his own writing as well as his psychotherapeutic practice.

In 1986, I was instrumental in securing honorary degrees from Saybrook University for both Rollo May and Carl Rogers. In 1991, I was asked to write a review of Rollo's book *The Cry for Myth*, which I was happy to do, never suspecting that such an honor would come my way when I first read his earlier works.

The Activism of Carl Rogers
Carl Rogers was the founder of person-centered psychotherapy and a co-founder of humanistic psychology. To improve the outcome for his patients, Rogers incorporated the ideas of congruence, empathic understanding, acceptance, and unconditional positive regard into therapeutic interaction. I was fortunate in getting to know all the founders of humanistic and transpersonal psychology, but Rogers was the first, as I had made an appointment to see him when I was teaching at Kent State University and he was teaching at the University of Wisconsin. I later discovered that Carl was committed to research studies that would evaluate his procedures, a pioneering project.

Carl's "person-centered approach to conflict resolution" brought antagonists together in a neutral setting, one in which they endeavored to state their opponent's point of view in terms that would be considered accurate. While they were attempting this assignment, the opponents were instructed to be aware of any issues, even minor ones, where there seemed to be some promise of accord. This development of empathy usually had positive results, notably in such overseas locations as Brazil, Northern Ireland, the Middle East, and the Soviet Union. At a 1985 conference in Rust, Austria, Rogers supervised a conflict resolution event for representatives of 17 different countries.

Carl was an early monitor of Wisconsin Senator Joseph McCarthy; moreover, his first post-doctoral position was to direct the Rochester, New York, Society for the Prevention of Cruelty to Children. One of his early books dealt with psychotherapy for service people returning from World War II. Carl originally described himself as an atheist, later as an agnostic, and still later as a believer in "spiritual realms." I recall a dinner event where we were sitting together, and Carl was eager to hear about the latest developments in parapsychology, implying that he had received "messages" from his late wife, Helen. I remarked that such post-mortem communications were not unusual, and that parapsychologists had begun taking an active interest in them, news that he appeared to find gratifying.

The Activism of Salma Hayek

In 1996, Gordon Melton, a scholar of religions and religious cults, contacted me, suggesting that I conduct a research study of J. Z. Knight, an Oregon-based author and speaker who claimed that she could "channel" an ancient warrior known as "Ramtha." I replied with great skepticism, telling him that what I had read about her suggested that she was directing a cult that was taking advantage of "New Age" aficionados. He shared that this had been his original opinion, but he had changed his mind after visiting her ranch in Yelm, Oregon, adding that he would find a way to cover my expenses. Once my colleagues and I arrived, we found Knight and her group to be extremely cooperative, and we took psychophysiological measurements of her cardiac, muscular, and brain activity. When compared with the same readings obtained when she was "channeling Ramtha," we discerned dramatic differences; although they did not establish the existence of Ramtha as an independent entity, they did portray a pattern that could not have been produced by role-playing or engaging in fraud.[4] I was invited to share our findings at a conference involving a variety of figures, ranging from the English quantum physicist B. J. Hiley to the American actor Linda Evans.

A few years later, I was invited to make another presentation, accompanied by my friend Sidian Morning Star Jones, who was eager to meet William Antz, director of the documentary "What the Bleep Do We Know?" that was a thinly disguised exposition of the philosophy of Ramtha. When Sidian and I arrived, our host told us that Salma Hayek also had just arrived and asked if I would like to meet her. I was ecstatic, as I had recently seen her Academy Award-nominated role as Frida Kahlo, the Mexican artist, and knew of her determination to carve out a career in the U.S. cinema. Within minutes, I saw the petite, beautiful actor at a distance and could not control my excitement, running up to her, embracing her, and exclaiming, "Salma Hayek, I love you." Never losing her aplomb, she hugged me back, whereupon I turned to Sidian, saying, "This lovely woman was the queen of Mexican soap operas and left it all behind to come to Hollywood where she studied English five hours a day so that she could get movie roles." Salma, listening in

---

[4] Krippner, S., Wickramasekera, I., Wickramasekera, J., & Winstead, C. W., III. (1998). The Ramtha phenomenon: Psychological, phenomenological, and geomagnetic data. *Journal of the American Society for Psychical Research, 92*, 1–24.

surprise, asked me how I knew so much about her. I replied, "I read that about you, thought it was a gutsy thing to do, and never forgot it."

Salma invited us to join her for lunch, and we were happy to do so. While Sidian was talking with William Antz, I told Salma that I had seen *Frida Still Life*, the 1983 Mexican biopic, before I had seen her movie. Salma asserted that the earlier film portrayed Kahlo as a victim, underplaying her strengths, something she had emphasized in her own film. Salma also shared that she had been invited to host the Nobel Peace Prize concert in 2005, and that she had been fighting for a greater range of film roles for Latina actors. She also told me that she was upset when her brother told her that he had been attending events at the Ramtha School of Enlightenment (RSE). But then she accompanied him to one of the RSE events, found it to be helpful, and returned for other events. At the end of dinner, Salma said that she would invite Sidian and me to spend a week at her ranch in southern California. Of course, I was eager to accept the invitation, but I did not have any of my business cards with me, so I told Salma she could get my contact information from the RSE office. Poor advice. It was my fault for not bringing my cards with me and for not giving Salma a handwritten account of my contact information. I am sure the invitation was sincere, but I needed to "strike while the iron was hot," knowing that once Sidian and I had left the RSE, there would be other matters that would occupy Salma's time.

When I told Salma about one of my "matchmaking" exploits, she mused, "I wish you could find a husband for me." I replied that I had just the guy for her, one who was funny, smart, good looking, and whom women seem to adore. Unfortunately, he was married. I was referring to Chris Ryan; he was amused when I told him this story. But there was no need for me to do anything more, as Salma soon met and married Henri Pinault, a business magnate who applauded her philanthropic work, her move into producing and directing, the establishment of her own cosmetics line, and her continued activism on behalf of women's empowerment. In 2023, Selma began using the name Salma Hayak Pinault. Chris was pleasantly surprised when I told him about my encounters with Salma because she was at the top of his list of female actors he would like to have met.

The Activism of Alan Watts
In January 1969, I had a telephone call from my Northwestern University professor Paul Witty, suggesting that we co-author an article on the environment. He had heard about the forthcoming "Earth Day"

in 1970, an event that launched the ecology movement in the United States; it resonated with his own worldview, which found inspiration in nature rather than in the bounds of organized religion. I told Paul that this was a great idea and suggested that he send me an outline so that I could start writing. One of my greatest regrets is that I did not take the initiative on this project, as it would have provided readers with a facet of Paul's psyche that had not been widely reported.

I took an early interest in environmental (or ecological) activism, thanks to my father who was an early practitioner of "organic agriculture," a procedure that eschewed chemical fertilizers and insecticides in favor of less toxic alternatives. Early in my explorations of Alan Watts's writings,[5] I discovered his interest in ecology; once I met him, we had several discussions on this topic. Alan preferred the term "ecological awareness" to "mystical experience," suggesting that these words described the same phenomenon.[6] In 1969 I was with Alan at the Esalen Institute, where we both were speakers at a forum and he proposed a "World Ecology Year." The following year marked the first "Earth Day," so Alan's proposal became part of the *Zeitgeist*. This may have been an example of Alan's conjecture that if one doesn't push too hard, things will happen when they are ready to happen. One can "go with the flow," but one needs to enter that flow.

Alan often compared Western and Eastern perspectives on nature, with the former seeing it as something to be "conquered" and "mastered." Eastern thought, on the other hand, sees people and the rest of Nature engaging in a "dance," during which the universe observes and enjoys itself. When discussing activism, Watts observed that those "activists" who were intent on making money were often miserable because they did not know what to spend it on or how to enjoy it. Watts's activism was directed toward helping his readers and listeners use philosophical insights to break "the taboo of understanding who you really are."

For two years, I taught a class on the psychology of alienation for the Metropolitan Leadership Program at New York University that was the result of student initiatives. I used *Anomie and Deviant Behavior*[7] as

---

[5] Columbus, P. J., & Rice, D. (Eds.). (2017). *Alan Watts in the Academy: Essays and lectures.* SUNY Press.
[6] Columbus, P. J., & Rice, D. (Eds.). (2012). *Alan Watts - Here and now: Contributions to psychology, philosophy, and religion.* SUNY Press.
[7] Clinard, M. B. (Ed.). (1964). *Anomie and deviant behavior.* Free Press of Glencoe.

one of the texts, as it had been compiled and edited by Marshall Clinard, a prominent sociologist I had known when I was studying at the University of Wisconsin. Students told me that one of the course highlights was attending a lecture by Alan Watts and visiting him after the program had ended. Alan was always eloquent and entertaining, whether his audience was in the triple digits (or higher) or single digits. In 2023, a group revealed that they had coalesced Alan's writings into an artificial intelligence (AI) site; I gave it a try and it was almost like talking with Alan directly. Almost, but not quite!

The Activism of Ethel Tobach
Ethel Tobach was an American psychologist, researcher, and political activist whose work was grounded in evolutionary biology. She was a co-founder of the Animal Behavior Society and the International Society for Comparative Psychology. Her passion for science was matched by her commitment to social justice, peace, and gender equality. Ethel published over 100 professional articles and books on a very wide range of topics, including effects of behavior and stress on animals' disease processes. In 2003, I was present when the American Psychological Association (APA) presented her with the Gold Medal Award for Lifetime Achievement in Psychology in the Public Interest, citing Ethyl's work against racism and sexism and her leadership in psychology groups dedicated to peace and nuclear disarmament. I first became aware of Ethel in 1979, when I read her book *The Four Horsemen: Racism, Sexism, Militarism, and Social Darwinism*[8], resonating with its point of view. I met Ethel at meetings of Psychologists for Social Responsibility, of which we were both members, and, later, when we joined APA Division 48, the Society for the Study of Peace, Conflict, and Violence. Her fellow social activist Marc Pilisuk and I invited her to join the faculty of Saybrook University, where she became a popular and valued professor, admired for her frank opinions. For example, she noted that Saybrook was offering a course on the writings of Carl Gustav Jung and insisted that it address his alleged anti-Semitic and pro-Nazi sentiments. I assured her that these issues would be addressed but noted that those statements of Jung's occurred early in his career and were not repeated once Hitler

---

[8] Tobach, E. (1979). *The four horsemen: Racism, sexism, militarism, and social Darwinism.* Behavioral Publications.

took power. I also reminded her that like many people considered to be "introverts," Jung focused on his inner life, tending to be relatively naïve about complex external issues.

When Saybrook put out a call for honorary degree nominations, Ethel nominated herself. Since I thought this was a gutsy thing for her to do, I supported Ethel's nomination, and she received her degree in 2009. Ethel spent most of her career as a research associate in the department of animal behavior of the American Museum of Natural History; whenever I visited New York City, she treated me for lunch at the museum, showed me some of its new exhibits, and introduced me to some of her fellow activists.

The Activism Of John C. Pierrakos
John C. Pierrakos was an American psychiatrist who founded "bioenergetic analysis" with Alexander Lowen, another psychiatrist. It became one of the first body-oriented psychotherapies. Later on, Pierrakos became the founder and director of the Institute of Core Energetics. With his wife, Eva, he also created the Pathwork Center in New York. I was introduced to John and Eva by my old friend Virginia Glenn, who had been attending their lectures; she invited me to their group gatherings.

Pierrakos and Lowen had been students of controversial psychoanalyst Wilhelm Reich, as had Allan Cott, a psychiatrist whose work with "megavitamin therapy" had been integrated into the program for learning disability students at the Churchill School, which I had helped to launch in 1972. Reich's concept of "body armoring," one's attempt to cope with trauma by blocking the "energy flow" in the body, is reflected in the work of all three psychiatrists as well as in Ida Rolf's practice of "structural integration." I underwent a dozen "Rolfing" sessions with Ida and her son, Richard Damerla. These sessions were characterized by a deep massage of the body's fascia tissue.

Siegmar Gerken studied with John Pierrakos for two decades. With his wife, Cornelia, he created the International Institute for Core Evolution in 1991. Siegmar and I have become close friends, and he visits me from time to time, bringing me up to date on his activism, including many overseas trainings in body-oriented and mindfulness-centered psychotherapy, as well as recurring Zen and management seminars, which were attended by the Norwegian Defense Ministry, among others.

I resonate with his work in the area of what Siegmar refers to as "embodied consciousness," and his collaboration with Professor Fritz-

Albert Popp, who conducted extensive research on the body's biophoton emission.[9] I had met with Popp several times when I was in Germany, thinking that biophoton measurement might be the key to understanding the energetic dynamics of one's psychophysiology, including the so-called "kundalini experiences" and their accompanying bodily phenomena.

The Activism of Gail Hayssen

Long before I met her, Gail Hayssen had been a student in Alexander Everett's course titled "Mind Dynamics," a course also taken by Werner Ehrhardt, who went on to create his own courses named "est," Latin for "it is." When Alexander asked me to conduct a review of the course's effectiveness, I administered a series of tests for the participants to take before and after the training, with additional follow-ups. Among the tests I used was Humphry Osmond's "Experiential World Inventory,"[10] an ingenious measure but one that had not been properly investigated. Much to my dismay, Alexander sold his course to another company that requested that I send them all my data, saying they would do the analysis. They never did, which was a great disappointment for me. At the time, I had no idea that I would meet Gail several years later.

Gail Hayssen's husband, David Levitt, was working at a think tank in Palo Alto, California, when it inaugurated a parapsychological project. Two prominent parapsychologists, Dean Radin and Russell Targ, were looking for research participants, and David encouraged Gail to apply. When she described her extraordinary experiences to Radin and Targ, they told her that she would be an "ideal subject" for their studies.

In one study, Gail attempted to describe images that would be selected a few hours after she had made her guesses. They were so impressed by her accuracy that she was invited to participate in several other studies, and she sometimes became the co-author when those results were published. In one study, chocolate that was "enhanced" by Gayle's "intention" had a significant positive effect on participants' mood when compared to the reactions to ordinary chocolate.

Dean Radin hired Gail as a research assistant at the Institute of Noetic Sciences (IONS), where she handled registration for conferences

---

[9] Popp, F-A. (2003). Properties of biophotons and their theoretical importance. *Indian Journal of Experimental Biology, 41,* 308–402.
[10] Osmond, H. (1981). *Predicting the past. Memos on the enticing universe of possibility.* Macmillan.

and answered letters and phone calls from people who were having unusual experiences and wanted to talk with someone who could help them fathom what had happened.

In the meantime, Gail continued to serve as a research participant at IONS, spending considerable time in a Faraday cage that blocked out electromagnetic radiation. In one experiment, Gail attempted to describe photographs being viewed in a different location in the laboratory. Radin described the remarkable results of that study in his best-selling book *Supernormal*.

At IONS, Gail also participated in a "double slit" experiment that attempted to determine whether a light source could ascertain whether it would be expressed as a particle or a wave. Gail's task was to interfere with the attempted pattern. On one occasion, she became so frustrated with the task that she cried out in agony. Her screams could not be heard, because she was in the Faraday cage, but at that moment all the power in the IONS laboratory shut down, as did the power source across the entire county.

When Gail was working at IONS, she attended a conference with other "remote viewers," during which Russell Targ brought in a large paper bag and asked if someone would like to guess its contents. Gail immediately speculated that it was a brass statuette of an eight-armed Shiva with a lotus at its base. When Targ opened the bag, the group discovered that Gail's guess had been a completely accurate description.

A few hours later, when another parapsychologist, Daryl Bem, was demonstrating sleight of hand, he produced another paper bag with undisclosed contents. Gail impulsively cried out, "There is a sand dollar in the bag," and again she was correct. Bem told the group, "What I was doing earlier today was magic, but what Gail just did was real."

Targ introduced Gail to Jean Millay, another research participant in one of his studies. Jean brought Gail to the annual International Shamanism Conference held in Marin County, where she befriended the conference organizer, Ruth-Inge Heinze. The two of them collaborated with Dean Radin on an experiment using a "token object," namely, a ring that Heinze had been wearing before she entered the Faraday cage. When Gail focused on the ring, she sensed that Heinze was thinking of Austria, but her demeanor was so serious that Gail wished that she would smile. On emerging from the Faraday cage, Heinze told Gail, "I know you wanted me to smile," and disclosed that she had recently spoken to a friend from Austria.

Gail easily established rapport with several featured guests at the shamanism conferences, including a Huichol shaman from Mexico, a female shaman from Siberia, and a Mongolian shaman who invited her to his country to learn about shamanism first-hand. Gail jumped at the chance, and her visit culminated in her initiation as a Mongolian shaman!

Jean introduced Gail to me at one of the shaman conferences, and we became close friends. I invited Gail to join me and a few of my friends at the home of Richard and Connie Adams, where we had been holding weekly "table tipping" sessions in which we attempted to levitate a table as we all sat around it with only our fingertips touching the tabletop. Gail was somewhat skeptical, but, after a few sessions, things started happening; there were sudden changes in temperature, and the table began rocking and moving around the room. It never levitated, so we could not rule out the possibility that small movements on our part were responsible for the effects. However, following one of the sessions, a vase in the room showed a large crack that it had not previously displayed.

Gail and her husband, David, hosted a weekend, enabling Jean Millay to greet her friends before leaving for Hawaii to spend the last few weeks of her life with her daughter Mara. Taking a cue from Aldous Huxley, she ingested LSD before she passed on. Sometime later, when members of our weekly "table tipping" group felt that we were being visited, Gail identified the visitor as Jean Millay.

This experience, and those like it, can have alternative explanations based on inadvertent verbal and physical cues and the vagaries of memory. But Gail had performed well in tightly controlled experiments, the results of which were published in *Explore,* a peer-reviewed journal. Gail's activism on behalf of parapsychology continued when she initiated her podcast, "A Small Medium at Large." I appeared on the podcast to discuss parapsychology, as did a number of my friends such as Sally Rhine Feather, Jeffrey Mishlove, and Stephan Schwartz. Gail's husband, David, had made a wise decision when he encouraged her to participate in these research studies.

The Activism of Gopi Krishna

Gopi Krishna was a yogi, mystic, teacher, writer and social activist, working with organizations that attempted to help poor families. His advocacy of women's rights began in the 1930s and included finding help for widows who were all too often encouraged to throw themselves upon their late husband's funeral pyre.

At the age of 34, Gopi Krishna experienced what he would later call "the rise of kundalini energy," from which it took him a dozen years to recover. He recalled:

> The illumination grew brighter and brighter, the roaring louder, I experienced a rocking sensation and then felt myself slipping out of my body, entirely enveloped in a halo of light ... I felt the point of consciousness that was myself growing wider, surrounded by waves of light ... I was now all consciousness, without any outline, without any idea of a corporeal appendage, without any feeling or sensation coming from the senses, immersed in a sea of light simultaneously conscious and aware of every point, spread out, as it were, in all directions without any barrier or material obstruction... bathed in light and in a state of exaltation and happiness impossible to describe.

Becoming an advocate of scientific attention to kundalini experiences, he spent the rest of his life urging scientific research on the topic, while authoring many books on the subject, a few of them in verse; some were translated into 17 languages. He was a visionary thinker who championed consciousness studies and later documented his experiences, which he posited as "a biological force driving human evolution." Gopi Krishna began his career as an activist for women (especially widows) and poor people. After his kundalini experience, he became an activist on behalf of consciousness research, writing and lecturing on the topic.

In 1972, our humanistic psychology tour group stopped to visit him at his home in Srinigar, a city in Kashmir, India. Gopi Krishna already had two visitors, Gay Gaer Luce, a science journalist who had written excellent books and articles about sleep and dreams, and Erik Peper, a pioneer practitioner of biofeedback and other means for stress reduction. They had taped hours of Gopi Krishna's recollections, hoping to discover some psychophysiological correlates of the kundalini experience. They concluded that this was no simple task because the technology to accomplish it had not been sufficiently developed. Nonetheless, Gopi Krishna regaled us with stories not only about his own experiences, but about how people with similar experiences could put them to good use through yoga and meditation.

I returned to Kashmir in 1974 with my wife, Lelie. and a group of Americans who had come to India for an international humanistic psychology conference. Gopi Krishna's home near Srinigar afforded us a stunning view of the area; we stayed in houseboats on Lake Dal, enjoying both the home-cooked Indian food and the floating lotus gardens. On land, we also toured the Shalimar Garden and visited Gopi Krishna at his home. He was no closer to finding psychophysiological correlates to kundalini experiences, but had located a number of historical figures who, he believed, had had experiences similar to his. Since my first visit, I had read several of Gopi Krishna's books as well as Carl Gustav Jung's writings on the topic. Jung considered the "kundalini awakening" as a path to "individuation," or the total integration of one's conscious and the unconscious. Jung and Gopi Krishna agreed that the kundalini awakening is so gradual and subtle that most people are not aware of what is happening. In retrospect, Gopi Krishna was active on behalf of consciousness research for decades, and his efforts probably spurred serious research on the topic.

The Activism of Kirk Schneider
I met Kirk Schneider during one of my annual visits to West Georgia College (later, the State University of West Georgia), and again when he arrived in California to begin his doctoral work at Saybrook, where I had arranged for him to be my assistant as part of a work–study program. Kirk has recalled his first time in my office, when he noted a large photograph of Rollo May on the wall, which resonated with his own interest in May's books. Little did either of us realize that he would develop a close working relationship with Rollo, culminating in their co-authored book *The Psychology of Existence,* published in 1995. Kirk served as president of the Society for Humanistic Psychology, editor of the *Journal of Humanistic Psychology,* and author of a dozen books that explored the interface of humanistic-existential psychology to such topics as psychotherapy, movies, and the psychology of awe.

Kirk and I shared an admiration for the work of Otto Rank, who profoundly impacted the work of Rollo May, Carl Rogers, Stanislav Grof, and Ernest Becker, among others, as well as the developing field of social work. Rank was the first to use the phrase "here and now" as applied to psychotherapy, and also described the role played by mythology in promoting both creativity and social cohesion.

Kirk cofounded the Existential-Humanistic Institute (an award-winning psychotherapy training center), and the "bridge-building" Experiential Democracy Dialogue, which uses humanistic psychological principles to make deep connections between people of highly contrasting backgrounds, including therapists and clients. He also received training in the Braver Angels conflict meditation approach that claims to assist "depolarizing the minds" of self-identified liberals and conservatives. When running for the presidency of the American Psychological Association, Kirk proposed a "National Corps of Psychologists" that would offer low-cost, high-quality psychological services, especially to underserved communities. Kirk did not win this election, possibly because his "corps" was considered to be too radical; nonetheless, he continued his activism both in the United States and overseas, where a dozen translations of his books have had salubrious effects.

The Activism of George M. Carter
Over the years, I have given several workshops at the Omega Institute in upstate New York, where I met George M. Carter. George and his mother had come to participate in my five-day course on dreams, shamanism, and personal mythology. The night before the workshop began, George had an upsetting nightmare featuring a threatening animal. He awakened, crying and in a cold sweat, something he had never done before, let alone with his mother in the room. That morning, I opened the course with a drumming ceremony and a guided imagery exercise for people to find a "power animal" that would assist them for the next several days. I told participants that there was no need to conjecture the source of that animal, whether it be archetypes, "spirits," or their own unconscious at work, and George later told me that he was impressed by this "agnostic" approach; the animal that appeared for him during the exercise was the same one that he had seen during his powerful nightmare. Upon working with this image, he was able to determine that it represented his own unacknowledged power, something he would need because he had just joined the AIDS Coalition to Unleash Power (ACT UP).

George spent the following decades as an AIDS activist, setting aside his work as a performance artist. He developed a comprehensive listing of interventions for managing HIV infections and, sometime later, managing side effects of treatment by antiretroviral drugs. In addition, he worked with one of New York's "buyers' clubs," the Direct AIDS Alternative Information Resources (DAAIR), which brought out unapproved but promising drug treatments as well as provided dietary supplements and other non-drug interventions. That work enabled George to examine the evidence, exploring the potential benefits, limitations, side effects, and interactions with other agents, and providing guidance for establishing whether use of the intervention was having an intended effect, such as managing fatigue. When DAAIR's founder closed the club in 2004, George and other activists started what would be the last AIDS buyers' club, the New York Buyers' Club (NYBC). As people with HIV increasingly began to use the Internet to find options, the need for NYBC diminished and it shut itself down in 2016.

George and other activists started the Foundation for Integrative AIDS Research (FIAR) in 2001 to design and implement studies of so-called "integrative therapies," assessing their benefit or lack thereof. These interventions were termed integrative as they combined pharmaceutical approaches with dietary, attitudinal, and lifestyle changes. In addition, FIAR worked with activists around the world to help develop HIV prevention programs, including Sunil Pant in Kathmandu, Nepal. FIAR sent Sunil Pant condoms and lubricants for LGBTQ Nepalis; later, Pant became the first openly gay member of Nepal's Parliament.

In collaboration with researchers at Mount Sinai Hospital, FIAR worked on three grants from the National Institutes of Health (NIH). One included working with a group of practitioners of Siddha (traditional medicine) in South India, while another undertook a review of existing therapeutics in managing HIV. The third analyzed the use of smoking marijuana in managing the side effects of AIDS. This led to focus groups that discussed the use of Schedule 1 drugs, such as LSD, psilocybin, and ibogaine. Later, George collaborated with groups in New York State to create a state-sponsored Institute for Psychedelic Research to explore topics of interest to local communities.

FIAR has also worked to help HIV refugees suffering in isolation camps in Kenya, a brutal situation for this highly vulnerable, stigmatized group, one ignored by larger international assistance groups. George also worked on a review of the treatments and vaccines for people who tested positive during the Covid-19 pandemic. Given that George plays the violin in chamber music sessions with a variety of musician friends, I suspect that his vitality is enhanced by his immersion in great music.

The Activism of Laura Huxley

Laura Archera Huxley, the second wife of Aldous Huxley, was a child prodigy who performed at Carnegie Hall for the first time while still in her teens and soon played the violin for the Los Angeles Philharmonic Orchestra. Later, she produced documentary films, was an assistant film editor at RKO, and began to study health, nutrition, and psychology. I first heard of Laura when she administered LSD to her dying husband, whose death in 1963 occurred on the same day as that of the essayist C. S. Lewis and President John F. Kennedy. She later wrote *This Timeless Moment*, a book describing life with her husband.[11] A previous book, *You Are Not the Target*, one of the best "self-help" books, contained exercises to help people cope with the stresses of a complicated world.[12]

Her nephew Pierre Ferrucci had studied under Roberto Assagioli, who had used the term "psychosynthesis" to describe his approach to psychotherapy. The term had already been used by Carl Gustav Jung and others, but Assagioli had created a broad-based intervention that included attention to clients' spiritual development, their subpersonalities, and their capacity for transformation. When Ferrucci heard of my visit to Florence to meet Assagioli, he invited me to have lunch at a vegetarian restaurant in Manhattan on November 11, 1970. He brought his aunt along for what turned out to be a stimulating conversation. I met Laura twice a year later, once at a dinner party hosted by my friends Henry and Sarane Drake in Los Angeles, and again when I attended a symposium on orthomolecular therapy, where she joined Linus Pauling and others to discuss the use of vitamin supplements and nutrition for therapeutic purposes (a practice that never quite lived up to its expectations). Pauling's work in biochemistry won him a Nobel Prize, and in 1982 he won a second Nobel Prize for his work on nuclear disarmament. Laura won several awards for her activism, notably the Peace Prize from the World Health Foundation for Development and Peace in 1990.

In 1991, we both spoke at a conference sponsored by the Message Company in Santa Fe, New Mexico. My talk focused on ayahuasca, the mind-altering brew that had recently gained considerable attention. When we dined together, she told me about her latest activism project, the founding of Children: Our Ultimate Investment, a non-profit organization. Laura told me that she used the term "ultimate investment" to differentiate positive investments from those characterizing alcohol, gun, and tobacco. In 1987, Laura wrote *The Child of Your Dreams*, in which she advised how one might approach conception and pregnancy from a spiritual perspective.[13]

---

[11] Huxley, L. (1991). *This timeless moment: A personal view of Aldous Huxley*. Mercury House.
[12] Huxley, L. (1963). *You are not the target*. Metamorphous Books.
[13] Huxley, L. (1987). *The child of your dreams: Approaching conception and pregnancy with inner peace and reverence for life*. Destiny Books.

The Huxleys' home, near the famed Hollywood sign, was destroyed by fire in 1961. Decades later, I visited Laura in her rebuilt home, a memorable occasion because my visit overlapped with that of a mutual friend, the artist Carolyn Mary Kleefield, whose work I had first seen at the Henry Miller Memorial Library in Big Sur, California. Laura invited me to her 80th birthday party held in a park with Baba Ram Dass and Al Huang, the noted martial artist, performing. Ram Dass was recovering from a stroke, so, when he was blocked for words, Al would finish the statement in dance and movement. When Ram Dass spotted me, he remarked that when he first met me, I was "completely into my head," but that, over the years, I had connected with my heart—a great compliment. I had brought my former nephew, John Graham, and his second wife to the event, and they expressed their delight in meeting people whom they found fascinating.

Laura was an activist for psychedelic research; she agreed with her husband that LSD and similar substances should be used only for research and for therapy and thought that Timothy Leary was wrong in advocating their indiscriminate use. But feeling that her most important advocacy was for children, she never tired of her work on their behalf. Laura was also an activist on behalf of women's role as visionaries. In 2021, I received the Laura Huxley Award for Services to the Visionary Community from the Women's Visionary Council, one of her many pioneering projects.

The Activism of Stephan Schwartz

In 1934, Manly Palmer Hall founded the Philosophical Research Institute Society in Los Angeles; in 1977, I was invited there for a lecture by its director, Henry Drake. Both Hall and Drake had authored books on humankind's "secret doctrines," and my talk focused on parapsychology because anomalous experiences had played a role in the formulation of several of those doctrines. My visit also gave me the opportunity to reconnect with Stephan Schwartz, who was then a senior fellow at the society. We had met briefly a decade earlier, in 1966, at the Edgar Cayce organization, the Association for Research and Enlightenment (ARE).

Stephan already had a long record of activism, going back to the 1950s and his participation in the civil rights movement, and later as the special assistant for research and analysis to the chief of naval operations, where he was part of the team that transformed the American military from the elitist conscription of the armed forces that was in effect during the Vietnam War era to an all-volunteer military meritocracy that was gender- and race-neutral. This work had earned him the Department of the Navy's Certificate of Commendation for Outstanding Performance.

Also in the early 1970s, Stephan had been appointed a member of a committee on innovation, technology, and the future sponsored by the U.S. Department of Defense and the Massachusetts Institute of Technology. In the 1980s, Stephan was one of the pioneers in the "Citizens' Diplomacy Movement" that entailed many visits to the Soviet Union. This early work impelled his studies on how individuals and small groups can create social transformation through activism.

Stephan pioneered several research initiatives in parapsychology. His Project Deep Quest, using a research submarine, had purportedly eliminated electromagnetic transmission as an explanation for parapsychological phenomena. He was also part of the small group that created what today we call "remote viewing," and he developed a consensus protocol for the practical application of the acquisition of information obtained in that manner. He used remote viewing to locate and describe in detail previously unknown sites that were later excavated. He conducted this research internationally, including the alleged location of sunken shipwrecks, Cleopatra's and Mark Antony's palaces in Alexandria, Egypt, remnants of the Lighthouse of Pharos, and the remains of Christopher Columbus's caravel from his fourth voyage. For this and similar work, he received the Parapsychological Association's Outstanding Contribution Award, and the German magazine OOOM named him one of the "100 Most Inspiring People in the World."

Stephan has been the columnist for the journal *Explore* since it began, and the editor of the *Schwartzreport,* a daily web publication. In both, he focuses on trends shaping the future, with an emphasis on creating social well-being and on the role consciousness plays in these attempts. He has written over 200 papers and book chapters, as well as both fiction and non-fiction books in several different disciplines, many of which won awards in their fields.

In 2019, *Explore* published my co-authored article on a remote viewing experiment I supervised, testing Stephan's ideas about numinosity and chaotic processes.[14] Without knowing participants'

---

[14] Krippner, S., Saunders, D. T., Morgan, A., & Quan, A. (2019). Remote viewing of concealed target pictures under light and dark conditions. *Explore, 15,* 27–37.

descriptions, Stephan evaluated all potential target pictures as to their "numinosity" (enchanting, wondrous) qualities, finding that the more "numinous" pictures were more correctly viewed by the participants. Over the course of several decades, Stephan and I have attended conferences together, giving me the opportunity to observe his activist experiences first-hand, especially those that foster well-being.

The Activism of Gloria Swanson

Lucille Kahn was a successful actor, who, following her marriage to David Kahn, a friend of the American seer Edgar Cayce, took an active role in fostering the work of Cayce's Association for Research and Enlightenment (ARE). In the 1970s, the Kahns hosted in their home small gatherings of people eager to have LSD sessions and to discuss such topics as parapsychology. Lucille was a regular attendee at the American Society for Psychical Research lectures, often bringing her friend Gloria Swanson with her. One night, I arrived to give a lecture and was surprised to see Gloria Swanson in the audience. Lucille introduced us, and I had the opportunity to visit later with the screen legend when she attended several other lectures.

In 1938, Swanson initiated Multiprises, a firm that ostensibly sought to find and support innovations in science and technology, although its unstated goal was to rescue some Jewish intellectuals from the Holocaust. She started her own production company, was a fashion icon, and wrote a best-selling autobiography, *Swanson on Swanson,* in which she described her romance with Joseph Kennedy, Sr., among others; one reviewer said the book had been written "without a trace of arrogance."[15] She was a pioneer vegetarian; her sixth husband, William Dufty, also a vegetarian, was the author of *Sugar Blues,*[16] which used the word *addiction* to describe America's overuse of sugar. She won a Golden Globes Best Actress Award for *Sunset Blvd.,* the film that had originally brought her to my attention.

In 1971, Swanson costarred in a Broadway production of *Butterflies Are Free*; following one of our encounters, I told her that I would be bringing my parents to see her show and asked if I could take them backstage to meet her. We enjoyed the show, in which Swanson played the role of a well-meaning but overly protective mother of a blind guy, and I took my father and mother backstage. She could not have been more gracious, and it gave my parents something to talk about with

---

[15] Swanson, G. (1980). *Swanson on Swanson*. Random House.
[16] Dufty, W. (1975). *Sugar blues*. Chilton.

their friends; I remember my mother telling one of them, "Gloria Swanson was not stuck up at all; she was just the same as you and me." Upon hearing this remark, I thought that it attested to Swanson's ability to "play to her audience," even off-stage and even to an audience of three.

The Activism of Albert Ellis

Albert Ellis was an American psychologist and psychotherapist who founded Rational Emotive Behavior Therapy (REBT). His contributions to the so-called *cognitive revolution* date back to the 1950s and included helping to develop and pioneer other cognitive–behavioral therapies.

On August 28, 1958, I attended the annual convention of the American Psychological Association (APA), held that year in Washington, DC. I had the opportunity to hear addresses by some of the psychologists whose work I had studied and overcame my shyness enough to chat with some of them. Their number included Wendell Johnson, whose writings on general semantics I had studied at the University of Wisconsin; Herbert Klausmeier and Horace Page, with whom I had studied at the University of Wisconsin; Robert Watson, with whom I had studied at Northwestern University; and my long-standing friends and mentors, Paul Witty and Gardner Murphy. I also visited with sociologist and social critic David Riesman; Wardell Pomeroy, the co-author of the "Kinsey Reports"; E. G. Boring, one of the first historians of psychology; Edward Tolman, who founded what is called "purposive behaviorism"; David Weschler, author of the intelligence tests I had learned how to administer; and Albert "Al" Ellis, whose groundbreaking book *Sex without Guilt*,[17] had just been published. This book had been a welcome tonic to me, as its postulates were both sensible and liberating. I wrote him asking for reprints; I received a few dozen of them, covering several of his contributions to theory and practice, with an emphasis on "Rational Therapy," which eventually became "Rational Emotive Behavior Therapy," an approach that made considerable sense to me.

I also had a chance encounter with the incoming APA president, Harry Harlow, who was standing outside the convention hall rehearsing his presidential address, "The Nature of Love." His talk summarized his maternal deprivation experiments with macaque monkeys, "cloth mothers," and "wire mothers." I congratulated Dr. Harlow on his election, noting that I had attended the University of

---

[17] Ellis, A. (1958). *Sex without guilt*. Lyle Stuart.

Wisconsin. I did not remind him that in 1963 he had objected to my attempts to bring J.B. Rhine to the campus. And I did not tell him that I had met one of his laboratory assistants who told me that she felt very sorry to see the monkeys suffering from maternal deprivation, so she hugged and cuddled them when nobody was looking. Years later, Harlow's experiments were criticized on ethical grounds and were a main impetus for the "animal rights" movement.

On June 7, 1970, the Reverend William "Bill" Glenesk of Spencer Church in Brooklyn gave a sermon on "The Sex Machine." I had suggested that he invite Al, who accepted the role of discussant, along with Jack Nichols, editor of the *Gay* newspaper. The lively discussion ranged from the work of sex therapists Masters and Johnson to *Playboy* magazine's nude photographs and Kenneth Tynan's Broadway play *Oh Calcutta*, which Bill had admired.

In 1967, David Smith, a local physician, inaugurated the Haight-Ashbury Free Clinic of San Francisco, funded by a series of rock musical concerts given by the Grateful Dead and several other groups. I befriended David and helped to publicize his efforts, which provided medical services for those in need. Bill Glenesk inaugurated a smaller scale version at Spencer Church, directed by Irving Oyle, a dynamic osteopathic physician who had already opened a free clinic in Mendocino, California, bringing in the inter-tribal medicine man Rolling Thunder to assist with some of the more intransigent cases, such as those allegedly due to negative thinking and poor health habits. I had personal knowledge regarding one case in which Rolling Thunder performed an "exorcism" accompanied by yells, screams, and strange odors that finally abated when the "negative spirit" was dispatched.

Years later, in 1980, the APA convention was highlighted by my inclusion on a panel discussing "holistic healing," which also included my friends Bernard Grad, the physiologist who had conducted healing research with mice and plants, demonstrating that their recovery could not be attributed to placebo effects, and Robert Becker, an orthopedic surgeon, who spoke on his study of the body's bioelectric fields and how they could facilitate tissue regeneration. I attended sessions in which Lloyd DeMause spoke on psychohistory and in which Karl Pribram discussed mind/brain interaction. I attended Otto Klineberg's talk on how psychology could impact public policy, after which he invited me to chat with him and his wife, Selma. His work on racial differences debunked the notion of "superiority" and was cited by the U.S. Supreme Court in its decision declaring school segregation unconstitutional. As usual, I attended all of Albert Ellis's presentations, especially the one focusing on the use of humor in psychotherapy.

My first contact with Al had stimulated a surprising string of letters from him, accompanied by reprints as well as tape recordings of some of his therapy sessions, the first of which arrived in October 1959, shortly after I had seen him again at another APA conference that featured Carl Rogers and Rollo May—two other psychologists who received priority when I made out my convention schedule. Some people were put off by Al's colorful language, but it made sense to me that some of his clients needed to be "shocked" out of their habitual—and irrational—beliefs and behaviors. Al would never use the expletive "fuck off" because of his admiration of sexual activity, whether it was heterosexual, bisexual, or homosexual in nature. Al jokingly suggested "*un-*fuck you" as a better term. He also, in typical witty fashion, advocated "masturbation" instead of "musturbation," the word he created that describes the irrational belief that something "must" be done or "must" be avoided.

In 2001, Stephan Kahn and Erika Fromm's co-edited book *Changes in the Therapist* was published.[18] I had contributed a chapter that focused on my use of hypnosis in counseling as well as my utilization of self-hypnosis. Much to my surprise, my chapter of the anthology appeared in a section for which Al had written the other chapter. Al had used hypnosis in his psychotherapy practice even before he developed REBT, and it involved an active, directive reinforcement of positive suggestions. Once he developed REBT, he still used hypnosis when it seemed appropriate, followed by the use of a more permissive approach. He also wrote about using self-hypnosis to help avoid the "musts" and "shoulds" in his own life. Both of us had been influenced by the writings of Epictetus, Marcus Aurelius, and Alfred Korzybski (among others), who asserted that it is not what happens to people that creates their emotions but what they tell themselves about those experiences.

From time to time, I attended Al's famous "Friday Night Sessions" in which he would provide "instant therapy" to volunteers, often leavening his demonstrations and advice with wit and humor. These sessions were held in the Manhattan Beaux Arts six-story townhouse

---

[18] Krippner, S. (2001). Myths in collision. In S. Kahn & E. Fromm (Eds.), *Changes in the therapist* (pp. 151–164). Lawrence Erlbaum.

building named "The Albert Ellis Institute," in which he had a private residence on the top floor. When I was living in New York, I was invited to make a presentation at the institute and to have dinner with Al following my talk. In 2002, I was resting in my Chicago hotel room, preparing to receive an award from APA for "distinguished contributions to the advancement of international psychology," when there was a knock on the door. Surprised to see Al, I asked him what had brought him to me room so early in the day; he replied, "A pretty girl talked me into it." Indeed, Tamara Gurbis, my roommate, pulled out her camera and started filming an interview with him, one in which he cited several topics on which the two of us agreed. He did not list parapsychology, a topic about which he was an extreme skeptic, but I was used to having disagreements with my friends on that controversy, as well as others.

When he celebrated his 90th birthday in 2003, Al received congratulatory notes from (among others), President George W. Bush, Bill and Hillary Clinton, New York Mayor Michael Bloomberg, and His Holiness the Dalai Lama. Two years later, the directors of the Albert Ellis Institute terminated all connections with Al, falsely accusing him of "gross mismanagement." Al did his best to obtain justice with the help of a lawyer who entered three lawsuits. Shortly before his death in 2007, he won the lawsuit addressing his being removed from the board of directors, with the judge stating that what was done to him was disingenuous. Unfortunately, he died before the other lawsuits on elder abuse and wrongful dismissal were completed.

Al did not use email, so I sent him several letters via postal mail expressing my support for his legal initiatives. Much to my delight, I received a typed letter from him expressing his gratitude and closing with the line, "We will be friends forever."

In 1982, the *American Psychologist* journal published a survey of U.S. and Canadian psychologists that named Al one of the three most influential psychotherapists of history, along with Carl Rogers and Sigmund Freud. Al and Carl had both received their doctorates from Columbia University, and much has been made of their differences. However, both emphasized unconditional self-acceptance as a significant and important step in successful psychotherapy, and I found them both to be exceptionally kind, genuine, and compassionate. Al's wife, Debbie Joffe Ellis, teaches courses on REBT and Comparative Psychotherapies at Columbia University, in the very same building in which Al studied, and continues to present on REBT throughout the USA and around the globe. She and I have made several presentations on REBT at various conferences and workshops. My friendship with Debbie was one of Al's most treasured gifts to me.

Debbie and I agreed that countless millions of lives have been enhanced, healed, and in some cases saved, due to the effectiveness of REBT, an approach that is no-nonsense, cognitive, and behavioral, and imbued thoroughly with compassion, providing insights regarding the understanding of emotions. When David Feinstein and I revised our workbook on "personal mythology,[19]" we gave credit to Al and REBT for their contributions. Al had been familiar with our approach and once told me that what David and I called "dysfunctional personal myths" was the same as what REBT refers to as "irrational beliefs." I considered this quite a compliment!

August 28, 1958, was a day when my life changed. I had read some of Al's work before I heard him speak at APA, but his presentation galvanized what I had read and added new material that I sensed would help people avoid being handicapped by irrational feelings that they were guilty and unworthy. When Al sent me reprints and tapes, I was pleasantly surprised, and it gave me the confidence to interact with other psychologists I had long admired, Rollo May and Carl Rogers among them.

---

[19] Feinstein, D., & Krippner, S. (2008). *Personal mythology: Using ritual, dreams, and imagination to discover your inner story* (3rd ed.). Energy Psychology Press/Elite Books.

Chapter 12

Bringing Order Out of Chaos
28 June 1959. A Day When My Life Changed

Chaos theory, which has its roots in mathematics, posits that systems are affected by their initial conditions, followed by tiny variations that can produce unpredictable, yet far-ranging, effects. It is the best-known example of *nonlinear dynamics*, a field of study that attempts to account for the behavior of complicated systems that appear random when linear cause-and-effect models are applied. The latter can be depicted with a straight line when portrayed graphically, but this is not possible when the effect is nonlinear. *Complexity theory* is a related example of nonlinear dynamics. It is also interdisciplinary but emphasizes relations between systems and the role played by "feedback loops" that further develop those relationships, applying the model to large-scale phenomena such as the world economy, global politics, and environmental crises.

Enter Ludwig von Bertalanffy

On June 28, 1959, when I was a graduate student at Northwestern University, I attended a lecture by Ludwig von Bertalanffy, having been introduced to him by one of my psychology professors, Donald Campbell, earlier in the week. Von Bertalanffy had proposed that general systems theory (GST) was a methodology, applicable to all the sciences, encompassing the cybernetic theory of feedback that represents a special class of self-regulating systems. But he discerned a fundamental difference between GST and cybernetics since the feedback mechanisms of the latter are controlled by constraints while dynamical systems display the free interplay of various forces. This perspective highlighted similarities (or *isomorphisms*) among cybernetic machines, living organisms, and social systems. In theory, at least, data from one scientific realm could be compared to those from another realm. Originally, von Bertalanffy had used the German term *Allgemeine Systemlehre,* which translates into "general theory of systems."

Although he was a biologist, von Bertalanffy geared his lecture to his audience of psychologists and graduate students. He noted that both psychoanalysis and behaviorism view human beings as chance products of nature and nurture, a mixture of genes and accidental events from infancy to maturity. To the contrary, asserted von Bertalanffy, humans and their world could better be seen as interacting organisms; therefore, he advocated an integration of the natural and social sciences to understand this system more fully. A *system,* he observed, is a pattern of two or more interacting components together with the relationships among them that permit the identification of a boundary-maintaining entity or process. All phenomena consist of interrelated systems, so the study of these relationships is needed to understand fully any given phenomenon. He emphasized the interdisciplinary nature of GST and how it searches for principles that apply to any number of those disciplines, so that data from one scientific realm could be compared to those of another one.

Von Bertalanffy's lecture was an event that changed my life. I began to consider the importance of GST in understanding post-traumatic stress disorder (PTSD), parapsychological experiences, and the interaction of human beings with the rest of nature. For example, I have charted the impact of geomagnetic fields (such as sunspot activity) on telepathy scores and other alleged parapsychological phenomena.

Chaos theory is a special adaptation of GST to systems that are "nonlinear." These systems cannot be understood by using a simple cause-and-effect "linear" model. In psychology, chaos theory is especially useful in describing and explaining complicated human activities such as family dynamics and creativity.

Chaos Theory and Self-Organization

The mathematician Edward Lorenz took a nonlinear approach when studying weather patterns. In 1975, David Yorke, another mathematician, coined the term *chaos theory* to describe the process, noting that ordinary statistical predictions were not useful when studying these phenomena. Decades later, some epidemiologists used chaos theory to study such disease outbreaks as Ebola and the Covid-19 pandemic, where the spread of disease did not seem to follow a linear pattern.

Kazimierz Dabrowski, the renowned Polish psychiatrist, observed how extreme behaviors, such as suicide, are often a by-product of the chaotic emotions and reactions that characterize a person's life.[1] The challenge for these individuals is to bring order out of this chaos. But the resulting order

---

[1] Tillier, W. (2018). *Personality development through positive disintegration: The work of Kazimierz Dabrowski.* Maurice Bassett.

needs to be life affirming because many people who engage in these actions are single-minded in their intention, motivation, and behavior. When I use the term *life affirming* as a description, I infer that support is given to choosing life rather than death, happiness rather than misery, and love rather than apathy. Bringing a meaningful life-affirming order into a chaotic life is a challenge because the chaos probably exists both inside and outside the awareness of an "at-risk" person.

But risky activities do not always follow simple rules; there is not always a linear progression from one level to the next. Moreover, there are likely to be unconscious conflicts of which the risk-taking person is only dimly aware; hence, these conflicts are often marked by ambivalence. When two belief systems regarding risk taking are in conflict, people may be torn between wanting to move on with their lives and being willing to remain "stuck." Psychotherapy can assist these people to become aware of this internal tug-of-war, reinforcing the life-affirming perspective and curtailing the life-denying perspective. In addition, self-regulation can help suicidal people bring at least a modicum of order into their awareness.

In early Greek mythology, Chaos was one of the original deities. Chaos her siblings, the most prominent of whom was Gaia (Earth) had no parents. In later Greek mythology, Chaos was not a deity at all but the "primal mud" from which everything emerged, thus bringing order out of chaos. Chaos theory also focuses on the unpredictable aspects of the cosmos and the seeming randomness of the creative process that actually mask an underlying order.

Self-organization can emerge from chaos. An example would be what happens when water is brought to a boil. As water is heated, the water at the bottom of a kettle rises to the top while cooler water at the top moves to the bottom. This causes turbulence, which takes the form of boiling water. What chaos theorists call a *bifurcation*, a shift that occurs at the point of transformation, is the moment at which the water starts to boil. This bifurcation point can occur when a connection is made and a shift occurs, as when someone's construction of "truth" or "reality" profoundly alters, creating a transition from one system to another.

This dynamic may be seen in an "at-risk" person living an emotional life filled with turbulence. Chris (not his real name) was a teenager whose inner life was turbulent, leading him to depend on his mother's affection for day-to-day support. When she died of an overdose of opiates, Chris's emotions reached a boiling point. When Chris, in a drunken state, claimed that he heard his deceased mother call to him, the water boiled over. This "call" was the bifurcation point that connected his inner turmoil with what he believed was reality and "the beyond." One evening Chris wrote a "goodbye" note and walked into the ocean; his body was never recovered. Suicide was his point of no return. When I began to study chaos theory, I was struck by how its postulates helped me to understand suicide, a topic that had interested me for decades because several friends and acquaintances, Chris among them, had taken their own lives.

Neurological networks are important examples of chaos at work, a way of looking at the world that avoids simple linear cause-and-effect reactions. These networks are complex and do not follow simple linear patterns, giving rise to a field of study called "complex network science." Many investigators study the various parts of a machine, or a person's body, or a culture. They believe that investigating parts of a whole is the best route to fathoming the whole. But chaos theorists maintain that a systems approach is needed, because the whole is more than the sum of its parts. Indeed, complexity theory goes a step further, holding that the whole is *different* from the sum of its parts. A system is complex when it is composed of subsystems for which the degree and nature of relationships are imperfectly known.

In psychology and psychotherapy, chaos theory often has been applied in the form of family therapy as focusing on each family member separately obscures the way in which the total family system functions. This has major implications for preventing destructive behavior because interviews with separate family members might not reveal family dynamics and how they affect a particular family member's irrational decisions. However, an adept family therapist watching the entire family interacting may perceive patterns that reveal unspoken rules and habits.

Revolutions and Their Impact

There have been at least three revolutions in Western culture that have impacted the way in which humans see their world and their place in it. The first revolution began in the early part of the 16th century, when Nicolaus Copernicus demonstrated that Earth is one of several planets that circle the sun. This assertion was not welcomed by the Catholic Church, which insisted that God had placed Earth and its inhabitants at the center of the universe. Copernicus's speculations were not published while he was alive, or he could have suffered the same fate as Galileo, who was sentenced to house arrest for the remainder of his life for postulating that the sun was the center of the solar system. Later, other astronomers produced results supporting the Copernican Revolution; eventually, Isaac Newton pulled everything together in his book on the laws of planetary motion, a book that was instrumental in forming the basis of the Western scientific method.

The second revolution had its roots in the 18th century, when careful observers began to publish their impressions that living creatures changed over time in ways that suggested they evolved. This idea was advanced by the 1859 publication of Charles Darwin's book *On the Origin of Species*. Many of Darwin's contemporaries, such as Robert Chamber and Alfred Russel Wallace, had similar ideas, but they were not as articulate as Darwin and their work did not have the same impact. Darwin's 1871 book *The Descent of Man* was even more radical, extending his theory to humans. Instead of being almost miraculously special, humans could be conceptualized as the product of "natural selection," the survival of those life forms that are best adapted to their natural environment. Unlike Copernican theory, Darwin's theory was not opposed by the Catholic Church, but many Protestant fundamentalists were hostile to the idea, and this opposition persists.

The publication in 1899 of Freud's book on dream interpretation launched the Freudian Revolution. Freud's publisher, however, put a 1900 date on it, because he felt that its importance would initiate the 20th century, even though it took eight years for the first 800 copies of the book to be sold. Freud cited the ways in which unconscious material influenced people's lives, even though they are rarely aware of this influence. Freud's atheism and Jewish ethnicity sparked opposition from many religious groups. Nonetheless, his 1909 visit to the United States was an enormous success; many Protestant members of the clergy began to take an interest in psychoanalysis, having been intrigued by Freud's ideas.

Some artists and playwrights began to incorporate psychoanalytic elements into their work, as can be observed in paintings by surrealists (such as Salvador Dali) and abstract expressionists (such as Jackson Pollock) as well as in such musicals as *Lady in the Dark* (which featured three dream sequences) and the plays of Eugene O'Neill (e.g., *Desire under the Elms*) and Thomas Mann (e.g., *Death in Venice*).

In a 1994 article, I suggested that chaos theory might be regarded as another revolution; one of my students, Sally Goerner, called it the "nonlinear revolution."[2] Chaos theory began as a mathematical paradigm, but soon was applied to many phenomena that do not follow a cause-and-effect formula. The original conditions of some things that begin as close often drift apart as time proceeds. Thus, it may be possible to predict what happens in the short term but not in the long term. On the other hand, those original conditions may respond to a stimulus that "ripples," as when a herd

---

[2] Krippner, S. (1994). Humanistic psychology and chaos theory: The third revolution and the third force. *Journal of Humanistic Psychology, 34*(3), 48–61.

of cattle is grazing peacefully until a bee stings one of its members. The herd's panicked reaction to this stimulus disrupts the "original condition," producing a stampede. Chaos theory also can be applied to several aspects of extreme behaviors; thus, an offhand comment by a teenager's acquaintance might initiate a series of negative reactions that eventually prove lethal to the teenager or the acquaintance. History will determine the full impact of chaos theory and whether it qualifies as a revolution.

In my 1994 article, I followed a customary distinction that lists humanistic psychology as the "third force" in psychology, following psychoanalysis (the first force) and behaviorism (the second force). I soon concluded that this appellation was in error. *Cognitive psychology* is a better choice for a "third force" because it became far more influential than humanistic psychology, both as a research endeavor in cognitive neuroscience and the cognitive unconscious, and as a psychotherapeutic application as in "cognitive psychotherapy" and "cognitive–behavioral psychotherapy." Hence, humanistic psychology is actually the "fourth force," if one wants to use those terms—a debatable move because the lines between psychological orientations are rarely clean-cut and are more often blurred.

The Butterfly Effect

Chaotic systems have some distinguishing features, such as being unpredictable from the perspective of linear cause and effect. However, they do have boundaries, so they can be identified, and studied. When that happens, investigators need to pay special attention to their initial conditions. Indeed, chaos theory emphasizes the way in which slight changes in the initial conditions of a chaotic system can trigger profound and unpredictable changes in the system. This "butterfly effect" metaphor proposes that a butterfly flapping its wings in one part of the world, such as Brazil, can initiate a chain reaction that cumulates in a tornado elsewhere in the world, as in Texas. An offhand compliment about a young person's informal artwork could initiate a chain of events that would send her to art school and, later, to eminence in the art world. The butterfly effect can also be observed when an artist decides to change one small part of the painting, and this leads to yet additional changes until the entire painting is altered.

Two 1998 movies, *Run Lola Run* and *Sliding Doors*, demonstrate the butterfly effect, as does a 2004 film aptly named *The Butterfly Effect*. In *Run Lola Run*, Franka Potente's character has 20 minutes to deliver a payment to her boyfriend or he will be killed. Three different endings depict how seemingly insignificant events assist or prevent her from achieving her goal. In *Sliding Doors*, the love life and career of Gwyneth Paltrow's character depend on whether or not she catches a train. She is unaware of the situation, while the film depicts two parallel stories and endings. Neither film mentions the butterfly effect, but several of the reviewers did.

J. B. Priestley's play *Dangerous Corner* illustrates the butterfly effect. A chance remark at a party evokes a cascade of revelations and recriminations that ends tragically. But then the scene is replayed. When it unfolds for the second time, the previously inoperative radio goes on and the music covers up the chance remark, which is never heard. Life goes on as before.

Practitioners of psychodrama often do something similar. After a practitioner recounts a troubling incident, a new ending is enacted by group members, an ending that may give the participant insights that can help resolve the stress. Practitioners of trauma therapy often ask their clients to rehearse their nightmare while awake, giving it a new ending. If they do this often enough with intensity and feeling, the nightmare begins to change, allowing for a better night's sleep.

At times, the butterfly effect manifests in ways that underscore and unpack the metaphor. Climate consists of a pattern of recurring climate changes over time. Weather is in constant flux due to the bifurcating that occurs. Positive and negative feedback loops are in ceaseless motion. Theoretically, somewhere in the system a "butterfly" loop might initiate minor changes. Eventually, one of these loops is amplified and a dramatic and unpredictable shift occurs. Chaos theory holds that even small shifts in initial conditions may influence large-scale phenomena, but not in a linear manner.

Chaos theory offers insight into human creativity; responding to chaos in a creative manner may well have been an adaptive trait that assisted humanity's survival. For instance, it ordinarily is more adaptive to "flow" with an unusual experience than to "fight" such an experience.

Psychologist Tobi Zausner has noted that chaotic processes are marked by both randomness and unpredictability.[3] There is a degree of randomness in every work of art, and there is no way of completely predicting its outcome. Without the random element, art can become rote and lifeless. However, if a work of art were only the result of randomness, it would be a product of disorder. Determination, purpose, and intent form the

---

[3] Zausner, T. (1996). The creative chaos: Speculations on the connection between non-linear dynamics and the creative process. In W. Sulis & A. Combs (Eds.), *Nonlinear dynamics and human behavior; Studies of nonlinear phenomena in the life sciences* (Vol. 5, pp. 343–349). World Scientific.

framework or attractors within which the random occurs. Randomness increases the irreversibility of a work of art.

"Copycat suicides" may be another example of the butterfly effect. The suicide of a person who is well known in a community or a nation sometimes triggers a "cluster" of suicides, typically in the same manner that characterized the original suicide. For example, Goethe's celebrated novel *The Sorrows of Young Werther*[4] was published in 1774. The novel's central character, Werther, shot himself after being rejected by the woman he loved. Young men throughout Germany began to dress like Werther, and some also shot themselves. This phenomenon led to the banning of the book in several German cities; moreover, in the 20th century, the term "the Werther Effect" was coined to describe what was also called "suicide contagion." Like the hypothetical flapping of a butterfly's wings triggering a distant tornado, a fictional death initiated a string of events that led to non-fictional tragedies.

Emulating, or copying, the publicized suicide of a local or national celebrity may serve as a trigger for highly susceptible and extremely emotional people to follow the example, sometimes in specific detail. The suicides of South Korean actress Choi Jin-Sil and American actor Marilyn Monroe were followed by hundreds of suicides, usually by young women wearing identical clothing to that worn during the original suicide. In the political arena, the self-immolation of a Tunisian street vendor named Mohamed Bouazizi in 2010 led to a rash of suicides that, in turn, swept a new government into office and triggered the so-called "Arab Spring" uprisings in the Middle East. Suicide proneness might be an individual's initial condition; under ordinary conditions, nothing dramatic would have occurred. But the suicide of a celebrity shifts or adds a new factor to those initial conditions, leaving other deaths in its wake.

In retrospect, most of the people committing these suicides were found to be suffering from mood disorders and substance abuse, with few or no protective buffers such as social support. What may have looked like a spontaneous act, if seen in a larger context, was the final level of Dabrowski's model, one in which drastic action is taken, albeit one in which that level might not have been reached without the final trigger.

---

[4] Goethe, J. W. v. (1774). The sorrows of young Werther.

Chaotic Attractors

An *attractor* pulls something toward it, as when the earth attracts objects to it by means of gravity. Many nighttime dreams have a "central image," one that represents the emotions of the dreamer and pulls additional material into it. A person who has experienced trauma will often have dreams in which an aspect of that trauma serves as an attractor. Leading dream scientist Ernest Hartmann had a client who had the following dream: "I was walking along a beach with a friend ... when suddenly a huge wave, maybe forty feet high, swept us away. I struggled and struggled in the water. I am not sure whether I made it out."

Hartmann disclosed that he had heard this dream, or something similar, from clients who had experienced trauma. Some had been raped; others had been attacked or had survived a disaster. One man had escaped a burning house in which his brother had died. He related, "I dreamed of a fire somewhere, in a house quite different from ours. In the dream my brother and everyone else escaped, but I was still in the house getting burned when I woke up." Hartmann suggested that the dreamer was coping with "survivor's guilt," trying to create a scenario where his brother survived but he did not.

A young boy was on a trip with his parents when he was accidentally locked alone in a room for a day and a half. He soon began to have dreams in which he was "locked in, enclosed and trapped in some way.... I also dreamed about being caught in a fire and of drowning in a tidal wave.... Sometimes scenes from my childhood entered into my dreams. My dreams were playing with the theme of being trapped in a room and bringing in all kinds of related stuff from my life, from stories I'd read, and from my imaginings." In these dreams, the trauma appears to take different forms, pulling in related material to supplement the central image; eventually, these dreams simply stopped. This is an example of emotional downloading and processing in dreams, one of their major functions. On the other hand, dreams that continually repeat the traumatic experience indicate that the dreamer has not sufficiently processed it.

Freud used the word *overdetermined* to describe an event or habit that had multiple causes, increasing the likelihood that it would occur. A therapist can keep this framework in mind, asking clients to narrate their traumatic experiences in many ways, connecting the trauma to various parts of their lives. In both the dreams and the therapist's office, the dreamer is making connections in a safe place, attempting to understand how a trauma may have been overdetermined not only by its connection with the obvious traumatizing event, such as combat horror, but with an earlier sexual assault, a severe bullying episode, or witnessing the hospitalization and death of a loved one. "Complex Post-Traumatic Stress Disorder," which acknowledges this overdetermination, is related to *complexity theory*, first "cousin" of chaos theory. Another "cousin" is *catastrophe theory*, in which major changes occur extremely rapidly in a nonlinear manner, as when a bridge collapses following a series of weights that are gradually increasing, or when a new species emerges following a rapid rearrangement of chromosomes.

Ernest Hartmann proposed that in dreams the brain's neural networks enable unfamiliar associations to occur in a broader and looser way than they would in waking life. When awake, one's thinking needs to be focused, but in dreaming, these broad, loose connections provide what is needed. Dreams serve many adaptive functions such as problem solving and emotional downloading, illustrating Darwin's thesis that adaptation is necessary for survival. However, a central image may sometimes be maladaptive, as in the cases of those who are prone to take violent action against themselves or others.

I have proposed that a "personal myth" may serve as a chaotic attractor. Once this idea becomes fixed, it begins to attract support from both internal and external sources, a process referred to as "antifragility." People who harbor the personal myth that "everyone is working against me" can find any number of experiences to support that impression. Someone may shove ahead of them in a line for tickets. A friend might make a sarcastic remark that is taken seriously. These incidents may seem trivial to an outsider, but to a vulnerable person they might result in a fatally aggressive act.

Living on the Edge of Chaos

Sometimes a system teeters on the edge of chaos; if it does not adapt to new challenges, it may fall off that edge. However, if it does adapt to demands in a novel way, it can emerge stronger and more resilient than ever. Newton's laws of motion described a universe that could be observed and measured, but it omitted the chaotic nonlinear world that is more difficult to comprehend.

Personal myths shape perceptions and behavior. If people have simplistic mythologies, such as believing that "everything happens for a reason," or "you get what you deserve," their behavior is likely to be mechanical. If people have nonlinear, chaotic mythologies, their behavior is likely to be evolutionary, adaptive, and organic, incorporating ambiguity and unpredictability. Before the birth of chaos theory, the great Danish philosopher Søren Kierkegaard wrote that people live in a nonlinear world, observing that life can only be understood backwards but it must be lived forwards. Chaos theorists contend that humans exist at the edge of chaos, hovering between structure and surprise. To fall too far into structure makes life routine and safe, but rigid. To yield wholly to surprise makes life interesting, but fragile. Either extreme may contribute to destructive behavior. In the former instance, a veteran may conclude," I killed innocent people and so now I must die." In the latter instance, news about the mass killing of schoolchildren might provoke an extreme reaction triggering self-harm in one who survived the horrors of combat, even though the traumatic war experience may have occurred years earlier.

From my perspective, many "at risk" people live at the edge of chaos. When the pain becomes too intense and the loss of hope too severe, they may find themselves pushed over the edge, engaging in behavior that is destructive to themselves or others. Successful therapy that recognizes this ambivalence attempts to save lives by supporting a precarious balance and strengthening it. Indeed, "balance" is a part of the cultural and personal mythologies of many Indigenous peoples, who avoid extreme behavior by withholding such actions unless they are needed for life-affirming purposes.

Archetypes as Chaotic Attractors

Jungian psychoanalyst Katherine Best[5] has described the archetypal ground of suicide, proposing that suicidal thoughts, images, and feelings may become dominant as time progresses. A person might become obsessed with the Christian martyr archetype, with the preoccupation manifesting in "stigmata," bodily wounds occurring in locations associated with the crucifixion of Jesus. But those thoughts might instead gravitate to the saints who killed themselves to avoid sexual assault by Roman soldiers or forced renunciation of their faith. The notion of suicide might seem to arise spontaneously, although it reflects a process that may have been building for a long time.

When suicide acts as a chaotic attractor, it pulls self-harm behaviors into its orbit. What begins as minor acts of self-harm can circle around the attractor site in similar acts. Their similar nature suggests the self-similarity of *fractals*, which are never-ending patterns that repeat themselves. Snowflakes have fractal patterns. Ferns and similar plants

---

[5] Best, K. (2013). *The archetype of suicide.* Runaway Press.

exhibit fractals. Fractals can be found in coastlines, in the heads of broccoli and similar plants, in video games, in blood vessels, and in neural networks. Fractals exist at the edge of chaos. When a critical *perturbation*, or shift, occurs, there may be a bifurcation to a point of no return. There may be a collapse into lethality, or there may be a life-affirming transformation. In the latter, a "spiritual emergency" becomes a "spiritual emergence." The former bifurcation results in a loss of balance and a deadly fall, while in the latter bifurcation, there is a positive rather than a negative shift.

The Golden Gate Bridge suicides and suicide attempts provide another point of departure. Between 1937 and 1971, 515 suicide attempters were pulled back from a protective net under the railing, few of whom made another attempt. For some, the protective net and the ensuing rescuers indicated that someone cared, that someone did not want them to end their lives. Bonds were formed, epiphanies were reported, and connections were made with a larger system. For others, coming close to death seemed to awaken them to life's wonders. When love, insight, and awe enter the chaotic process, they may well become game changers.

Dreaming and the Self-Organizing Brain

My major contribution to this field was a series of articles I co-authored with psychologists David Kahn and Leslie Combs on the topic of dreaming as a function of chaos-like processes in the brain.[6,7] We proposed that the brain is a self-organizing system made up of several self-organizing subsystems. These neural networks are constantly changing, not only due to their own development but also due to everyday learning and other environmental interactions. Not only are these networks self-organizing, but they are also self-creating, producing something new (a process called *auto-poesis*). In this respect, the brain is like the weather, and like the weather changes can result from exceedingly small disturbances or perturbations (as in the butterfly effect). Some systems, such as rocks, are "closed," allowing for minimal outside influence. Others, such as the brain, are "open," and this is the basis for their constant development.

When EEG rhythms are studied, they can be divided into alpha, beta, delta, gamma, and theta, as determined by cycles per second. On closer

---

[6] Kahn, D., Krippner, S., & Combs, A. (2002). Dreaming as a function of chaos-like stochastic processes in the self-organizing brain. *Nonlinear Dynamics, Psychology, and Life Sciences, 6,* 311–322.

[7] Kahn, D. L. (2020, Winter). Trauma dreams of transgender youth. *Dreamtime,* 12–13.

examination, however, the actual waveform changes from cycle to cycle, and it is impossible to predict the future of a particular brain wave. While people are awake, their brain activity is largely constrained by sensory input. In sleep, however, these attractors are basically internal rather than external, even though brain activity is comparable to that in wakefulness. In addition, the information being processed during sleep emphasizes emotions and memories, as can be discerned by examining dream content. During rapid eye movement (REM) sleep, brain neurons containing serotonin cease firing while those containing acetylcholine become more active, decreasing heart rate and breathing.

Not only do the brain chemicals differ from those manifesting during wakefulness; the sleeping brain also engages in a different type of self-organization, resulting in diminished memory, logical thinking, and self-reflection. The activation of the pons, which serves to connect the brain stem to the rest of the body, plays a key role in initiating dreaming. It triggers a chain of events that arouse the dreamer's visual cortex, where meaning is assigned to internal stimuli that are otherwise meaningless. Because the brain is virtually isolated from external stimulation, some parts of the brain communicate more readily with some areas and less so with other areas. Subtle influences that would be ignored during wakefulness take on a significant role, often creating a butterfly effect, in which an initial image triggers activity that unleashes a dramatic dream narrative.

Dream narratives rarely follow logical development; rather, they make up their own rules, changing the scenario as new input is created that the brain cortex attempts to weave into the story. Sometimes the story makes a shift, one that is nonlinear rather than linear. Dreams that occur in non-REM sleep tend to be more logical, with fewer interruptions in the narrative because they are less affected by the new input. In REM dreams, new material can be triggered by shifts in the activity of the pons and associated areas, eventually reaching the visual as well as the motor and the auditory cortex, albeit to a lesser extent. A bifurcation often results, as the narrative divides into two branches, or "plot twists." These shifts and other transitions are made easily due to diminished short-term memory, the loss of a continuous "sense of self," and a proclivity to form bizarre associations, also due to the reduced activity of the prefrontal cortex that engages in logical, linear thinking during wakefulness. It is not so much that rules are abandoned during REM sleep; they are simply changed. The dreamer's waking experiences are stretched, turned about, and parceled out in fragments, indicating that nonlinear dynamics are at work.

David, Leslie, and I proposed that in dreaming the brain's ordinary reasoning and logic go offline, with these functions now carried out by what has been called a *default mode network*, in which the brain can talk to itself. The healthy brain is always active, even during sleep. When brain activity initiates a dream, it is likely that the first image is a chaotic attractor that brings in other images to create a narrative that is meaningful but not foreordained. When the dreamer shifts bodily position, brain activity also shifts, and the dream reflects these changes, often by marking a radically different point of departure.

In 2020, British psychologist Sue Llewellyn's book *What Do Dreams Do?*[8] was published. Llewellyn maintained that during dreaming the brain's visual cortex defends its domain from encroachment from other brain areas. In developing her thesis, Llewellyn cited our chaotic theory of dreaming, noting its use in detecting underlying patterns in seemingly unrelated dream reports. Llewellyn stated that the human brain is poised "at the edge of chaos," which is an optimal condition for processing information to meet unexpected dilemmas. Too much order blocks anything new; too much disorder disrupts the self-organization process. What Llewellyn calls "self-organized criticality" is the optimal zone for creativity, producing novel solutions to artistic and scientific challenges as well as to everyday issues.

Phase transitions, an essential element in chaos theory, occur when a system shifts from one position to another. Creative people make many phase transitions, resulting in more "aha!" moments. Those incidents are preceded by a chaotic exploration of past memories in a search for unusual solutions to a problem. After the insight, another chaotic process integrates the new associations and puts the novel idea to use.

In a chaotic system, brain states arise out of many local interactions; slight changes in neurotransmitter activity can have far-reaching impacts due to the butterfly effect. When someone is awake, the neural "gates" are open to input from the external world, but the sleeping brain closes those gates and opens others to the internal world of memories, emotions, and intuitions, all of which can be detected in dreams. However, too much disorder can lead to mental illness, marked by a loss of boundaries between waking and sleeping as well as by severely diminished criticality. The brain is trapped in chaotic disorder; it swings among several attractors, and the result often leads to multiple diagnoses by mental health practitioners as the disorders seem to transmute from one to another.

Llewellyn concluded that "dreaming is a private world." Most dreamers are not concerned with the loss of control and the diminished "sense of self"

---

[8] Llewelyn, S. (2020). *What do dreams do?* Oxford University Press.

that often characterize dreams. When mentally ill people feel that they are not in control during wakefulness, they may blame other people, governmental agencies, or alien invaders for controlling their behavior. This misattribution typically results from the lack of "top-down" control that characterizes many dreams but can be terrifying during wakefulness. Psychotherapists, therefore, attempt to reinforce patients' "sense of self" and bolster their ability to master everyday tasks.

Llewellyn suggested that for early humans dreams were "survival kits" that helped them find food, detect threats from wild animals and enemy tribes, and formulate creative solutions to life challenges. Those men and women who put their dreams to practical use survived, passing on their genes to future generations. Her book is one of the best introductions to dream science; Kahn, Combs, and I were gratified that our chaotic theory of dreaming was an integral part of it.

Precursors of Chaos Theory

If one reads the philosophical literature carefully, one can find precursors of chaos theory in various ancient speculations. Perhaps this is most evident in the work of Epicurus, the Roman philosopher who counseled that the fear of divine punishment is the main cause of human anxiety. Epicurean philosophy imploded the concept of divine punishment, stating that there were no gods; moreover, if there were, they would not take an interest in human concerns. Two centuries later, an Epicurean, the Roman philosopher Lucretius, authored his epic poem, *De Rerum Natura* (*On the Nature of Things*),[9] in which he integrated this dictum into a theory that bypassed divine judgment and emphasized human relationships. Some readers of Lucretius's poem see it as a forerunner of humanism and Darwinian evolution as well as chaos theory, especially in his concept of "swerve," an abrupt change of direction that results from human decision making, not the intervention of deities. Lucretius also described how slight changes in atoms can evoke larger changes, as they do in the butterfly effect.

De Rerum Natura was lost for centuries, and its rediscovery may also exemplify the butterfly effect. In 1417, a clerk named Poggio Broccolini was rummaging among manuscripts in a German monastery when he discovered what proved to be the last remaining full copy of *The Nature of Things*. Fascinated by the multivolume poem, Broccolini translated it, after

---

[9] Lucretius Carus, T., & Mantinband, J. H. (1965). *On the nature of the universe (De rerum natura): A new verse translation.* Ungar.

which its focus on human, as opposed to divine, values became a major cornerstone of Renaissance philosophy.

The *I Ching*, the Chinese "Book of Changes," can be seen as a nonlinear work based on the assumption of constant change. To obtain a six-line hexagram that will yield useful advice, one tosses coins (or sticks) six times. This ritual resembles chaos theory in that it is process oriented, not goal-oriented, and nonlinear rather than linear. The composer John Cage once described music as "a purposeless play"; later, when he read the *I Ching*, he recognized its ability to identify order in chance events by proposing a question and using the resulting hexagram as the basis for a new composition. This is illustrated in Cage's "Music of Changes" for piano, and in virtually all his electronic music.

William Bevan[10] mentioned nonlinear dynamics in his presidential address to the American Psychological Association (APA) in 1982, which was the first time the term was used in the *American Psychologist*, APA's flagship journal. In 1994, a feature article on chaos theory was published; then in 2018 a symposium on the topic was held at APA's annual convention. I was part of this symposium, organized by my colleague Ruth Richards, who drew upon chaos theory in her books, such as *Everyday Creativity and The Healthy Mind*,[11] published in 2018.

Founding the Society

The Society for Chaos Theory in Psychology and the Life Sciences had its inaugural meeting at Saybrook University in August 1991. Leslie Combs and I were instrumental in the selection of Saybrook as the host of this historic event, but credit must also go to our colleagues Bela Banathy and Arne Collen. From Banathy, I learned about *systems inquiry*, an epistemology or "way of knowing" that is grounded in a systems view of the world, one that formulates theoretical postulates, conceptual paradigms, and such tools as "systems design" with its concern for the "goodness of fit" and its impact on future generations. From Collen, I discovered the differences among *mono-disciplinarity* (the typical, albeit fragmented approach to knowledge), *multi-disciplinarity* (the combination of several

---

[10] Bevan, W. (1991). Contemporary psychology: A tour inside the onion. *American Psychologist, 46*, 475–483.
[11] Richards, R. (2018). *Everyday creativity and the healthy mind: Dynamic new paths for self and society.* Palgrave Macmillan.

disciplines by one manager), *inter-disciplinarity* (the interaction among several disciplines by various specialists), and *trans-disciplinarity* (the attempt at a synthesis but with "meaning and harmony" rather than "finding the ultimate truth" as a viable strategy). I suspect that someday chaos theory, complexity theory, and catastrophe theory will lead to a transdisciplinary field of study that our 1991 conference helped to inaugurate.

I have made several presentations at subsequent meetings of the society, including one at its twentieth anniversary meeting in Milwaukee, Wisconsin. Our chaos theory of dreaming was published in several journals, including the Society's *Nonlinear Dynamics, Psychology, and Life Sciences*.

I suspect that Dabrowski was correct when he wrote that suicide is complicated. No two suicides are the same, but almost all contain rational and irrational as well as conscious and unconscious elements. Anyone eager to assist suicide-prone people needs to take a systems approach, one that recognizes the milieu in which those people live and in which they might die. It may be challenging to exist at the edge of chaos, but adapting to that circumstance improves the odds of survival. Living at the edge of chaos presents risks for those who are suicidal, but social connections may make the difference between death and survival.

For me, chaos theory provides a useful framework for studying the variability of traits manifested by humans. Bifurcations, fractals, self-organization, emergence, auto-poesis, and transformation provide for human agency, a human's ability to attribute meaning and to make choices regarding possible outcomes. My chance encounter with Ludwig von Bertalanffy in 1959 introduced me to general systems theory, and later I discovered chaos theory. Both provided me with a perspective that has impacted my entire professional career.

Chapter 13

Fran Dillon Comes to The Rescue
12 August 1961. A Day When My Life Changed

Based in Chicago, Science Research Associates (SRA) was a publisher of educational materials and classroom-based reading comprehension products. Founded in 1938 with an occupational focus, it moved into individualized classroom instruction in 1951 with the SRA Reading Laboratory Kit, a format that was later applied to mathematics and other school subjects. Each kit was a large box filled with color-coded cardboard sheets, each of which contained a reading exercise for the student, who would work on it independently from other students. The exercise ended with multiple-choice tests, and those students who passed moved on to the next exercise, which was a bit more difficult than that which preceded it. Students in the same classroom could work at their own levels, calling upon their teacher only if they ran into trouble. The emphasis on "individualized instruction" was a boon to teachers who might have several levels of reading mastery in their class.

IBM purchased SRA in 1964, at a time when mathematics education became extremely crucial due to the so-called "Space Race" and the perception that Soviet students were outdistancing their American rivals. When McGraw-Hill purchased SRA in 1989, it continued manufacturing educational materials such as the SRA Open Court Reading program, first introduced in 2009.

The SRA Reading Lab

I remember the day in 1956 when Paul Witty, one of my professors at Northwestern University, walked into our classroom holding an SRA Reading Laboratory Kit. Beaming, he announced, "This box is going to individualize classroom reading instruction!" He went on to demonstrate how the reading exercises were based on high-interest stories ranging from outer space to wild animals, from foreign travel to automobile design. If students did not find the exercise on outer space interesting, they could simply request a different exercise at the same reading level. Later, I purchased a sample Reading Lab and used it for demonstration purposes for my classes on reading instruction at Kent State University.

Frances "Fran" Dillon, like Cora Lynn McCormick, was one of my early students at Kent State University. She volunteered to be an unpaid teaching assistant for my other classes. I remember that Paul Witty had an assistant, Anne Coomer, who had earned her PhD in Education and had a position with the Chicago Public Schools, but assisted Professor Witty in her spare time, which seemed to have been considerable. Fran and her husband, George, often drove me to various meetings and also coordinated activities involving my frequent guests. Cora Lynn also provided invaluable assistance, but she lived too far away to do many of the daily tasks that required attention.

On August 12, 1961, I told Fran that SRA had invited me to give a seminar on reading difficulties at a nearby Ohio school district, but that I could not accept because it conflicted with a class meeting. When Fran heard the amount of money I would be paid, she said that she would run my classes on those dates. This was an unexpected offer, which I immediately accepted. The feedback from the Ohio school teachers was so positive that SRA began to send other invitations my way. I continued to lead seminars and workshops for SRA during my tenure at Kent State as well as when I worked at Maimonides Medical Center. Sometimes I worked for SRA two or three times a month at various locations in the eastern part of the United States and, on occasion, in Canada.

My presentations did not focus on the SRA Reading Lab; in fact, I rarely mentioned the lab. The sponsors of my programs brought along samples of the lab and other SRA publications, which were put on exhibit, but I was not asked to mention or endorse them. SRA had researched my background and was aware of my experience when making the assignments. My major domain was that of reading difficulty – specifically, its diagnosis and its remediation. I tended to avoid generalities, instead giving specific examples of instruments, such as the Kent State University Informal Reading Survey, an item that I had developed. I also provided examples of remedial procedures such as "experience stories," in which a member of the workshop would assume the role of an elementary school pupil, describe an actual life experience, and then write it as a story, using both novel words and those already in the hypothetical pupil's vocabulary. At other times, the requested seminar would focus on reading instruction for the "culturally disadvantaged reader," the "gifted or talented reader," or the "low-performing high school reader." I also gave seminars on initiating counseling and guidance programs and the psychoneurological aspects of reading difficulties. The difference between a workshop and a seminar was that the former utilized participation by attendees, often in the form of role-playing.

My presentations on the neuropsychology of learning disabilities were warmly greeted by seminar participants, given that they had been offered so little information on the topic in their previous training. However, I had audited two courses led by Helmer Myklebust at Northwestern, one of the pioneers in the field. His earlier work with deafness and aphasia launched him into a consideration of the entire spectrum of learning disabilities. In the classic volume he edited with Doris Johnson, the statement is made that children may have trouble learning to read, write, speak, or calculate without any reference to mental retardation, sensory deficits, or emotional disturbance.[1] This contention was controversial at the time, but subsequent research has supported it as data established how small neurological defects could have major effects on language learning. In addition, since I had been impressed by the earlier writings by Ralph D. Rabinovitch on what he called "primary" learning disabilities, I assigned some of his articles to my Kent State University students. One if his most important articles had been published in the *Bulletin of the Orton Society*,[2] and I was flattered when the Canadian branch of the society invited me to give a presentation in 1966.

Samuel Orton was a pioneer in this field, hypothesizing that many reading problems resulted from the failure of the left hemisphere of the brain (thought to be predominantly verbal) to attain superiority over the right hemisphere (thought to be predominately nonverbal)—a hypothesis later found to be of value but overly simplistic. Orton also introduced "multisensory" remedial approaches that combined tactile and kinesthetic modes of instruction along with those that were visual and auditory. Some of his colleagues advocated that discovering the "learning style" of a pupil could enable teachers to use visual, auditory, or tactile–kinesthetic teaching methods, a practice that seemed to make little measurable difference in remedial efforts but often motivated

---

[1] Johnson, D. J., & Myklebust, H. (1967). *Learning disabilities: Educational principles and remedial approaches.* Grune & Stratton.

[2] Rabinovitch, R. D. (1964). Educational attainment in children with psychiatric problems (including incidence of those with primary learning disability) at Hawthorn Center: A preliminary report. *Bulletin of the Orton Society, 14,* 1–5.

both teacher and pupil because of its use of innovative methods that neither had experienced previously.

The term *neuropsychology* refers to the scientific approach that combines neurology and psychology. Neuropsychological tests assess nervous system-based cognitive impairments such as those affecting attention, language, learning, memory, and visuospatial functioning. Some writers prefer the term *psychoneurology* to highlight the psychological aspects of the condition.

The Institutes

On January 28, 1964, I attended a one-day seminar at the Institutes for the Advancement of Human Potential (IAHP) in Philadelphia, a clinic known for its radical psychoneurological approaches to remediation from brain damage. The Institutes were founded in 1955 by Glenn Doman and Carl Delacato, two clinicians who posited that brain damage could be reversed by diet, exercise, and "patterning" procedures such as "cross-pattern" creeping, crawling, and walking. Temple Fay, a neurosurgeon who had developed many of these procedures, worked with the Institutes during their earliest years.

Having found the first seminar valuable, I returned to the Institutes in April for a two-day seminar that featured the director of a Brazilian offshoot of IAHP and his film, which showed an auditorium in which dozens of parents were industriously "patterning" their children. My bias was to welcome the "patterners" to the ranks of those helping brain-injured children function better, although their claims were presented with few reservations or nuances. Nevertheless, I was impressed by the appearance of Raymond Dart during one of the seminars, as I was aware of his 1924 discovery of Australopithecus africanus, an early human ancestor. Dart told the group that IAHP's procedures made sense to him from a psychoneurological perspective, although his terminology was so technical that I doubt that anyone in the seminar completely understood it. To check whether I had grasped what he had meant, I wrote him a letter asking for clarification, receiving a long, hand-written letter in return confirming his appreciation of the Institute's work and giving details that answered my questions. Later I discovered that Dart's son, Galen, had sustained brain injury during his birth in 1941, which might have provoked his interest. Dart continued to commute to Philadelphia to consult with IAHP until his death in 1988.

13. Fran Dillon Comes to The Rescue

Before making final arrangements for a speaking engagement in Dallas in 1968, I made an appointment to tour the nearby University of Plano, a private liberal arts college that had opened in 1965. The school was the brainchild of Robert J. Morris, a lawyer who had served earlier as the president of the University of Dallas. Morris had an ambitious goal: the creation of a "politically conservative" liberal arts college that would incorporate the Doman and Delacato interventions for the stimulation of brain development, especially for those students whose birth and/or brain injuries had hampered their learning process. During my visit, my host took me to the school's auditorium, where a "crawling session" was in process. I watched in awe as about 200 male and female students engaged in "cross-pattern crawling," their right arms moving forward in tandem with their left legs, after which they shifted to the opposite pair of limbs. The classes in which these exercises transpired were named The College of Neurological Organization to highlight its pivotal role in the educational process. By sheer serendipity, my arrival coincided with Dr. Dart's visit; I knew that both Dart and Morris had sons who were neurologically impaired, and that Morris credited his son's improvement to the Institute's procedures.

I found the morale at the University of Plano to be quite high on the part of both students and instructors. In a creative gesture, President Morris had bought the Malaysian Pavilion from the recent New York-based World's Fair, and I recognized the graceful, elegant pagoda that had become the central building of the campus. Morris had planned to finance his school by land speculation; indeed, he was able to sell one swath of land as a shopping center and another as a venue for small businesses. But the land boom fizzled out in 1975. In 1976, the University of Plano closed its doors, and Morris turned to running for office and writing on various political topics.

Maimonides, Coney Island, San Juan, and Juarez

Maimonides Medical Center was unique in having several educational therapists on its staff. One of them, Cecelia "Cele" Pollack, the director of Learning Rehabilitation Services for Maimonides' patients, became a close friend of mine. Dr. Pollack had developed an "inter-sensory approach" to remediation, and her colleague, Lilly Pope, had inaugurated a similar approach at the Coney Island Hospital. On March 8, 1966, Dr. Pollack and I had lunch and discussed the ways in which I might serve as a consultant to her program given my background in learning disabilities and my favorable reaction to her inter-sensory approach. Like other methods with similar titles, Cele's approach integrated coordinated muscle movements into the program and used cut-out letters and words that students could touch and feel as well as see and hear. Cele and I collaborated on several projects in the following years; she was a specialist in diagnosing children with "minimal brain injury" and designing appropriate remedial programs. Years later, Cele and I co-authored an article on auditory perception with Joseph Nahem, another of Maimonides' educational therapists.

Cele, who corresponded extensively with her counterparts in the U.S.S.R. and Eastern Europe, eventually received an invitation to lecture in East Germany. On her return, she described the huge bouquet of roses she had received from the welcoming committee, as well as the enthusiastic groups that attended each of her presentations. Cele's emphasis on the psychoneurological correlates of learning disabilities coincided with the perspective of her hosts, who found it more palatable to posit neurological damage over general intelligence because Marxist ideology downplayed individual differences in the latter.

I visited Coney Island Hospital numerous times at Lily Pope's invitation, consulting with educational therapists and participating in case discussions. Most notable was a borough-wide conference on the topic of learning disabilities, for which the title of my presentation was "Time, Space, and Dyslexia."[3] In that presentation, I attempted to make a connection between Lily's description of temporal and spatial distortions by students with learning disabilities and the diagnostic label of *dyslexia*, a term for reading difficulties with a psychoneurological base.

Both Cele and Lily drew from the writings of Lev Vygotsky, a prominent Soviet educational psychologist, and from classic texts by Samuel Orton, Alexander Luria, Ivan P. Pavlov, and others. The intersensory approach to reading remediation is often used in association with the Illinois Test of Psycholinguistic Abilities, the scores of which I tended to cite in my case studies as they pointed to specific areas needing attention such as grammar, semantics, spelling, vocabulary, and sound–symbol relationships. Instruction is considered "intersensory" if a single stimulus, such as the letter M, is taught by

---

[3] Krippner, S. (1971). Time, space, and dyslexia: Central nervous system factors in reading disability. *Journal of the Reading Specialist, 10*, 128–148.

having a student say the letter while holding a three-dimensional model of the letter.

On October 20, 1966, Montague Ullman presided over a meeting in which he described how Maimonides' Department of Psychiatry would transition to the Maimonides Community Mental Health Center. Three years earlier, President John Kennedy had signed the Community Mental Health Act, which funded centers for community mental health care, positing that the services would be superior to institutionalization and would allow people with mental illness to remain at home, coming to the centers for treatment. It soon became obvious that addiction disorders needed to be included among the criteria for those treated, and the term *behavioral health care* came into vogue to cover the diverse services offered by the Maimonides Community Mental Health Center, including its learning rehabilitation program.

In January of that year, I had been in San Juan, Puerto Rico, for a speaking engagement, after which I saw my first bullfight. The bullfight was part of an attempt to bring the sport to Puerto Rico, depending on local reaction. For better or for worse, the reaction was not favorable. The "bull" looked more like a "calf," and was so frightened that it jumped into the stands, prompting immediate shock from those with the premium "front-row" seats. Years later, I attended another bullfight in Juarez, Mexico, one in which the bull fought valiantly and had its life spared. However, attendance at the Juarez event was slight, and the bullfight ring was subsequently converted into a venue for rock concerts. I was not dismayed because my sympathies had always been with the bull.

My host, Celinda Madera de Nido, introduced me to Efren Ramirez, the director of the Addiction Research Center. His approach, based on existential psychotherapy, focused on reinforcing clients' positive choices. Instead of telling clients how they became addicted, Dr. Ramirez told me that he allowed them to disclose the reasons themselves. I told him about how I had referred some friends of mine to Alcoholics Anonymous, and how one of them, Morgan McNeel, also took me to meetings of Narcotics Anonymous and Sex and Love Addicts Anonymous. Morgan was "multiply addicted" but overcame all three issues with the help of "twelve-step programs." After Morgan retired from a successful teaching career in Hawaii and Guam, he moved to Los Angeles and established Gramercy House, a low-cost "transitional" facility for gay men who were recovering alcoholics attending weekly "step" programs. I stayed there frequently when I was in the area, and it was inspiring to hear the stories of those men whose lives had been saved by their AA memberships.

For years, I worked part time at a hospital in Juarez, seeing a variety of clients, including several with substance abuse issues. In addition to my long-time interest in the field and my consultations with various "LSD rescue" operations in the 1960s and 1970s, I attended workshops and lectures on the topic to keep abreast of recent developments, especially regarding employing hypnosis to support smoking cessation, something I had done successfully for years. In 2010, I received the Advanced Alcohol and Other Abuse Counselor Certificate from the International Certification and Reciprocity Consortium for Alcohol and Other Drug Abuse. I received another certificate from the Mexican Certification Board for Professionals on Addictions, Alcohol, and Tobacco. These are not credentials I have often employed but they give me "gravitas" and "authority" when I author articles about addictive behaviors and their treatment.

Four Projects

Early in 1967, my background in special education gleaned me four professional invitations, all of which were welcome because I needed the money to make home repairs and to pay my stepchildren's private school tuition. On January 13, I had a phone call from David Cleland of the University of Pittsburgh, whose specialty was project management. He asked if I would be willing to head a study of a summer remedial program for middle-grade school students in Baltimore's low-income schools. I expressed my interest and correctly assessed that this was another Science Research Associates (SRA) project.

On January 28, I attended a conference at Wagner College to discuss its invitation for me to teach their course Educating the Exceptional Child. Wagner College was within walking distance of our home, and only a short drive during inclement weather. I accepted their offer and trekked to the college every Monday night during the years that my family and I lived in Staten Island.

Joseph Rubin was the local attorney who guided our year-long search for a manageable mortgage and, later, our lawsuits when the flood repairs on our home did not hold up. When Mr. Rubin discovered my background in special education, he asked me to do a psychological workup on his son. He was pleased with the results, and on February 20 we had a meeting with Susan Silberstein of the Staten Island Mental Health Center to discuss organizing a clinic for diagnosing and treating brain-injured children. We named our facility the Staten Island Developmental Evaluation Center, and I was on duty every Wednesday night, evaluating children and sharing the results with their parents. It turned out that my training in tests and measurements was superior to that of any of the other clinicians, having been rooted in courses I had taken at both the University of Wisconsin and Northwestern University, my assistantship in Northwestern's Psychoeducational Clinic, and the courses I had taught at Kent State University.

Also in January 1967, I met with Harry Valentine, a New York investments counselor who had been a long-time supporter of the Institutes for the Advancement of Human Potential (IAHP). He was eager to open a Manhattan branch of the IAHP, and I agreed to be the consulting psychologist. He soon enlisted the aid of Alan Levin, a local physician and neurologist. The three of us spent considerable time planning and publicizing the Institute, as well as organizing evaluation projects.

A number of doctoral dissertations had examined *patterning therapy*, producing positive results; but they were vulnerable to criticism due to lack of control groups as well as an absence of long-term follow-up. I planned and executed my own study with the assistance of Stuart Fischer, a medical student who was a Dream Lab assistant, and published the results in 1973.[4] In addition to "patterning" by the parents of the research participants, we included a "megavitamin" dietary supplement. I administered the Illinois Test of Psycholinguistic Abilities at the beginning of the intervention, two months after the intervention, and six months after that. Why did I do two follow-up tests? When someone whose scores are somewhat below the average is evaluated, a re-test frequently shows an improvement. This may not be due to an intervention; more likely it is a "regression toward the mean," a common occurrence in psychological testing, when either high or low scores disappear or lessen in subsequent testing. The first follow-up test was to allow for the occurrence of the expected regression. The second follow-up was an attempt to discern actual improvements, if any. The earlier doctoral dissertations had ignored the regression effect, and it is likely that most of the improvements noted were simply the result of data regression toward the mean, as

---

[4] Krippner, S., & Fischer, S. (1973). A study of neurological organization procedures and megavitamin treatment for children with brain dysfunction. *Journal of Orthomolecular Psychiatry, 1,* 121–132.

well as the lack of comparison groups and long-term follow-up evaluation.

Once backing for the New York Institute had been obtained, Harry Valentine began to improve public relations. Because of the controversial nature of IAHP, Harry named our new facility, The Churchill School, honoring the British statesman who supposedly overcame childhood learning disabilities to attain eminence. (Churchill's biographers have noted that he exaggerated his school problems to impress his readers, but the legend remains.) In addition, Harry shifted away from the remediation favored by the Philadelphia institutes, as it had been negatively evaluated by the American Academy of Pediatrics and other professional groups.

Harry favored the more focused sensory integration method of Jeanne Ayers,[5] whose procedures resembled those of Cele Pollack at Maimonides in that they attempted to integrate visual, auditory, and tactile–kinesthetic means of learning with motor expression. For example, poor balance and improper left-right directional knowledge can impair a student's ability to pay attention in class; poor handwriting can affect the ability to express one's ideas. Remedial efforts often included jumping, swinging, and matching a printed word with one presented auditorily. In 1966, Jeanne Chall's book *Learning to Read: The Great Debate*[6] had emphasized the superiority of "coding" methods of learning to read, many of which impacted sensory integration interventions. The sensory integration method attempts to coordinate the better known senses such as vision, hearing, taste, and smell, with the lesser known senses such as balance, coordination, posture, and muscle, tendon, and joint movement. Ayers' work was challenged, but not to the extent that had befallen that of Doman and Delacato. After all these years, I am puzzled as to why there is so little conclusive research on this approach.

Nonetheless, The Churchill School was extremely successful, developing into a kindergarten through 12th-grade facility, with most of its graduates entering college. I stayed connected with the school administrators, and in 2021 had a Zoom conference with the current director to obtain an update on the school's current activities and future plans. I was delighted to see the school's active presence on the Internet, as evidenced by the newsletter it sends to friends and

---

[5] Ayers, A. J. (1972). *Sensory integration and learning disorders*. Western Psychological Services.
[6] Chall, J. S. (1966). *Learning to read: The Great Debate*. Harcourt, Brace.

supporters, often announcing quiz shows, style shows, and other unique events for the Churchill community.

I kept abreast of the activities of the Staten Island Developmental Evaluation Clinic until Susan Silberstein left. In 1969, the clinic's functions were assumed by the Staten Island Developmental Disabilities Council, which had a full list of special education professionals on its staff. A new staff member told me that the case reports I had written on many children were still in the files and were used as examples for neophyte psychologists. Why not? I had written case reports for one of my psychology classes at the University of Wisconsin, wrote several more for Dr. Witty when I assisted him at Northwestern University's psychoeducational clinic, and prepared dozens more when I directed the Child Study Center at Kent State University. When I returned to Kent State University in March 1967 for a visit, I discovered that there was a surprise party for me, attended by over fifty of my former students. I also learned that there had been another name change, from the Reading Center to the Educational Child Study Center, and then to the Kent State University Reading and Writing Development Center. I told the staff members that they had finally gotten the name right!

One Summer in Baltimore

One of my most memorable SRA workshops was the one that took place in Memphis, Tennessee, in March 1967. I had brought Bob Harris, my stepson, with me, and we toured the city before I began work. We saw Elvis Presley's home, "Graceland," and the St. Jude Children's Research Hospital, which featured a bust of Danny Thomas, the hospital's sponsor, sculpted by Margaret Sanders, the daughter of Colonel Harlan Sanders of Kentucky Fried Chicken fame. When Bob and I arrived at the airport for our return flight, we noticed Chuck Berry, the eminent "rocker," asleep on a bench—but did not disturb him. And when we arrived back in New York, we had an offer from a couple to share expenses for a taxicab ride into Manhattan. Bob and I recognized the male half of the couple as the musician, producer, and manager Peter Asher; since I was authoring a book chapter on psychedelics and creativity, I did an impromptu interview with Asher, finding his comments both perceptive and articulate. Asher observed that a simple cause-and-effect model does not operate when it comes to art; one never knows exactly what effect LSD or any other unique experience will have on a painter, a poet, or a musician.

Science Research Associates, which had been receiving positive notices about my seminars and workshops, offered me the directorship of a reading project in Baltimore's inner schools. Since SRA would pay for three assistant directors, I chose Margaret Hudson, my long-time friend and colleague from the Richmond, Virginia, Public Schools; Lee Ross, a social psychologist who had just received his PhD from Columbia University; and Fred Phelps, a classmate at Northwestern University and a fellow dormitory counselor. Lee and Fred ended up creating the experimental design with which we would evaluate the effects of our intensive summer reading program, one that emphasized imagination and creativity along with fundamental word recognition and comprehension skills.

I also enlisted the help of some of our summer Dream Lab assistants to collate records and score the reading achievement tests we used to evaluate the program. I brought one of them, Gayle Miree, to Baltimore with me for a special assignment. Gayle was a petite African American woman who looked much younger than her actual age. I placed her on a school bus of senior high school students who were going to be given a tour of the local colleges, with the instruction to pay special attention both to the students' reactions and those of the guidance counselor who was accompanying them. Margaret Hudson had told the bus driver to stop at her alma mater, Goucher College, and he was happy to do so. He also stopped at various community colleges and four-year public universities. But Gayle reported that the guidance counselor would not let the students get out of the bus and walk around, even when there was a host waiting for them. The counselor told the host in a voice loud enough that the students could not help but hear it, "These boys and girls simply are not college material. You might as well save your time and just drive on." We were shocked to hear this and made a major issue of this incident in our final report as it served as a splendid example on how lowered expectations often influence student outcomes.

On September 20, 1968, Margaret, Lee, Fred, and I checked into a Manhattan hotel to spend three days drafting our report on the Baltimore project. Before she left Richmond, Margaret had asked me to write to Wayne Dennis, a professor of psychology at Brooklyn College, the only other man she had slept with while married to her late husband, Bill Hudson. Their tryst occurred when Margaret was in one of Wayne's summer classes, and once summer school was over, they had never seen each other again. But Margaret had stayed aware of Wayne's life, knowing that his first wife had died and that his second marriage was on the rocks.

I wrote to Wayne but did not receive a reply, so I thought that he had forgotten Margaret following their "one summer of happiness" (the title of a risqué Swedish film most of us had seen). Once Margaret arrived at our hotel, however, she found Wayne waiting for her. Lee, Fred, and I didn't see the two of them for almost three days, but they did join us for a goodbye lunch, after which Wayne took Margaret to the airport. In all fairness, I need to note that Margaret did not totally play hooky during the trip; she edited the final copy of our report and had copies made for our final presentation in Baltimore. Lee Ross presented the results of our project to the Baltimore educational staff, noting that the overall reading achievement scores had neither improved nor gotten worse. However, the students were fairly enthusiastic about the program, and there were few absences while it was ongoing. I had interspersed various games and role-playing stints to foster critical thinking with the reading instruction, and the standardized tests we used simply did not catch those outcomes. In retrospect, I noted that the retests had not anticipated the regression-toward-the-mean effect; a second re-test would have been a useful addition, and I have always regretted not having offered it.

Lee Ross went on to join the Stanford University faculty, where he became well known for his development of the "fundamental attribution error," an investigator's failure to consider the setting of an experiment and the role it might play in the outcome. Those researchers who commit this error tend to overemphasize the personal characteristics of the people they are studying while ignoring the impact of the surrounding situation. Lee and I remained friends until he passed on in 2021. Fred Phelps became a popular instructor at Lehman College, teaching courses on counseling and guidance.

Wayne Dennis wasted no time in moving to "Sam Hill," the farm that Margaret had bought a few years earlier, naming it after the expression, "What in Sam Hill?" I visited them several times and rejoiced to see how happy they were together. The farm sported crops of sweet corn, squash, cucumbers, and other vegetables that Margaret transformed into her tasty mélange of Southern, Italian, and Irish dishes. I felt bad for Father Patrick, who had to explain to Margaret why they could never get married. It was less the opposition of the church and more the fact that Father Patrick had no marketable skills other than the priesthood. The courses he taught at his parish's parochial school would not have found their way into the curriculum of a public school.

Margaret and Wayne married and traveled to Lebanon, where Wayne had conducted an earlier student enrichment program. He and his team discovered that adopted children made a significant jump on intelligence score tests when compared with those who had not been adopted, as did those living in a group home where cognitive stimulation was highlighted as opposed to those living in a group home with minimal cognitive stimulation. Social skills also improved significantly in the "enriched" groups when compared to the "control" groups. The IQ scores of many of the children in "enriched" groups improved one standard deviation or more, an increase virtually unheard of in previous literature. Wayne's book titled *Children of the Crèche*,[7] or "cradle," referred to the name of one of the "enriched" settings. Wayne knew about my interest in psychic phenomena, so when I asked him to autograph the book, he wrote "environment changes IQ by 50 points—This is parapsychology!"

Later, Wayne and Margaret co-edited a book, *The Intellectually Gifted*,[8] and I was the first person to provide a glowing review. One of the book chapters, written by Anne Roe, was titled, "A psychologist examines 64 eminent scientists"; when I was conducting my doctoral research at Northwestern University, I had made use of her vocational assessment scale. Another chapter was written by Julian Stanley, who, in 1953, when J. B. Rhine was scheduled to speak at the University of Wisconsin, had told his class, "If you are interested in ESP, you might as well hear about it from the horse's mouth, from the biggest horse's ass of them all." Needless to say, I did not mention the incident in my review.

Glenn Doman passed on in 2013, and his daughter, Janet Doman, took over the directorship of the Institutes for the Achievement of Human Potential; I stay in touch with their activities through their newsletter. I also follow the activities of the Churchill School and the Staten Island Developmental Disabilities Council, happy for the success of those two agencies that I helped found in the 1960s, and for Fran Dillon's rescue that initiated my longtime contact with SRA. Not too bad for all concerned!

---

[7] Dennis, W. (1973). *Children of the Crèche.* Appleton-Century-Crofts.
[8] Dennis, W., & Dennis, M. W. (Eds.). (1976). *The intellectually gifted: An overview.* Grune and Stratton.

Chapter 14

A Turbulent Sea
24 March 1962. A Day When My Life Changed

The American Psychological Association held its annual convention in New York City in September 1961, and I spent some informal time with Gardner Murphy, Don Hayakawa, and Albert Ellis. I had looked forward to two symposia. One was on creativity, featuring the author James T. Farrell, the playwright Arthur Miller, and Paul Freeman, a founder of Gestalt therapy. The other was a presentation on "The Sacred Mushroom," featuring Timothy Leary. When I reached the meeting room for the latter, there were no chairs available, so I sat on the windowsill. It was close to the front of the room, allowing me to see and hear Leary and the other panelists—Frank Barron, a psychologist who was a pioneer in creativity studies, and the writers William Burroughs and Gerald Heard.

Enter Timothy Leary

A striking figure with a flashing smile and salt and pepper hair, Leary hailed psilocybin's potential to encourage major breakthroughs in the social sciences. He stressed the importance of one's frame of mind (the "set") and physical surroundings (the "setting") if one were to have a positive experience. He also observed that the researcher who guides the participant is not merely an observer but a "collaborator," working with the participant toward mutually agreed-upon goals.

Leary had dropped out of a Roman Catholic college as well as West Point Military Academy before taking an interest in psychology. He transferred to the University of Alabama in late 1941 but was expelled a year later for spending a night in the female dormitory. He also lost his student deferment in the midst of World War II; Leary was drafted into the U.S. Army and underwent basic training in 1943. For the duration of his military career, he was assigned as a staff psychometrician. Later he was reinstated at the University of Alabama and soon thereafter completed his degree via correspondence courses, graduating in August 1945. Not much later he became the research director for the Kaiser Foundation Hospital in Oakland, California. After the suicide of his first wife and the breakup of his second marriage, he resigned his position at Kaiser and left for Europe with his two children, Jack and Susan, settling in a villa in Spain's Costa del Sol. Harvard professor David McClelland, who had been impressed with Leary's work at Kaiser, tracked him down and persuaded him to return to academia, securing a position for him at Harvard University.

Barron, who had introduced Leary to the "sacred mushroom" in Mexico in 1960, discussed the implications of using psilocybin and similar substances to facilitate creativity. Burroughs and Heard described their own experiences. I had previously read *The Yagé Letters*, co-authored with Allen Ginsberg,[1] about their South American adventures, notably with yagé, better known as ayahuasca. Gerald Heard, author of *The Ascent of Humanity* and numerous other books, had taken mescaline and LSD in the 1950s, and was impressed by their potential for personal transformation. After listening to these accounts, I decided that I would volunteer for Leary's research project.

I had a friend, Steve Klineberg, who was studying psychology at Harvard; he suggested that he also volunteer for Leary's study. Steve's session went well, so I wrote Leary a letter of application. I was delighted when I received a conditional acceptance, depending on my physician's statement that I was in good health and my responses to a personality test that accompanied the letter. I was given a date for my appointment with Leary and made my flight reservations. I arrived at the Harvard campus on March 23, 1962, just in time to accompany Steve to a presentation by Jack Kerouac at a university dormitory. Along with Burroughs and Ginsberg, Kerouac was considered a seminal voice of the so-called "Beat Generation." His best-known book, *On the Road*, had a major cultural impact, notably on musicians such as Bob Dylan, who claimed that the book inspired him to write his protest songs. The next day, I joined Steve for a lecture by the psychologist Erik Erikson on "Reality and Unreality," a pertinent topic, in retrospect, for the events that were to unfold.

Steve took me to Leary's office, where Leary greeted me warmly. Having studied my physician's statement and my responses to the personality test I had taken, he remarked, "You are just the type of person we want in our study," adding that our session would be the

---

[1] Burroughs, W., & Ginsberg, A. (1963). *The Yage letters*. City Lights.

following night. Knowing of my interest in parapsychology, he told me about his recent visit to the parapsychology laboratory at Duke University, where he and his colleague Richard Alpert had given psilocybin to the staff, with the exception of J. B. and Louisa Rhine, who preferred to participate as observers. Leary recalled how the researchers were testing each other's ESP with standard decks of "Zener cards," depicting a circle, a cross, a square, a pyramid, and a set of wavy lines. Leary chuckled that the neophytes could barely keep their attention focused; one of them actually slipped away, returning with a rose that he presented to Louisa Rhine.

Enter Alan Watts

Leary also invited me to dinner at his home that evening in honor of Alan Watts, who had obtained a travel and study grant from Harvard's Department of Social Relations. I eagerly accepted the invitation, having read Watts's book *The Way of Zen*.[2] While at Northwestern, I had discovered that Watts had been chaplain at Canterbury House for five years after being ordained as an Episcopalian priest in 1945. However, he became dissatisfied with his role and retreated to a farmhouse near Millbrook, New York, where he went through a period of deep contemplation. In 1950, Watts left the ministry and joined the faculty of the American Academy of Asian Studies in San Francisco. A prolific author and gifted lecturer on Eastern philosophy, Watts expressed skepticism that a genuine spiritual experience could be evoked by chemicals. He soon changed his mind, however, stating that LSD had given him an "undeniably mystical state of consciousness." I was literally sitting at Watts's feet during the discussion session that followed the potluck dinner, delighted by his responses to questions with both wit and profundity. He urged caution in the use of LSD and other psychedelics, although predicting that many people in Leary's psilocybin experiments would never see the world in the same way again once the "veil had been lifted."

Leary drove me back to Steve's apartment, noting that he would not be able to stay with me during my entire session the following evening. The State Medical Commission wanted to speak with him about a number of complaints that he had been drugging Harvard students, and he had no choice but to comply. But I almost did not make it to that

---

[2] Watts, A. W. (1962). *The way of Zen.* Penguin.

session. I awoke in the middle of the night, my body wracked with pain. I spent hours in the bathroom, heaving the food from the potluck dinner, one part of which had obviously triggered my distress. The next morning, Steve and I arrived at the research office early so that Leary's assistants would not sense my fragile condition. Once his two assistants arrived, they did a fine job preparing me for the evening session. As soon as they left, I headed to the bathroom for more vomiting.

The Session

I spent the rest of the day at Steve's apartment trying to recuperate but was still in pain when we arrived at the venue for our psilocybin session on March 24. Leary arrived, gave each of us a 30-milligram tablet of psilocybin, and then went off to his appointment, leaving his telephone number so that we could let him know how the session went. It was 5:30 in the afternoon. Once the chemical began to unleash its magic, my malaise disappeared, not to return during the next several hours. Leary's two assistants proved to be excellent guides, both having taken a small amount of psilocybin, supposedly to enhance rapport.

Steve and I had brought an intelligence test with us, thinking that the results under psilocybin might differ from the expected results. But once I started to administer the test to Steve, we broke out in laughter and put the test away for the rest of the night. I recalled Leary's account of the Duke University session so was not surprised by our reaction. I left the table and reclined on a sofa. Having dispensed with the test, I closed my eyes and was treated to a kaleidoscopic array of shapes and colors. When I opened my eyes, the room seemed to be vibrating and all of the colors became more vivid. My fingers were tingling, and my limbs were trembling. It was 5:57 PM.

I closed my eyes and visualized a giant mushroom encompassing me like an umbrella. A spiral of letters, words, and numbers blew away, as if a tornado had struck. Perhaps these images represented the verbal world, the framework imposed by culture. Without it, I felt closer to my senses, my feelings, and my direct impressions.

One of my guides gave me some apple slices. The process of chewing seemed interminable. My mouth was a cavern, and I felt the pulp moving slowly down my esophagus. Intrigued by the apple's intense taste, I groped my way to the kitchen, hoping to find other substances I could explore. I was not disappointed. I located a spice cabinet and sampled the cloves, cinnamon, and other herbs. The smells and tastes were intense but pleasant. I could understand why medieval merchants were motivated to take risky journeys to faraway Eastern locales in order to satisfy the cravings of their customers.

Having removed my shoes, I worked my way back to the sofa, enjoying the texture of the carpet. Once there, I caressed the pillows, the afghan, and the breasts of Leary's female assistant. None of them complained! We had been listening to Mussorgsky's "Pictures at an Exhibition," and I imagined seeing each picture. Once the final movement, "The Great Gate of Kiev," had ended, an assistant changed the record to Beethoven's "Seventh Symphony." I felt as if I were inside the music, surrounded by its chords and tones.

When I closed my eyes, I was faced with delicate arabesques and Persian miniature paintings. Once I opened my eyes, it seemed as if everything in the apartment had become transformed. An alarm clock became a work of art from Cellini's studio. The gaudy necklace on the dresser became a strand of gems on loan from the Empress Josephine.

The other three people in the room seemed to radiate light. Auras surrounded their bodies, and I felt an incredible closeness to them. But then they started to talk, and I crawled into the bedroom, taking some cinnamon sticks and peppermint candy with me to maintain my gustatory and olfactory sensations. A whirlwind appeared to pick me up and take me into a whirlpool. I emerged from a giant Yin/Yang design to find myself at the court of Kublai Khan. I was struck by the elaborate brocade of the emperor's robe, observing that even courtiers wore gowns that had been painstakingly embroidered. Just then, a peacock walked by, its natural plumage putting the human-made raiments to shame.

The scene shifted to an auditorium, constructed as a geodesic dome by Buckminster Fuller. The orchestra was playing the Beethoven symphony that was currently on the turntable. But I could see the orchestra members, each of whom was dressed in an ostentatious scarlet uniform with bright gold epaulets. I could zoom in and out of the scene, getting a close-up of any performer I chose.

In an instant, I was at the French court of Versailles. Benjamin Franklin, the U.S. Ambassador, was regaling the French monarchs with humorous stories, but I knew his ultimate goal was to seek financial assistance to help the colonies fight their war of independence. Every member of the court was wearing elaborate costumes of fur, silk, satin, and jewels. Franklin was modestly dressed, but his sparkling wit elicited more attention that any number of gowns and robes.

When it was time to change records again, the assistants chose a collection of flamenco music. Immediately, I was in Spain, being entertained by a troupe of colorful dancers at what appeared to be a gypsy encampment. One black-haired, jet-eyed dancer threw a bouquet of roses into the air, where they exploded like firecrackers.

The scene shifted to the New World and Monticello, where Thomas Jefferson was revealing his latest invention to a group of friends. It was a four-sided music stand, enabling members of a string quartet to read copies of the same musical score simultaneously. Suddenly, four musicians were in place, and I could see how well Jefferson's invention performed. Traveling north to Baltimore, I found myself consoling Edgar Allen Poe, who had just lost his young bride. His pale complexion and dark eyes conveyed the impression that he would like nothing better than to join her.

The somber feelings persisted as I moved to Washington, DC, where I gazed on a bust of Lincoln. Lincoln's features began to darken, and I noticed a revolver on the floor. At the same time, someone was shouting, "He was shot. The President was shot," I noticed a wisp of smoke emerging from the gun, curling into the air. But the bust was no longer Abraham Lincoln; the image of John F. Kennedy had taken its place. The voice repeated, "He was shot. The President was shot." My eyes were filled with tears.

Wiping my eyes, I closed them to find myself on a raft in a "turbulent sea." My two fellow travelers were with me, trying to keep our small craft afloat and survive the storm. We came upon a gigantic figure, one that resembled the statues of Hindu deities I had seen in books and movies. The figure was standing waist deep in the churning waters. He smiled, and I felt his compassion, concern and love. He was unable—or unwilling—to alter our course or provide us with help. But we knew that his caring was genuine, and that was all we needed to navigate our way to safety. The verse "God helps those who help themselves" came to mind, and then I realized that my session had ended. Like it or not, I had returned to the world of cultural conditioning, and the verse that ended the session seemed like a transition between worlds. It was about 11:00 PM. The image of the "turbulent sea" stayed with me, as it was an accurate metaphor for our lives on this Earth. Nonetheless, we have at least a modicum of skill to wend our way through that sea, arriving at a safe port, or at least a port that provides security until the next challenge arises.

I telephoned Leary, who said that he had just returned from his meeting and that my session was probably the last one that could be held. The state had asked for further documentation before the project could continue. I gave Leary a brief recap of my experiences, and Steve did the same. We returned to Steve's apartment, and the next day I left for New York City. In reviewing my session, I recalled reading about presidential deaths when I was about ten years of age, noting that they had occurred at 20-year intervals. William Henry Harrison was elected to the presidency in 1840, dying of pneumonia early in his term. Abraham Lincoln was elected in 1860, dying early in his second term. James Garfield was elected in 1880, and William McKinley was re-elected in 1900; like Lincoln, they were assassinated. Warren Harding, elected in 1920, allegedly died of food poisoning. Franklin Delano Roosevelt was re-elected in 1940 and died shortly after beginning his fourth term in office. John F. Kennedy was elected in 1960, and—as foreshadowed by my psilocybin image – did not live out his term. However, the 1848 election of Zachary Taylor, who died in office, did not fit the mold. Nor did Richard Nixon's 1974 resignation, or Ronald Reagan's election in 1980. Some pundits claim that it was Reagan's survival of an assassination attempt that finally broke the pattern.

So how did my life change on March 24, 1962? I had a memorable initiation into psychedelic experience, maintaining my interest therein ever since; I have written articles and book chapters about the potential value of psychedelics. The final segment of my journey introduced nothing new to my personal philosophy, but certainly confirmed my conviction that we cannot depend upon outside agencies, metaphysical or not, to solve our problems. Frank Lloyd Wright was fond of citing the Biblical injunction "The Kingdom of God is within you," and for me that is our basic resource. But when we stay afloat on a turbulent sea and draw upon our inner resources to express concern, compassion, and love, we are partaking in divinity.

Enter Jean Houston and Robert E. L. Masters

In 1966, Robert E. L. Masters and his wife, Jean Houston, published *The Varieties of Psychedelic Experience*, a book that became a classic in the field. The "varieties" are based on reports from 206 volunteer participants and interviews with another 214 who took psychedelics in other sessions. Four levels of mental functioning emerged, namely, (1) sensory, (2) recollective–analytic, (3) symbolic, and (4) integral. My 1962 session can be used to illustrate these levels.

1) At the sensory level, they noted, the participant may report altered awareness of the body, unusual ways of experiencing space and time, heightened sensory impressions, and—with

eyes closed—intense visual imagery. This framework matches my report that "the room seemed to be vibrating; all of the colors became more vivid. My fingers were tingling, and my limbs were trembling.... I closed my eyes and visualized a giant mushroom encompassing me like an umbrella. A spiral of letters, words, and numbers blew away as if a tornado had struck." As noted above, upon eating an apple slice, "My mouth was a cavern, and I felt the pulp moving slowly down my esophagus. I was intrigued by the apple's intense taste and groped my way to the kitchen, hoping to find other substances I could explore. I was not disappointed. I located a spice cabinet and sampled the cloves, cinnamon, and other herbs. The smells and tastes were intense but pleasant."

2) As part of recollective–analytic functioning were the visits to the court of Kublai Khan, the scarlet uniform-clad orchestra members, and the French court of Versailles. The gypsy encampment in Spain, as well as visits to Monticello, and Washington, DC, occurred at this level. One could make the case that my images of the Lincoln and Kennedy assassinations appeared at the recollective–analytic level, as I had made a connection with my childhood discovery of this pattern. Of course, I had not been the only one to detect this "death cycle," but my own childhood speculation had been on my mind ever since Kennedy's election. The premonition may or may not have been coincidence, but it reflected a recurring concern that I had harbored since the 1960 elections.

3) At the symbolic level, as I found myself "on a raft in a turbulent sea," my sense of a Hindu god may have been Krishna, the alleged reincarnation of Vishnu, the "preserver." Vishnu is called upon by the faithful whenever there is a crisis or imbalance in their lives or in their milieu. Vishnu symbolizes protection and balance, qualities desperately needed in the aftermath of the assassinations of Martin Luther King, Jr., and the two Kennedys, and the Vietnam disaster.

4) As for the integral level, I had no images that I can connect to it. Vishnu does not play a passive role in Indian mythology but embodies compassion, concern, and love. It was not until after the session that I had the insight that people embody the Divine whenever they help, assist, protect, and preserve. I did not take this correspondence too far, noting much later that Masters and Houston criticized those who would superimpose Eastern

philosophy and its archetypes upon a Westerner's psychedelic experience. Indeed, in terms of the integral level, Masters and Houston have noted that that is where psychedelic religious, and mystical experiences occur. They defined religious experiences as those in which there is an encounter with God, the "Ground of Being," or whatever rests at the deepest level of a person's psyche. Mystical experiences, on the other hand, involve the dissolution of one's self-concept and integration with the Cosmos. These definitions, which would appear in Masters' and Houston's other writings, provided a framework for other researchers who needed a template to guide them in mapping their discoveries.

No participant in Masters' and Houston's research studies exhibited serious psychiatric breakdowns or deleterious side effects after their experiences. This successful track record did not matter to government bureaucrats, however, who shut down all psychedelic research in the early 1970s. Coincidentally, Leary was arrested in 1972, charged with possession of marijuana. Decades later, there was a "psychedelic renaissance," and research was resumed. Robert Masters did not live long enough to enjoy this breakthrough, nor did Leary, although both were confident that it would occur.

Psychedelic Art

My psilocybin session on March 24, 1962, had changed my life in a number of ways. It came to the attention of Robert Masters and Jean Houston, who attended the seminar Virginia Glenn had arranged for me in New York City. Masters and Houston were preparing a book titled *Psychedelic Art*, and on January 6, 1967, Masters invited me to write a chapter about psychedelic artists. The book, which sold out almost immediately, was translated into several languages.

In the years to come, I updated my original work, adding several additional artists, writers, and musicians who referred to their artistic productions as psychedelic because they had some connection with their occasional or frequent use of these substances. The final report appeared in the *Journal of Humanistic Psychology* in 2017, where I observed that humanistic psychologists had taken an early interest in psychedelics.

I defined psychedelic art as artwork produced in the context of the ingestion of LSD-type drugs and related substances. There is a long history of such work, dating back to ancient times (picturing mushrooms and other plants with psychedelic effects), as well as more recent anecdotal first-person accounts and various collections of psychological data resulting from experiments and interviews. My research participants were some 200 professional artists, writers, and musicians, who referred to their artistic productions as psychedelic because they had some connection with their occasional or frequent use of these substances. Although there were no commonalities characterizing all of their paintings, films, poems, novels, songs, or other works, several frequent themes were noted following content analysis of the interview reports or their responses to a questionnaire I had sent out by postal mail.

Using thematic analysis, I grouped the artists' responses into three categories: the impact of psychedelics on the content of their work, on the approach they took to their work, and on the technique they used to manifest their work. Regarding content, one artist observed, "I have seen sights more beautiful than words can describe and have tried to incorporate these visions into my art." In respect to approach, a fabric designer noted, "The loosening-up effect offered by the psychedelic experience has been very useful, but without the balance of persistently directed effort, no art could be produced." A graphic artist added, "It is difficult for me to produce anything more than sketches during an LSD session; my mind is too active to maintain a prolonged artistic effort.' In discussing technique, a research participant noted, "I always had been afraid to use color in my work, but a single LSD session helped to conquer that fear."

There were a few dozen musicians in my group of research participants, both instrumentalists and vocalists, most of them rock performers. All had smoked marijuana, and most had taken LSD. When I conducted a separate thematic analysis for this group, I found three major themes that ran through my interviews: lyrics, texture, and mood. Because pop music encompasses many aspects of contemporary culture, it was natural that references to drugs should appear in some of the lyrics. Well-known references to psychedelics include the Byrd's' *Eight Miles High*, the Beatles' *Magical Mystery Tour*, and the Electric Prunes' *I Had Too Much to Dream*. Even without drug-oriented lyrics, psychedelic influence was still present in the pop music of those years. Such influence can be found in the texture or the physical properties of the music, influencing one's mental state, often reminding listeners of their own drug experiences. Jimi Hendrix created music with unique textural characteristics. Blue Cheer utilized 15 amplifiers to produce a distinctive texture. The Beatles combined simple lyrics with a complex texture, as in "Strawberry Fields Forever."

"Mood" was mentioned by many musicians, some of whom admitted that they enjoyed uplifting the mood of their audiences. I interviewed most of the members of the Grateful Dead rock group, beginning with Bob Weir, who observed that it was difficult to identify specific drug effects in a musician's work since creative artists will manifest songs, paintings, or poems out of the totality of their lives. Mickey Hart, one of the band's two drummers, added that linear dimensions of time and space do not typify many types of creativity. Regarding mood, he mentioned that there are three "dances": the personal, the cultural, and the cosmic. If a technique works, the reward is a new dimension of rhythm, and the ensuing mood can be "sacred" in nature.

One of the musicians suggested that I listen to the song *Tomorrow Never Knows* by John Lennon and Paul McCartney. I discovered that it was a vivid description of a psychedelic trip, beginning with "Turn off your mind, relax, and float downstream," and I wanted to include it in my chapter. I also realized that I would need permission from the publisher, Northern Songs, Ltd. in London. It took me some time to locate the address and write a letter (those were the days before the Internet and e-mails). Once I had made contact, I received a very gracious letter of permission from them, as long as I included "used by permission" in a footnote, which I was delighted to do.

My research project had been inspired by earlier accounts in the psychological literature on psychedelics and creativity. For example, in 1963 psychologist Frank Barron[3] administered psilocybin to a number of individuals he deemed to be "highly creative" and recorded their impressions. A composer wrote, "Every corner is alive in a silent intimacy." But a painter observed, "I have seldom known such absolute identification with neither what I was doing—nor such a lack of concern with it afterwards." In his 1963 book on creativity, Barron concluded, "What psilocybin does is to...dissolve many definitions and melt many boundaries, permit greater intensities or more extreme values of experience to occur in many dimensions."

---

[3] Barron, F. X. (1963). *Creativity and psychological health: Origins of personal vitality and creative freedom.* Van Nostrand.

During the half century between my chapter in *Psychedelic Art*[4] and my article in the *Journal of Humanistic Psychology*,[5] I was invited to speak on the topic at various colleges, universities, and conferences, and to publish various updates. I was not a psychotherapist, so I did not write or lecture on first-hand experiences in psychedelic-facilitated psychotherapy. But I was comfortable with my niche regarding the impact of psychedelics on creativity—a niche that would have remained vacant were it not for the events that transpired at Harvard on March 24, 1962.

---

[4] Krippner, S. (1968). The psychedelic artist. In R. E. L. Masters & J. Houston, *Psychedelic art* (pp. 163–182). Grove/Balance House.
[5] Krippner, S. (2017). Ecstatic landscapes: The manifestation of psychedelic art. *Journal of Humanistic Psychology, 57*, 415–435.

References[1]

A Course in Miracles. (1975). Foundation for Inner Peace.

Abzug, R. H. (2021). *Psyche and soul in America: The spiritual odyssey of Rollo May.* Oxford University Press.

American Psychiatric Association (1980). *Diagnostic and Statistical Manual of Mental Disorders* (3rd ed.).

American Psychiatric Association (2013). *Diagnostic and Statistical Manual of Mental Disorders* (5th ed.).

American Psychological Association (2007). *APA Dictionary of Psychology* (pp. 436. 457, 907). American Psychological Association.

Arthur, G. (1966). *The circle of sex.* University Books.

Ayers, A. J. (1972). *Sensory integration and learning disorders.* Western Psychological Services.

Barber, T. X. (1969). *Hypnosis: A scientific approach.* Van Nostrand Reinhold.

Barber, T. X. (1993). *The human nature of birds: A scientific discovery with startling implications.* Penguin.

Barrett. D. (2001). *The Committee of Sleep: How artists, scientists, and athletes use their dreams for creative problem solving—and how you can too.* Crown.

Barron, F. X. (1963). *Creativity and psychological health: Origins of personal vitality and creative freedom.* Van Nostrand.

Barušs, I., & Mossbridge, J. (2017). *Transcendent mind: Rethinking the science of consciousness.* American Psychological Association.

Beck, W. & Purdy, C. (1909). *On, Wisconsin!* (song). Hillison, McCormack & Company

Benjamin, H. (1964). Introduction. In R.E.L. Masters, *Forbidden sexual behavior and morality: An objective reexamination of perverse sexual practices in different cultures.* Julian Press.

Benjamin, H. (1964). Introduction. In R.E.L. Masters, *Prostitution and morality: A definitive report on the prostitute in contemporary society and an analysis of the costs of the suppression.* Julian Press.

Benjamin, H. (1966). *The transsexual phenomenon: A scientific report on transsexualism and sexual conversion in the human male and female.* Julian Press.

Benjamin, H. (1967). Introduction. *Christine Jorgensen: A personal autobiography,* by C. Jorgensen. Bantam Books.

Berger, E. (2020). Contextualizing monuments and movies: Iconoclasm through the lens of media ecology and general semantics. *ETC: A Review of General Semantics, 77,* 47–53.

Bertinelli, V. (2022, March). What I know now. *Time* magazine, p. 18.

Best, K. (2013). *The archetype of suicide.* Runaway Press.

---

[1] All three volumes contain a combined reference section for all three volumes.

Bevan, W. (1991). Contemporary psychology: A tour inside the onion. *American Psychologist, 46*, 475–483.

Blair, W. A. (2014). *With malice toward some: Treason and loyalty in the Civil War Era.* University of North Carolina Press.

Boal, I., Stone, J., Watts, M., Winslow, C. (Eds.). (2012). *West of Eden: Communes and utopias in Northern California.* PM Press.

Bohm, D., & Peat, D. (1988). Consciousness and the Implicate Order. *Psychological Perspectives, 19*, 31–43.

Bouse, K. J. (2017). *Neo-shamanism as a developmental, spiritual matrix for contemporary magical discovery and practice.* Available from Dissertations & Theses @ Saybrook University; ProQuest One Academic.

Bouse, K. (2019). *Neo-shamanism and mental health.* Palgrave/Macmillan.

Bowersock, M. (2011). *Marcia Gates: Angel of Bataan.* New Moon Publishing.

Brandelius, J. L. (1989). *The Grateful Dead family album.* Warner.

Braude, S. E. (2003). *Immortal remains: The evidence for life after death.* Rowman and Littlefield.

Burr, H. S. (1973). *The fields of life: Our links with the universe.* Ballantine.

Burroughs, W., & Ginsberg, A. (1963). *The Yage letters.* City Lights.

Calvet, C. (1983). *Has Corinne Been a Good Girl?* St Martins.

Campbell, J. (1949). *The hero with a thousand faces.* Pantheon Books.

Campbell, J. (1993). *Myths to live by.* Arkana.

Cardeña, E., Lynn, S. J., & Krippner, S. (Eds.). (2014). *Varieties of anomalous experience: Examining the scientific evidence* (2nd ed.). American Psychological Association.

Cardeña, E., Lynn, S. J., & Krippner, S. (2017). The varieties of anomalous experience: A rediscovery. *Psychology of Consciousness: Research, Theory, and Practice, 4*, 4–22.

Carpenter, B., & Krippner, S. (1989, Fall). Spice island shaman: A Torajan healer in Sulawesi. *Shaman's Drum,* 47–52.

Castañeda, C. (1993). *The art of dreaming.* HarperPerennial.

Castaneda, C. (1998). *The teachings of Don Juan: a Yaqui way of knowledge.* Berkeley, University of California Press.

Chall, J. S. (1966). *Learning to read: The Great Debate.* Harcourt, Brace.

Chopra, D. (2022). *Abundance: The inner path to wealth.* Harmony Books.

Clinard, M. B. (Ed.). (1964). *Anomie and deviant behavior.* Free Press of Glencoe.

Clottes, J., & Lewis-Williams, D. (1998). *The Shamans of prehistory: Trance and magic in the painted caves.* Harry N. Abrams.

Cohen, T., & Skutch, J. (1985). *Double vision.* Celestial Arts.

Columbus, P. J., & Rice, D. (Eds.). (2012). *Alan Watts—Here and now: Contributions to psychology, philosophy, and religion.* SUNY Press.

Columbus, P. J., & Rice, D. (Eds.). (2017). *Alan Watts in the Academy: Essays and lectures.* SUNY Press.

Combs, A. (1995). *The Radiance of being: Complexity, chaos, and the evolution of consciousness.* Floris Books.

Combs, A. (2009). *Consciousness explained better: Towards an integral understanding of the multifaceted nature of consciousness.* Paragon House.

Combs, A. (2014). My life in chaos. In A. Montuori (Ed.). *Journeys in complexity: Autobiographical accounts by leading systems and complexity thinkers.* Routledge.

Combs, A. (Ed.), Laszlo, E., Artigiani, R., & Csányi, V. (1996). *Changing visions: Human cognitive maps, past, present and future.* Praeger.

Combs, A., Winkler, M., & Daley, C. (1994). A chaotic systems analysis of circadian rhythms in feeling states. *Psychological Record, 44,* 359–368.

Cooper, D. (2000). *Death of the family.* Random House.

Daily Jefferson County Union. (1939). https://www.dailyunion.com/

Davies, J.A. (1942). *Mission to Moscow: A Record of Confidential Dispatches to the State Department, Official and Personal Correspondence, Current Diary and Journal Entries, Including Notes and Comment Up to October, 1941.* Victor Gollancz Limited.

Davies, J. A., & Pitchford, D. B. (Eds.). (2015). *Stanley Krippner: A life of dreams, myths, and visions.* University Professors Press.

Delaney, G. (2006). *Your sleeping genius: Harnessing the hidden power of your dreams.* Gildan Audio.

Dennis, W. (1973). *Children of the Crèche.* Appleton-Century-Crofts.

Dennis, W., & Dennis, M. W. (Eds.). (1976). *The intellectually gifted: An overview.* Grune and Stratton.

de Mille, R. (1976). *Castaneda's Journey: The Power and the Allegory.* Ironwood Hills

de Mille, R. (1980). *The Don Juan papers: Further Castaneda controversies.* Ross-Erickson.

Devor, A. H. (2003). Erickson Educational Foundation. In M. Stein (Ed.), *The Encyclopedia of Lesbian, Gay, Bisexual, and Transgender History in America.* Charles Scribner's Sons.

Devor, A. H. (2016). *FTM: Female to male transsexuals in society* (2nd ed.) Indiana University Press.

Dhiegh, K. A. (1973). *The eleventh wing: An exposition of the dynamics of I Ching for Now.* Nash Publishers.

Dias del Castillo, B. (1963). *The true history of the conquest of New Spain.* Penguin. (Original Spanish publication 1632).

Dickens, C. & Dunn, H. (1921) *A Tale of Two Cities.* New York, Cosmopolitan Book Corporation.

Domhoff, W.A. (2017). *The emergence of dreaming: Mind-wandering, embodied simulation, and the default mode network.* Oxford University Press.

Dos Passos, J. (1937). *U.S.A.* Modern Library.

Dufresne, I. (1988). *Famous for 15 minutes, My years with Andy Warhol.* Harcourt Brace Jovanovich.

Dufty, W. (1975). *Sugar blues.* Chilton.

Easton, H., & Krippner, S. (1966). Disability, rehabilitation, and existentialism. In C. E. Beck (Ed.), *Guidelines for guidance: Readings in the philosophy of guidance* (pp. 427–433). Wm. C. Brown.

Easton, H., & Krippner, S. (1971). Disability, rehabilitation, and existentialism. In H. A. Moses & C. H. Patterson (Eds.), *Readings in rehabilitation counseling* (2nd ed., pp.144–149). Stipes.

Eden, D. (with D. Feinstein), (2008). *Energy medicine* (rev. ed.). Tarcher/Penguin.

Eden, D., & Feinstein, D. (2014): The energies of love: Using energy medicine to keep your relationship thriving. Tarcher/Penguin.

Eggleston, G. (2015). A new mourning: Discovering the gifts in grief. Balboa Press.

Ehrenreich, B. (2014). *Living with a wild god: A nonbeliever's search for the truth.* Grand Central.

Ellis, A. (1958). *Sex without guilt.* Lyle Stuart.

Ellis, A., & Joffe Ellis, D. (2019). *Rational Emotive Behaviour Therapy.* American Psychological Association.

Ellis, A., & Yeager, R. J. (1989). *Why some therapies don't work: The dangers of transpersonal psychology.* Prometheus Books.

Ellsberg, D. (2000). *Secrets: A memoir of Vietnam and the Pentagon Papers.* Viking/Penguin.

Eskenazi, J. (2012, April 25-May 1). The psychic world of Stanley Krippner: A quest to document ESP. *San Francisco Weekly*, 9–14.

Estrada, A. (1981). *María Sabina: Her life and chants.* Ross-Erikson.

Evans, B. (1954). *The spoor of spooks, and other nonsense.* A. A. Knopf.

Evans, B., & Evans, C. (1957). *A Dictionary of Contemporary American Usage.* Random House.

Farrell, J. T. (2004). *Studs Lonigan.* Library of America.

Feinstein, D., & Krippner, S. (1987). *Personaliche Mythologie: Die psychologische Entwicklung des selbst.* Sphinx Verlag.

Feinstein, D., & Krippner, S. (1988). *Personal mythology: The Psychology of your evolving self.* Jeremy P. Tarcher.

Feinstein, D., & Krippner, S. (2008). *Personal mythology: Using ritual, dreams, and imagination to discover your inner story* (3rd ed.). Energy Psychology Press/Elite Books.

Feinstein, D., Krippner, S., & Granger, D. (1988). Mythmaking and human development. *Journal of Humanistic Psychology, 28*, 23–50.

Foreman, M. et al. (2019). Genetic link between gender dysphoria and sex hormone signaling. *Journal of Clinical Endocrinology & Metabolism, 104*, 390–396.

Frankl, V. E. (1959). *From death camp to existentialism: A psychiatrist's path to a new therapy.* Beacon Press.

Frankl, V. E. (2006). *Man's search for meaning: An introduction to logotherapy.* Beacon Press. (Original German publication 1946).

Friedman, H. (1983). The Self-Expansiveness Level Form: A conceptualization and measurement of a transpersonal construct. *Journal of Transpersonal Psychology, 15,* 37–50.
Friedman, H. L. (2018). Transpersonal psychology as a heterodox approach to psychological science: Focus on the construct of self-expansiveness and its measure. *Archives of Scientific Psychology, 6,* 230–242.
Gardner, H. (1983). *Multiple intelligences: New horizons.* Basic Books.
Garfield, P. (1975). *Creative dreaming: Plan and control your dreams to develop creativity, overcome fears, solve problems, and create a better self.* Simon & Schuster.
Garfield, P. (2001). *The universal dream key: The twelve most common dream themes around the world.* Cliff Street Books.
Garnett, A. C. (1942). *A realistic philosophy of religion.* Harper and Brothers.
Garnett, A. C. (1952). *The moral nature of man: A critical evaluation of ethical principles.* Ronald Press.
Gauquelin, M., & Gauquelin, F. (1979). Star U.S. sportsmen display the Mars effect. *Skeptical Inquirer, 4* (2), 31–43.
Gildzen, A. (1965). *Monday night in Brooklyn.*
Ginsburg, T. (2022). *Breath of spirit: Integration methodology: breathing practices as tool for self-actualization.* Author.
Goerner, S. (1999). *After the clockwork universe: The emerging science and culture of integral society.* Floris Books.
Goerner, S. J. (1993). *The evolving ecological universe: A study in the science and human implications for a new world hypothesis.* Gordon & Breach.
Gould, S. J. (2002). *Rock of Ages: Science, religion, and the fullness of life.* Random House.
Gowan, J. C. (1974). *Development of the psychedelic individual.* Author.
Gowan, J. C. (1975). *Trance, art, and creativity.* Creative Education Foundation.
Gowan, J. C., & Bruch, C. B. (1971). *The doubtful gift: Strategies for educating gifted children in the regular classroom.* Houghton Mifflin.
Graboi, N. (1991). *One foot in the future: A woman's spiritual quest.* Aerial Press.
Great teachers: U.S. college students select 1950's outstanding professors. (1950, Oct 16). *Life, 29*(16). 109–116.
Guinness, A. (1999). *A positively last appearance.* Gardner Books.
Halpern, S. (1977). *The human instrument.* Halpern Sounds.
Hardy, C. (1988). *Networks of meaning: A bridge between mind and matter.* Praeger.
Hastings, A., & Krippner, S. (1961). Expectancy set and "poltergeist" phenomena. *ETC: A Review of General Semantics, 18*(3), 349–360.
Havens, R. (2005). *The Wisdom of Milton H. Erickson.* Crown House.
Hayakawa, S. I. (1949). *Language in thought and action.* Harcourt, Brace.
Hieronimus, R. R. (1989). *America's secret destiny: Spiritual visions and the founding of a nation.* Destiny Books.

Hoard's Dairyman. (n.d.). https://hoards.com
Hutchings, R. M. (Ed.). (1968). *On the nature of things* (Vol. 12). University of Chicago Press.
Huxley, A. (1954, Jan 11). The case for ESP, PK and PSI. *Life, 36*(2). 96–108.
Huxley, L. (1963). *You are not the target.* Metamorphous Books.
Huxley, L. (1987). *The child of your dreams: Approaching conception and pregnancy with inner peace and reverence for life.* Destiny Books.
Huxley, L. (1991). *This timeless moment: A personal view of Aldous Huxley.* Mercury House.
Iljas, J., & Krippner, S. (2017). *Sex and love in the 21st century: An introduction to sexology for young people.* Sentia Publishing.
Inyushin, V. M. (1977). Bioplasma: The fifth state of matter. In J. White & S. Krippner (Eds.), *Future science: Life energies and the physics of paranormal phenomena* (pp, 103–120). Anchor Books.
Ireland, R. (2011). *Your psychic potential: A guide to psychic development.* North Atlantic Books.
Irwin, L. (2022). *Dreams beyond time: On sacred encounter and spiritual transformation.* Lexington Books.
Jackovich, K. G., & Sennet, M. (2009, March 22). The children of John Wayne, Susan Hayward, and Dick Powell fear that fallout killed their parents. *People.*
Janesville Daily Gazette. (1933). https://www.gazetteextra.com
Johnson, D. J., & Myklebust, H. (1967). *Learning disabilities: Educational principles and remedial approaches.* Grune & Stratton.
Jones, S. M. S., & Krippner, S. (2012). *The voice of Rolling Thunder: A medicine man's wisdom for walking the red road.* Bear.
Jones, S. M. S., & Krippner, S. (Eds.). (2016). *The shamanic powers of Rolling Thunder.* Bear.
Jorgensen, C. (1967). *Christine Jorgensen: A personal autobiography.* Bantam.
Joyce, J. (1976/1939). Finnegans wake. Penguin Books.
Jung, C. G. (1963). In A. Jaffé (Ed.), *Memories, dreams, reflections.* Pantheon.
Kahn, D. L. (2020). Trauma dreams of transgender youth. *Dreamtime,* Winter, pp. 12-13.
Kahn, D., Krippner, S., & Combs, A. (2002). Dreaming as a function of chaos-like stochastic processes in the self-organizing brain. *Nonlinear dynamics, psychology, and life sciences, 6,* 311–322.
Kaiser, D. (2011). *How the hippies saved physics*: Science, counterculture, and the quantum revival. W. W. Norton.
Katz, L. (1945, April). Art and archaeology in the Aztec figure of Coatlicue. *Magazine of Art.*
Kaufman, J. B. (2009). *South of the border: Walt Disney and the Good Neighbor Program (1941–1948).* Disney Editions.
Keen, S., & Valley-Fox, A. (1989). *Your mythic journey: Finding meaning in your life through writing and storytelling.* J. P. Tarcher/St. Martin's Press.

Kesselring, J. (1942). Arsenic and old lace: play in three acts. [New York], Dramatists play Service, Inc.
Kilner, W. J. (1920). *The human atmosphere* (2nd ed.). K. Paul Trench.
Kinsey, A. C., Pomeroy, W. B., & Martin, C. E. (1948). Sexual behavior in the human male. Saunders.
Kirsch, I. (2009). *The emperor's new drugs: Exploding the anti-depressant myth.* Random House.
Kostyuk, N. et al. (2011). Gaseous discharge visualization: An imagery making tool for medical biometrics. *International Journal of Medical Imagery, 20*, 1–6.
Kripal, J. (2010). *Authors of the impossible: The paranormal and the sacred.* University of Chicago Press.
Krippner, S. (1961). The vocational preferences of high-achieving and low-achieving junior high school students. *Gifted Child Quarterly, 5*, 88–90.
Krippner, S. (1963). Hypnosis and reading improvement among university students. *American Journal of Clinical Hypnosis, 5*, 187–193.
Krippner, S. (1963). Sociopathic tendencies and reading retardation in children. *Exceptional Children, 29*, 258–266.
Krippner, S. (1963). The boy who read at eighteen months. *Exceptional Children, 30*, 105–109.
Krippner, S. (1965). Consciousness-expansion and the extensional world. *ETC: A Review of General Semantics, 22*, 463–474.
Krippner, S. (1965). Hypnosis and creativity. *American Journal of Clinical Hypnosis, 8*, 94–99.
Krippner, S. (1966). The use of hypnosis with elementary and secondary school children in a summer reading clinic. *American Journal of Clinical Hypnosis, 8*, 261–266.
Krippner, S. (1967). Relationship of reading improvement to scores on the Holtzman Inkblot Technique. *Journal of Clinical Psychology, 23*, 114–115.
Krippner, S. (1967). Review of *The varieties of psychedelic experience* by R. E. L. Masters and J. Houston. *American Journal of Clinical Hypnosis, 9*, 220–221.
Krippner, S. (1967). The Ten Commandments that block creativity. *Gifted Child Quarterly, 11*, 144–156.
Krippner, S. (1968). An experimental study in hypnosis and telepathy. *American Journal of Clinical Hypnosis, 11*, 45–54.
Krippner, S. (1968). The psychedelic artist. In R. E. L. Masters & J. Houston, *Psychedelic art* (pp. 163–182). Grove/Balance House.
Krippner, S. (1970). Race, intelligence, and segregation: The misuse of scientific data. In B. N. Schwartz & R. Disch (Eds.), *White Racism* (pp. 452–464). Dell/Laurel.
Krippner, S. (1971). On research in visual training and reading disabilities. *Journal of Learning Disabilities, 4*(2), 6–17.
Krippner, S. (1971). *The Tragicall Historie of Shamlet Prince of Denmark: A Literary Parody.* Exposition Press.

Krippner, S. (1971). Time, space, and dyslexia: Central nervous system factors in reading disability. *Journal of the Reading Specialist, 10,* 128–148.

Krippner, S. (Ed.). (1972). The plateau experience: A. H. Maslow and others. *Journal of Transpersonal Psychology, 4,* 107–120.

Krippner, S. (1972). Marijuana and Viet Nam: Twin dilemmas for American youth. In R. S. Parker (Ed.), *The emotional stress of war, violence, and peace* (pp. 176–225). Stanwix House.

Krippner, S. (1973). Foreword. In K. A. Dhiegh, *The eleventh wing: An exposition of the dynamics of I Ching for now* (pp. xii–xx). Nash Publishers.

Krippner, S. (1975). *Song of the Siren: A parapsychological odyssey.* Harper & Row.

Krippner, S. (1976). Hypnosis as verbal programming in educational therapy. In E. Dengrove (Ed.), *Hypnosis and behavioral therapy* (pp. 235–243). Charles C. Thomas.

Krippner, S. (1976). Kirlian photography: A new frontier in science techniques for the creative. *Creative Child and Adult Quarterly, 1,* 150–154, 238–241.

Krippner, S. (1976). The plateau experience: A. H. Maslow and others. In T. X. Barber (Ed.), *Advances in altered states of consciousness and human potentialities* (Vol. 1, pp. 651–664). Psychological Dimensions.

Krippner, S. (1977). A first-hand look at the psychotronic generators. In J. White & S. Krippner (Eds.), *Future science: Life energies and the physics of paranormal phenomena* (pp. 420–430). Anchor Books.

Krippner, S. (1977). Preliminary investigations of Kirlian photography as a technique in detecting psychokinetic effects. *International Journal of Paraphysics, 11,* 69–73.

Krippner, S. (1990). Personal mythology: An introduction to the concept. *The Humanistic Psychologist, 18,* 137–142.

Krippner, S. (1994). Foreword. In D. S. Paulson, *Walking the point: Male initiation and the Vietnam experience* (pp. ii–iv). Distinctive Publishing.

Krippner, S. (1994). Humanistic psychology and chaos theory: The third revolution and the third force. *Journal of Humanistic Psychology, 34*(3), 48-61.

Krippner, S. (1999). Psychological research methods and anomalous shamanic experiences and reports. In V. I. Kharitonova & D. A. Funk (Eds.), *Proceedings of the International Congress on Shamanism and other Indigenous Spiritual Beliefs and Practices* (pp. 150–164). Institute of Ethnology and Anthropology, Russian Academy of Science/V. Maritonova.

Krippner, S. (1999, Summer). Protecting Indigenous knowledge from ecopiratism. *Shaman's Drum,* pp. 8, 10-11.

Krippner, S. (2001). Introduction. In D. A. Sisk & E. P. Torrance, *Spiritual intelligence: Developing higher consciousness* (pp. ix–xii). Creative Education Foundation Press.

Krippner, S. (2001). Myths in collision. In S. Kahn & E. Fromm (Eds.), *Changes in the therapist* (pp. 151–164). Lawrence Erlbaum.

Krippner, S. (2002). Stigmatic phenomena: An alleged case in Brazil. *Journal of Scientific Exploration, 16*, 207–224.

Krippner, S. (2004). Trance and the trickster: Hypnosis as a liminal phenomenon. *Journal of Clinical and Experimental Hypnosis, 53*, 97–118.

Krippner, S. (2009). The future of ethnomedicine. In L. Freeman, *Mosby's complementary and alternative medicine: A research-based approach* (3rd ed., pp. 574–580). Mosby/Elsevier.

Krippner, S. (2011). *Mysteries: An investigation into the occult, the paranormal, and the supernatural: A retrospective look at mysteries from the perspective of parapsychology.* In C. Stanley (Ed.), *Around the outsider: Essays presented to Colin Wilson on the occasion of his 80th birthday* (pp. 160–178). O Books.

Krippner, S. (2013). Encounter with a wizard. *World Futures, 69*(4–6), 290-310.

Krippner, S. (2013). Four loose stitches: Anomalous healing data and a Ouija Board ritual. In D. Eulert (Ed.), *Ritual & healing: Stories of ordinary and extraordinary transformation* (pp. 269–275). Motivational Press.

Krippner, S. (2014). The mind-body-spirit paradigm: Crisis or opportunity? *American Journal of Clinical Hypnosis, 56*, 210–215.

Krippner, S. (2017). A unique partnership: Examining information in dreams about deceased veterans. *Journal of the Society for Psychical Research, 81*(3), 180–193.

Krippner, S. (2017). Ecstatic landscapes: The manifestation of psychedelic art. *Journal of Humanistic Psychology, 57*, 415–435.

Krippner, S. (2018). Transpersonal transformative experiences: Spiritual and secular. *NeuroQuantology, 16*(10), 60–77.

Krippner, S. (2020). Altered and transitional states. In M. A. Runco & S. R. Pritzker (Eds.), *Encyclopedia of creativity*, 3rd ed. (Vol. 1, pp. 29–36). Academic Press.

Krippner, S. (2020). Dreams. In M. A. Runco & S. R. Pritzker (Eds.), *Encyclopedia of creativity*, 3rd ed. (Vol. 1, pp. 383–389). Academic Press.

Krippner, S. (2021). Anomalies in Brasilia: Physiological and geomagnetic correlates 1993–2019. *Magazine of the Society for Psychical Research, 3*, pp. 18–20.

Krippner, S. (2022). Changes in psychology, chaos theory, and complexity theory in the last 25 years: A conversation with Stanley Krippner. In D. Schuldberg, R. Richards, & S. Guisinger (Eds.), *Chaos and nonlinear psychology: Keys to creativity in mind and life* (pp. 165–183). Oxford University Press.

Krippner, S., & Bindler, P. R. (1974). Hypnosis and attention: A review. *American Journal of Clinical Hypnosis, 16*, 166–177.

Krippner, S., & Blickenstaff, R. (1970). The development of self-concept as part of an art workshop for the gifted. *Gifted Child Quarterly, 14*, 163–166.

Krippner, S., & Bova, M. (2018). Folk healing in Calabria, Italy: A colorful tradition. In D. Eigner & J. Kremer (Eds.), *Cultural and medical traditions: Contributions to medical anthropology* (Vol. 2, pp. 165–200). Schriftenreihe der Landesverteidigungsakademie.

Krippner, S., & Bova, M. (2020). Exploring realities: Honoring Lawrence LeShan on his 100th birthday. *Journal of Transpersonal Psychology, 52*(2), 167–187

Krippner, S., & Brown, D. P. (1973). Field independence/dependence and Electrosone-50 induced altered states of consciousness. *Journal of Clinical Psychology, 29*, 316–319.

Krippner, S., & Carpenter, B. (1985, Winter). Three Balinese dreams: Cultural and personal myths in the life of a Balinese artist. *Shaman's Drum*, 29–33.

Krippner, S., & Davidson, R. (1972, March). Parapsychology in the U.S.S.R. *Saturday Review*, 56–60.

Krippner, S., & Dillard, J. (1988). *Dreamworking: How to use your dreams for creative problem-solving*. Bearly.

Krippner, S., & Easton, H. (1970). The existential themes in Jungian psychology. *Journal of Contemporary Psychotherapy, 3*, 19–26.

Krippner, S., & Ellis, D. J. (Eds.). (2009). *Perchance to dream: The frontiers of dream psychology*. Nova Science Publishers.

Krippner, S., & Fersh, D. (1970). Paranormal experience among members of American contra-cultural groups. *Journal of Psychedelic Drugs, 3*, 109–114.

Krippner, S., & Fersh, D. (1972). Spontaneous paranormal experience among members of intentional communities. In G. B. Carr (Ed.), *Marriage and family in a decade of change* (pp. 220–233). Addison-Wesley.

Krippner, S., & Fischer, S. (1973). A study of neurological organization procedures and megavitamin treatment for children with brain dysfunction. *Journal of Orthomolecular Psychiatry, 1*, 121–132.

Krippner, S., & Grossman, G. (1972). The hypnotic power of Coatlicue: A psychological interpretation. *Revista InterAmerican, 2*, 224–230.

Krippner, S., & Hastings, A. (1981). Parapsychology. In A. Villoldo & K. Dychtwald (Eds.), *Millennium: Glimpses into the 21st century* (pp. 104–119). Jeremy P. Tarcher.

Krippner, S., & Herald, C. (1964). Reading disabilities among the academically talented. *Gifted Child Quarterly, 8*, 12–20.

Krippner, S., & Murphy, G. (1973). Humanistic psychology and parapsychology. *Journal of Humanistic Psychology, 13*(4), 3–24.

Krippner, S., & Paulson, D. S. (2006). Posttraumatic stress disorder among U.S. combat veterans. In T. G. Plante (Ed.), *Mental disorders of the new millennium: Public and social problems* (Vol. 2, pp. 1–23). Praeger.

Krippner, S., & Persinger, M. (1998). Enhancement of accuracy of telepathic dreams during periods of decreased geomagnetic activity: The William Erwin experiments. In N. L. Zingrone, M. J. Schlitz, C. S. Alvarado, & J.

Milton (Eds.), *Research in parapsychology 1993* (pp. 39–40). Scarecrow Press.

Krippner, S., & Persinger, M. A. (2008). Evidence for enhanced congruence between dreams and distant target material during periods of decreased geomagnetic activity. In A. D. Basiago & E. M. Thompson (Eds.), *Fatima revisited: The apparition phenomenon in ufology, psychology, and science* (pp. 79–86). Anomalous Books.

Krippner, S., & Pitchford, D. (2018). Humanistic and existential approaches in the treatment of PTSD. In R. House, D. Kalish, & J. Maidman (Eds.), *Humanistic psychology: Current trends and future prospects* (pp. 174–185). Routledge.

Krippner, S., & Rubin, D. (Eds.), (1973). *Galaxies of life: The human aura in acupuncture and Kirlian photography.* Gordon & Breach.

Krippner, S., & Rubin, D. (Eds.). (1974). *The Kirlian aura: Photographing the galaxies of life.* Anchor Books.

Krippner, S., & Rubin, D. (Eds.). (1976). *The energies of consciousness: Explorations in acupuncture, Kirlian photography, and the human aura.* Gordon & Breech.

Krippner, S., & Taitz, I. (2017). Psychotherapeutic approaches for post-traumatic stress disorder nightmares. *International Journal of Dream Research, 10*, 101–109.

Krippner, S., & Thompson, A. (1996). A 10-facet model of dreaming applied to dream practices of sixteen Native American cultural groups. *Dreaming, 6*, 71–96.

Krippner, S., & Weinhold, J. (2001). Gender differences in the content analysis of 240 dream reports from Brazilian participants in dream seminars. *Dreaming, 11*, 35–42.

Krippner, S., & Welch. P. (1992). *The spiritual dimensions of healing: From native shamanism to contemporary health care.* Irvington.

Krippner, S., & Winkler, M. (1995). Post modernity and consciousness studies. *Journal of Mind and Behavior, 16*, 255–280.

Krippner, S., Benjamin, H., & Allen, V. (1973). *Case –history data from 392 male and 71 female transsexuals.* American Society of Psychosomatic Dentistry and Medicine.

Krippner, S., Bogzaran, F., & de Carvalho, A. P. (2002). *Extraordinary dreams and how to work with them.* SUNY Press.

Krippner, S., Honorton, C., & Ullman, M. (1973). An experiment in dream telepathy with "The Grateful Dead." *Journal of the American Society of Psychosomatic Dentistry and Medicine, 20*, 9–17.

Krippner, S., Jaeger, C., & Faith, L. (2001). Identifying and utilizing spiritual content in dream reports. *Dreaming, 11*, 127–147.

Krippner, S., Lenz, G., Barksdale, W., & Davidson, R. (1974). *Content analysis of 30 dreams from 10 pre-operative male transsexuals.* American Society of Psychosomatic Dentistry and Medicine.

Krippner, S., Pitchford, D. B., & Davies, J. (2012). *Post-traumatic stress disorder: Biographies of disease*. Greenwood/ABC-CLIO.

Krippner, S., Saunders, D. T., Morgan, A., & Quan, A. (2019). Remote viewing of concealed target pictures under light and dark conditions. *Explore, 15*, 27–37.

Krippner, S., Wickramasekera, I., Wickramasekera, J., & Winstead, C. W., III. (1998). The Ramtha phenomenon: Psychological, phenomenological, and geomagnetic data. *Journal of the American Society for Psychical Research, 92*, 1–24.

Kris, E. (1956). The personal myth: A problem in psychoanalytic technique. *Journal of the American Psychoanalytic Association, 4*, 653–681.

Krivorotov, K. (2012). *The energy of consciousness*. CreateSpace.

Lanza, R. (2010). *Biocentrism: How life and consciousness are the keys to understanding the true nature of the universe*. BenBella Books.

Larsen, S. (1990). *The mythic imagination: The quest for meaning through personal mythology*. Bantam Books.

Laszlo, E. (1987). *Evolution: The grand synthesis*. Shambhala.

Leger, R. R. (July 24, 1978). "Scientists are aglow over a photo process with vast potential." *Wall Street Journal*, 1–2.

Lehman, H. C., & Witty, P. A. (1927). Play activity and school progress. *Journal of Educational Psychology, 18*, 318–326.

Leonard, G. (1972). *The transformation: A guide to the inevitable changes in humankind*. Tarcher.

Letheby, C. (2021). *Philosophy of psychedelics*. Oxford.

Lévi-Strauss, C. (1978). *Myth and meaning: Cracking the code of culture*. University of Toronto Press.

Litvag, I. (1972). *Singer in the shadows: The strange story of Patience Worth*. Popular Books.

Llewelyn, S. (2020). *What do dreams do?* Oxford University Press.

Loye, D. (1998). *The sphinx and the rainbow: Brain, mind, and future vision*. iUniverse.

Lucretius Carus, T., & Mantinband, J. H. (1965). *On the nature of the universe: (De rerum natura) A New verse translation*. Ungar.

Maliszewski, M., Vaughan, B., Krippner, S., Holler, G., & Fracasso, C. (2011). Altering consciousness through sexual activity. In E. Cardeña & M. Winkelman (Eds.), *Altering consciousness: Multidisciplinary perspectives* (Vol. 2, pp. 190–209). Praeger/ABC-CLIO.

Maslow, A. (1962). Toward a psychology of being. Van Nostrand.

Maslow, A. (1976). *Religions, values, and peak experiences* (2nd ed.). Compass.

Masters, R. E. L. (1964). *Forbidden sexual practices and morality: An objective re-examination of perverse sex practices in different cultures*. Julian Press.

Masters, R. E. L. (1964). *Prostitution and morality: A definitive report on the prostitute in contemporary society and an analysis of the causes and effects of the suppression*. Julian Press.

Masters, R. E. L. (1988). *The Goddess Sekhmet: Psycho-spiritual exercises of the fifth way*. Amity House.
Matte. N., & Devor, A. H. (2007). Building a better world for transpeople: Reed Erickson and the Erickson Educational Foundation. *International Journal of Transgenderism, 10,* 47–68.
May, E. C., & Marwaha, S. B. (Eds.). (2014). *Anomalous cognition: Remote viewing research and theory*. McFarland.
May, E. C., & Marwaha, S. B. (Eds.). (2019). *The Stargate Archives: Reports of the United States government-sponsored psi program, 1972–1995*. McFarland.
May, E., Rubel, V., McMonagle, W. J., & Auerbach, L. (2014). *ESP wars: East & West: An account of the military use of psychic espionage as narrated by the key Russian and American players*. CreateSpace Independent Publishing Platform.
May, L. J. (1991). *Lola May Who?* Author.
May, R., Angel, E., & Ellenberger, H. F. (Eds.). (1958). *Existence: A new dimension in psychiatry and psychology*. Basic Books.
May, R. (1969). *Love and will*. W. W. Norton.
Melvoin, N. (2021, May 24-31). Kids need summer camps. *Time* magazine, 31.
Metzner, R. (2009). *Sacred vine of the spirits: Ayahuasca*. Park Street Press.
Mikhalevskii, V. L., & Frantov, G. S. (1966). Photographing surfaces of metal ores by means of high-frequency currents. *Russian Journal of Scientific and Applied Photography and Cinematography, 2,* 380–381.
Millay, J. (2000). *Multidimensional mind: Remote viewing in hyperspace*. North Atlantic Books.
Moreira-Almeida, A., Moreira de Almeida, T., Gollner, A. M., & Krippner, S. (2009). A study of the mediumistic surgery of John of God. *Journal of Shamanic Practice, 2*(1), 21–31.
Morgan, N. (2020). *Someone left the cake out in the rain: A memoir by Nancy Morgan*. One Street Press.
Mundy, J. (2004). *Missouri mystic*. Royal Fireworks Press.
Murphy, G. (1958). *Human potentialities*. Basic Books.
Naranjo, C. (1973). *The techniques of Gestalt Therapy*. SAT Press.
Naranjo, C. (1974). *The healing journey*. Pantheon.
Naranjo, C. (1997). *Transformations through insight: Enneatypes in life*. Holm.
Narby, J. (2005). *Intelligence in nature: An inquiry into knowledge*. Jeremy P Tarcher/Penguin.
Narby, J., & Huxley, F. (Eds.). (2000). *Shamans through time: 500 years on the path to knowledge*. Penguin/Random House.
Nelson, R. D. (2019). *Connected: The emergence of global consciousness*. ICRL Press.
Newland, C. A. (1962). *Myself and I*. Coward-McCann.
Nitsch, T. (1997). *Creature teachers: A guide to the spirit animals of the Native American tradition*. Bloomsbury.

Noel, W., & Wang, J. (2018). *Is Cannabis a gateway drug? Key findings and a literature review.* Federal Research Division, Department of Justice.

Osmond, H. (1981). *Predicting the past: Memos on the enticing universe of possibility.* Macmillan.

Ostrander, S., & Schroeder, L. (1970). *Psychic discoveries behind the Iron Curtain.* Prentice-Hall.

Pallamary, M. J. (2017). *n0thing: A sequel to Dreamland.* Mystic Ink Press.

Paulson, D. (1994). *Walking the point: Male initiation and the Vietnam experience.* Distinctive Pub. Corp.

Paulson, D., & Krippner, S. (2007). *Haunted by combat: Understanding PTSD in war veterans including women, reservists, and those coming back from Iraq.* Praeger Security International.

Peck, D. (Ed.). (1993). *The very special raspberry cookbook.* Wimmer Book Distributor.

Penrose, R. R., Hameroff, S., Kak, S., & Tao, L. (2011). *Consciousness and the universe: Quantum physics, evolution, brain & mind.* Cosmology Science.

Persinger, M. A., & Krippner, S. (1989). Dream ESP experiments and geomagnetic activity. *Journal of the American Society for Psychical Research, 83*, 101–116.

Pieracci, M. (1990). The mythopoesis of psychotherapy. *The Humanistic Psychologist, 18*, 208–224.

Pierre, J. M., Ganlal, M., & Son, M. (2016). Cannabis-induced psychosis associated with high potency "wax dabs." *Schizophrenia Research, 172*, 211–212.

Pink, D. H. (2022). *The power of regret: How looking backward moves us forward.* Riverhead.

Piotrowski, Z. A. (1973). The Piotrowski Dream Interpretation System. *Psychiatric Quarterly, 47*, 609–622.

Pipes, K. S. (2004). *Ike's final battle: The road to Little Rock and the challenge of equality.* World Ahead Publishing.

Pollan, M. (2018). *How to change your mind.* Penguin.

Pollan, M. (2021). *This is your mind on plants.* Penguin.

Popp, F-A. (2003). Properties of biophotons and their theoretical importance. *Indian Journal of Experimental Biology, 41*, 308–402.

Presman, A. S. (1970). *Electromagnetic fields and life.* Basic Books.

Price-Williams, D. (2008). *Life Dreams: Field notes on psi, synchronicity, and shamanism.* Pioneer Imprints.

Rabinovitch, R. D. (1964). Educational attainment in children with psychiatric problems (including incidence of those with primary learning disability) at Hawthorn Center: A preliminary report. *Bulletin of the Orton Society, 14*, 1–5.

Radha, S. S. (2004). *Realities of the dreaming mind: An introduction to dream yoga.* Timeless Books.

Radin, D., Hayssen, G., & Walsh, J. (2007). Effects of intentionally enhanced chocolate on mood. *Explore, 3*, 405–492.

Rao, K. R. (Ed.). (1985). *Charles Honorton and the impoverished state of skepticism: Essays on a parapsychological pioneer.* McFarland.

Reid, H. O. (1956). The Supreme Court and interposition. *Journal of Negro Education, 25,* 109-117.

Reisman, F. R. et al. (Eds.). (2021). *Giants and trailblazers in creativity research and related fields.* KIE Book Series.

Rhine, J. B. (1953). *New world of the mind.* William Sloane.

Rhine, J. B., & Pratt, J. G. (1959). *Parapsychology: Frontier science of the mind.* Duke University Press.

Rhine, L. E. (1961). *Hidden channels of the mind.* Time–Life Books.

Rhine, L. E. (1969). *ESP in life and lab.* McMillan.

Rhine, L. E. (1981). *The invisible picture: A study of psychic experiences.* McFarland.

Richards, R. (2018). *Everyday creativity and the healthy mind: Dynamic new paths for self and society.* Palgrave Macmillan.

Rock, A., & Krippner, S. (2011). *Demystifying shamans and their world: A multidisciplinary study.* Imprint Academic.

Rogers, C. R. (1961). *On becoming a person.* Houghton-Mifflin.

Rogers, C. R., Lyon, H. C., & Tausch, R. (2013). *On becoming an effective teacher.* Routledge.

Russell, R. (2022, August). "Say it out loud! Behind the debate over abortion, there lies a troubling truth." *Church and State,* p. 22

Ryan, C., & Jetha, C. (2010). *Sex at dawn: The Prehistoric origins of modern sexuality.* HarperCollins.

Sanchez, D. W. (2009). *The Killing Fields; Harvest of Women.* St Marks Press.

Sanders, M. (1996). *The Colonel's secret: Eleven herbs and a spicy daughter.* Ibis Foundation.

Saxon, L. (2012.) *Sex at dusk: Lifting the shiny wrappings from Sex at Dawn.* Create Space Independent Publishing.

Scherer, J. J. (1991, Winter). The role of chaos in the creation of change. *Creative Change, The Journal of Religion and Applied Behavioral Science.*

Sheldrake, R. (1981). *A New Science of Life: The Hypothesis of Formative Causation.* J.P. Tarcher.

Siewert, H., & Du Bois, C. (2022). *My dream of democracy: My flight, my life.* A Place in Time Press.

Simonton, D. K. (1986). Presidential greatness: The historical consensus and its psychological consequences. *Political Psychology, 7,* 259–283.

Singh, T. (1990). *How to learn from a Course in Miracles* (3rd ed.). Harper San Francisco.

Singh, T. (1994). *Moments outside of time: My journeys to Israel, Japan, and India.* Life Action Press.

Smith, D. E., & Gay, G. R. (Eds.) *It's so good, don't even try it once: Heroin in perspective.* Basic Books.

Storm, L., Sherwood, S. J., Roe, C. A., Tressoldi, P. E., Rock, A. J., & Di Risio, L. (2019). On the correspondence between dream content and target material under laboratory conditions: A meta-analysis of dream-ESP studies, 1966-2016. *International Journal of Dream Research, 10,* 120–140.

Stowell, M. S. (1997). Precognitive dreams: A phenomenological study. Part I: Methodology and sample cases. *Journal of the American Society for Psychical Research, 91,* 163–220.

Stowell, M. S. (1997). Precognitive dreams: A phenomenological study. Part II: Discussion. *Journal of the American Society for Psychical Research, 91,* 255–304.

Swanson, G. (1980). *Swanson on Swanson.* Random House.

Sword, R. (2019) Time-focused psychotherapy: Time perspective therapy. In I. A. Serlin, S. Krippner, & K. Rockefeller (Eds.), *Integrated care for the traumatized: A whole-person approach* (pp. 109–125). Rowman & Littlefield.

Tart, C. T. (1968). A psychophysiological study of out-of-the-body experiences in a selected subject. *Journal of the American Society for Psychical Research, 62,* 3–75). *Transpersonal psychologies.* Harper and Row.

Tart, C.T. (1975). *States of consciousness.* Dutton.

Taves, A., Barley, M. (2023). A feature-based approach to the comparative study of "nonordinary" experiences. *American Psychologist, 78,* 50–61.

Tenen, S. (2011). *The alphabet that changed the world: How Genesis preserves a science of consciousness in geometry and gesture.* North Atlantic Books.

Thong, D., with Carpenter, B., & Krippner, S. (1993). *A psychiatrist in paradise: Treating mental illness in Bali.* White Lotus Press.

Thorne, F. C. (1967). *Integrative psychology.* Florence Calvet Books.

Tiller, W. A., Dibble, W. E., & Fandel, J. G. (2005). *Some science adventures with real magic.* Pavior.

Tillich, P. (1952). *The courage to be.* Nisbet.

Tillier, W. (2018). *Personality development through positive disintegration: The work of Kazimierz Dabrowski.* Maurice Bassett.

Timsit, Y., Youri, L., Valiadi, M., & Not, F. (2021). Bioluminescence and photoreception in unicellular organisms: Light signaling in a bio-communication perspective. *International Journal of Molecular Sciences, 22,* 1–16.

Tobach, E. (1979). *The four horsemen: Racism, sexism, militarism, and social Darwinism.* Behavioral Publications.

Trinklein, F. (1971). *The God of Science.* William B. Eerdmans.

Turner, L. (1982). *Lana: The lady, the legend, the truth.* E. P. Dutton.

Tye, L. (2020). *Demagogue: The life and long shadow of Senator Joe McCarthy.* Houghton-Mifflin Harcourt.

Ullman, M. (1973). Social factors in dreaming. *Contemporary Psychoanalysis, 9,* pp. 186-196.

Ullman, M. (2006). The Dream: In search of a new abode. *Dream Network Journal,* pp. 2–16.

Ullman, M., & Krippner, S. (1970). *Dream studies and telepathy: An experimental approach.* Parapsychology Foundation Monograph 12.

Ullman, M., Krippner, S. & Vaughan. A. (2023). *Dream telepathy: The landmark ESP experiments.* 50th Anniversary Edition. Afterworlds Press. (Originally published in 1973.)

Vallee, J. (2014). *Passport to Mongolia: From folklore to flying saucers.* Daily Grail.

Van Wijk, R., van Aken, H., Mei, W., & Popp, F. A. (1993). Light-induced photon emission by mammalian cells. *Journal of Photochemistry and Photobiology, B: Biology, 18,* 75–79.

Vaughan, F. (2002). What is spiritual intelligence? *Journal of Humanistic Psychology, 42,* 2, 16–33.

Villoldo, A. (2015). *One spirit medicine: Ancient ways to ultimate well-being.* Hay House.

Villoldo, A. (2018). *The heart of the shaman: Stories and practices of the luminous warrior.* Hay House.

Villoldo, A., & Krippner, S. (1987). *Healing states.* Fireside/Simon & Schuster.

Walker, E. H. (2000). *The physics of consciousness.* Perseus Books.

Walker, H. B. (1966). *Thoughts to live by.* Aspley House.

Wasson, R. G. (1957, May 13). Seeking the magic mushroom. *Life magazine,* 100–120.

Watson, L. (1982). *Lightning Bird: The story of one man's journey into Africa.* Dutton.

Weil, P., Amiden, A., Krippner, S., Lal Arora, H., Winkler, M., Kelson, R., & Crema, R. (1995). The magenta phenomena, Part III: An hermeneutic and phenomenological investigation. *Exceptional Human Experience, 13,* 54–63.

Wiessner, I. et al. (2022). LSD and creativity: Increased novelty and symbolic thinking, decreased utility and convergent thinking. *Journal of Psychopharmacology, 3,* 348–-359.

Williams, C. (1980). *I'm alive: An autobiography.* Harper and Row.

Williams, W. (1986). *The spirit and the flesh: Sexual diversity in American Indian culture.* Beacon Press.

Wilson, C. (2005). *Dreaming to some purpose.* AbeBooks.

Winkler, M., & Krippner, S. (1994). Persuasion. In V. S. Ramachandran (Ed.), *Encyclopedia of human behavior* (Vol. 3, pp. 481–-488). Academic Press.

Witty, P. A. (1940). Contributions to the IQ controversy from the study of superior deviates. *Self & Society, 51,* 503–508.

Witty, P. A. (Ed.). (1951). *The gifted child.* D. C. Heath.

Wright, F. L. (1943). *Frank Lloyd Wright: An autobiography.* Horizon.

Wright, F. L. (1957). *A Testament.* Horizon.

Wright, O. L. (1878). *Frank Lloyd Wright.* Horizon.

Young, A. (1976). *The reflexive universe: Evolution of consciousness* (rev. ed.). Amdos.

Young, C., Conard, P. L., Armstrong, M. L., & Lacey, P. (2018). Older military veteran care: Many still believe they are forgotten. *Holistic Nursing, 36,* 291–300.

Zausner, T. (1996). The creative chaos: Speculations on the connection between non-linear dynamics and the creative process. In W. Sulis & A. Combs (Eds.), *Nonlinear dynamics and human behavior; Studies of nonlinear phenomena in the life sciences* (Vol. 5, pp. 343–349). World Scientific.

Zimbardo, P. G. (2007). *The Lucifer effect: Understanding how good people turn evil.* Random House.

Zimbardo, P., Haney, C., Banks, C. W., & Jaffe, D. (1971). Stanford Prison Experiment.

Zimbardo, P., Sword, R. K. M., & Sword, R. M. (2012). *The time cure: Overcoming PTSD with the new perspective of Time Perspective Psychotherapy.* John Wiley & Sons.

Zinchenko, V. P., Leontiev, A. N., Lomov, B. F., & Luria, A. R. (1973). Parapsychology: Fiction or reality?" *Questions of Philosophy, 27,* 129–136. (original version in Russian)

Zingrone, N. L., Alvarado, C. S., & Agee, N. (2009). Psychological correlates of aura vision: Psychic experiences, dissociation, absorption, and synesthesia-like experiences. *Australian Journal of Clinical and Experimental Hypnosis, 37,* 131–168.

Zion, S. (1988). *The autobiography of Roy Cohn.* Lyle Stuart.

www.ingramcontent.com/pod-product-compliance
Lightning Source LLC
Chambersburg PA
CBHW070322240426
43671CB00013BA/2335